D0230134

MURDER IN PRINT

REF 823.09
DEC 2000

BAR

CHECKED   JUL 2008

SOLIHULL
SFC   LIBRARY
RECEIVED
49027
STOCK   823.09

Ref

BARNES

This book is due for return or before the date shown below.

Don Gresswell Ltd., London, N.21 Cat. No. 1208   DG 02242/71

CHECKED   JUL 2008

CHECKED -- JUL 2002

Solihull Sixth Form College

49027

49027

SOLIHULL
SIXTH FORM
COLLEGE

MURDER IN PRINT

A GUIDE TO
TWO CENTURIES OF
CRIME FICTION

MELVYN BARNES

SOLIHULL SFC	LIBRARY
RECEIVED	'93
STOCK NO.	49027
CLASS NO.	823·09
14·95	Ref.

BARN OWL BOOKS

© Melvyn Barnes 1986

First published 1986 by
Barn Owl Books
3 Ranelagh Gardens
Stamford Brook Avenue
London W6 OYE

British Library Cataloguing in Publication Data

Barnes, Melvyn
   Murder in print: a guide to two centuries of crime fiction.
   1. Detective and mystery stories, English——Bibliography
   I. Title
   016.823'0872   Z2024.D4

   ISBN 0-9509057-4-7

All Rights Reserved. No part of this publication may be
reproduced, stored in a retrieval system, or transmitted in any
form or by any means, electronic, photocopying, recording, or
otherwise, without the prior permission of Barn Owl Books.

Set in 11/12 pt English Times
by Colset Private Limited, Singapore
Printed and bound by Richard Clay (The Chaucer Press) Ltd,
Bungay, Suffolk

CONTENTS

AUTHOR'S PREFACE

Over ten years ago I produced *Best detective fiction: a guide from Godwin to the present* (Clive Bingley 1975; Hamden, Connecticut: Linnet Books 1975). The present volume was originally intended to be the second edition, but it soon became obvious that something far more extensive was required. Whereas the original book was largely confined to the classic and conventional form of detective fiction, the field has changed over the years to a degree that cannot be ignored. If the full picture is to be shown, there must be greater coverage of the modern crime novel in all its manifestations. Similarly, various subgenres, while mentioned in the earlier book, now warrant considerable sections of their own.

We are here dealing with arguably the most popular type of fiction, and one on which its devotees have strong opinions. It was gratifying to receive letters after the publication of *Best detective fiction*, drawing attention to old favourites who had been overlooked and new writers who had established themselves as heirs apparent. These views have been taken into account in the compilation of the present volume, which is also the result of further extensive research and an examination of the best authors to have emerged in the past twenty years. All material which appeared in the original volume has similarly been comprehensively revised, reorganized and expanded.

The final product is therefore a new book, with a new title to reflect its wider coverage. *Murder in print* deals with some 260 authors, compared with 122 in the original volume. Almost 500 titles are featured, compared with only 220 in *Best detective fiction*.

Nevertheless, the creation of this new guide has still involved a large measure of personal choice. Although a considerable proportion of the featured books are held by most authorities to be key contributions to the field, there are others whose inclusion might provoke disagreement from among the vast army of crime fiction enthusiasts. In the case of new authors, time will place them in perspective among their fellow crime writers, and in some cases it may transpire that their 'best' books are yet to come.

As with *Best detective fiction*, each selected title in this guide fulfils one or more of the following criteria: excellence of plot, writing and/or characterization, or a degree of innovation which has established or enhanced a trend. Thousands of crime stories therefore find no place here; in common with all branches of literature, the field has produced many examples which are mediocre, unoriginal or just bad. In a few cases it has been necessary to bring a further criterion into play – sheer durability, in that public demand has been sustained to an extent which identifies the works concerned as something exceptional.

Clearly some parameters have had to be drawn – not an easy task, nor one which is ever universally regarded as successfully achieved. In general, I have excluded the 'thriller' from this book. This form, although it may indeed have a detective as its central character, nevertheless relies for its effect primarily upon pace and action and poses the questions 'what is going to happen next?' or 'how will the hero get out of this fix?' To give but two examples, this criterion disqualifies the novels of Leslie Charteris and John Creasey, but admits Creasey's realistic police procedural stories as 'J. J. Marric'. Spy stories have similarly been excluded.

Regarding citation, each title is listed in its first British and first American edition, although there are naturally some examples of books which have been published on only one side of the Atlantic. Place of publication is London unless stated otherwise. Transatlantic title changes, which are common and often unaccountable, are also given. The citation of the first edition will be useful to serious collectors, but it also provides a standard point of reference. Reprints and new editions of many of the titles have been published in hardback and/or paperback, and will still be

49027

available through bookshops and libraries. Finally it must be mentioned that all pseudonymous works – which represent a large proportion of the field – are cited under the pseudonym, with the authors' actual names, however, mentioned in the text.

The narrative form of this volume, together with the arrangement of related titles, combine to give a picture of the development of crime fiction from its earliest days to the present. I offer it principally as a guide to the genre, showing its history through the finest examples, rather than as a detailed academic analysis. The librarian, the researcher and, of course, the crime fiction addict will find here the acknowledged classics of the field, while significant authors of the past twenty years are represented by works which will service as good introductions to their styles and techniques for readers who might not have sampled them before.

March 1986   Melvyn Barnes

SELECT BIBLIOGRAPHY

There now exist many analytical and historical accounts of crime fiction, and the past ten years in particular have seen a spate of such publications. The fact that crime fiction has at long last been considered worthy of serious study is to be applauded, and the reader might find the following examples of interest for further reference. It is a selective list only.

In addition, there are now many detailed studies of individual authors. All this, together with the growth in book dealers who specialize in crime fiction, signifies a coming of age which is long overdue.

John Ball (editor), *The mystery story*. Del Mar, California: Publisher's Inc., 1976; Penguin, 1978.

Earl F. Bargainnier (editor), *Ten women of mystery*. Bowling Green, Ohio: Popular Press, 1981.

Jacques Barzun and Wendell Hertig Taylor, *A catalogue of crime*. New York: Harper & Row, 1971.

John C. Carr, *The craft of crime: conversations with crime writers*. Boston: Houghton Mifflin, 1983.

Diana Cooper-Clark, *Designs of darkness: interviews with detective novelists*. Bowling Green, Ohio: Popular Press, 1983.

Patricia Craig and Mary Cadogan, *The lady investigates: women detectives and spies in fiction*. Gollancz, 1981; New York: St Martin's Press, 1982.

George N. Dove, *The police procedural*. Bowling Green, Ohio: Popular Press, 1982.

Lucy Freeman (editor), *The murder mystique: crime writers on their art*. New York: Ungar, 1982.

David Geherin, *Sons of Sam Spade: the private eye novel in the 70s*. New York: Ungar, 1980.

Howard Haycraft, *Murder for pleasure: the life and times of the detective story*. New York: Appleton-Century, 1941; Peter Davies, 1942. Reprinted, New York: Biblo & Tannen, 1968.

Howard Haycraft (editor), *The art of the mystery story: a collection of critical essays*. New York: Simon & Schuster, 1946. Reprinted, New York: Grosset & Dunlap, 1961.

H. R. F. Keating, *Murder must appetize*. Lemon Tree Press, 1975; New York: Mysterious Press, 1981.

H. R. F. Keating (editor), *Crime writers: reflections on crime fiction*. British Broadcasting Corporation, 1978.

H. R. F. Keating (editor), *Whodunit? a guide to crime, suspense and spy fiction*. Windward, 1982; New York: Van Nostrand Reinhold, 1982.

Stephen Knight, *Form and ideology in crime fiction*. Macmillan, 1980; Bloomington, Indiana: Indiana University Press, 1980.

Tage la Cour and Harald Mogensen, *The murder book: an illustrated history of the detective story*. Allen & Unwin, 1971; New York: Herder, 1971.

Jessica Mann, *Deadlier than the male: an investigation into feminine crime writing*. David & Charles, 1981; New York: Macmillan, 1981.

A. E. Murch, *The development of the detective novel*. Peter Owen, 1958; New York: Philosophical Library, 1958.

Francis M. Nevins Jnr. (editor), *The mystery writer's art*. Bowling Green, Ohio: Popular Press, 1970.

Ian Ousby, *Bloodhounds of heaven: the detective in English fiction from Godwin to Doyle*. Cambridge, Massachusetts: Harvard University Press, 1976.

Leroy Panek, *Watteau's shepherds: the detective novel in Britain 1914-1940*. Bowling Green, Ohio: Popular Press, 1979.

Otto Penzler (editor), *The great detectives*. Boston: Little, Brown, 1978.

Otto Penzler, Chris Steinbrunner and Marvin Lachman (editors), *Detectionary: a biographical dictionary of leading characters in detective and mystery fiction*. New York: Overlook Press, 1977.

Eric Quayle, *The collector's book of detective fiction*. Studio Vista, 1972.

Ellery Queen, *Queen's quorum: a history of the detective-crime short story*. Boston: Little, Brown, 1951; Gollancz, 1953. Revised edition, New York: Biblo & Tannen, 1969; Greenhill, 1986.

John M. Reilly (editor), *Twentieth-century crime and mystery writers*. New York: St Martin's Press, 1980; Macmillan, 1980. Second edition, New York: St Martin's Press, 1985; St James Press, 1985.

Erik Routley, *The puritan pleasures of the detective story*. Gollancz, 1972.

Sutherland Scott, *Blood in their ink: the march of the modern mystery novel*. Stanley Paul, 1953.

Chris Steinbrunner and Otto Penzler (editors), *Encyclopedia of mystery and detection*. New York: McGraw-Hill, 1976; Routledge & Kegan Paul, 1976.

R. F. Stewart, . . . *And always a detective: chapters on the history of detective fiction*. David & Charles, 1980.

Julian Symons, *Bloody murder: from the detective story to the crime novel*. Faber & Faber, 1972. Published in New York as *Mortal consequences*, Harper & Row, 1972; second edition as *Bloody murder*, London and New York: Viking Press, 1985.

Colin Watson, *Snobbery with violence: crime stories and their audience*. Eyre & Spottiswoode, 1971; New York: St Martin's Press, 1971. Revised and reprinted, Eyre Methuen, 1979.

Robin W. Winks (editor), *Detective fiction: a collection of critical essays*. Englewood Cliffs, New Jersey: Prentice-Hall, 1980.

Dilys Winn (editor), *Murder ink: the mystery reader's companion*. New York: Workman, 1977; Westbridge, 1978. New edition, New York: Workman, 1984.

Dilys Winn (editor), *Murderess ink: the better half of the mystery*. New York: Workman, 1979.

1

FROM THE BEGINNINGS

The classical detective story dates from 1841 with the first publication of Poe's *The murders in the Rue Morgue*, but various authorities have identified elements of detection in the literature of a far earlier age. Examples have been quoted from the Apocryphal scriptures concerning the exploits of Daniel, from Virgil's *Aeneid*, from Herodotus, and from Chaucer's *Canterbury tales*. In each of these there are puzzles presented, some involving crime, and solutions are reached by the crude employment of techniques which detective novelists of the twentieth century were to enchance with the elaborations of our modern age.

It must be stressed, however, that there was no clear intention in any of these early works to present a detective story in the sense that readers have now come to understand the term, and their interest to the crime fiction enthusiast is purely academic. They are therefore excluded from this guide, together with *The Arabian nights entertainments* and Voltaire's *Zadig*. Also excluded are the works of the picaresque novelists, the Gothic novelists, Fenimore Cooper, Balzac, Eugène Sue and Dumas. The extent to which such writers employed the conventions of detective fiction is a fascinating study in itself, and interested readers are referred to the books quoted in the Select Bibliography, particularly that by A. E. Murch.

Mention must nevertheless be made of two key works which greatly influenced the literature that was to come. Considerably predating Poe, but so important that they must be cited as the earliest examples of pure detection, were the works of Godwin and Vidocq.

William Godwin (1756-1836), philosopher and atheist, wrote

Godwin, William
Things as they are; or, the adventures of Caleb Williams
Three volumes
B. Crosby, 1794

primarily as a propagandist novel, but contained within it is a classic of detective fiction. A murder is committed, and an amateur detective identifies the criminal by the analysis of clues which the author has deliberately contrived. Generally known by its subtitle, this novel may be defined as a Gothic romance, although not one that is specially remembered today. Godwin set out to demonstrate the need for social and political reform rather than to tell a straightforward story of murder and its consequences, and of course the term 'detective story' was not at that time in common usage. The tyranny of rich landlords, the abuse of power by the few in authority, and the wretchedness of the penal system were depicted here by Godwin before ever Dickens came on the scene, and it is sad that Godwin's chief claim to fame today is that his daughter created Frankenstein.

Furthermore, Godwin's propaganda is in no sense obtrusive. Caleb Williams investigates the murder of an obnoxious landlord for which two tenants have been hanged, and discovers that his own employer is guilty. In order to do this, Williams uses methods which were later adopted by countless investigators in the field of which Poe became the acknowledged founder. Following his successful enquiries, Williams is hounded by the murderer through a series of adventures involving prison, various disguises, and numerous scenes depicting the glaring social iniquities of the age. The theme of the pursuer pursued has been subsequently used by scores of thriller writers, as has Godwin's technique (described in his preface) of planning the story backwards. As an example of propagandist fiction, as a picaresque novel, or as the first pure detective story, this work merits further study today.

When Godwin was writing *Caleb Williams*, much of his research into the activities of criminals was conducted with the aid of *The Newgate calendar*. These annals of the gaol wherein resided the most notorious villains, as well as the saddest cases of degraded humanity, provided material for many novelists of the picaresque school. In some cases the pursuit of the criminal, as narrated in *The Newgate calendar*, involved something approaching detective work, but it was not until the publication of Vidocq's memoirs that latent writers of detective fiction were provided with accounts of authentic criminal investigation of a kind which could inspire them.

Eugène François Vidocq (1775–1857) was the first head of the Paris Sûreté and later a private detective, but at the outset of his career he was the hunted rather than the hunter. His progression from criminal to detective was to be reflected in such fictional characters as Gaboriau's Lecoq, Leblanc's Arsène Lupin, and Chesterton's Flambeau.

Vidocq, Eugène François
Memoirs of Vidocq, principal agent of the French police until 1827
Four volumes
Hunt & Clarke, 1828–9

was later published in one volume in Philadelphia and Baltimore (Carey & Hart, 1834). I have included it here in spite of its apparently factual status, because there is little doubt that it was highly coloured and heavily fictionalized. Vidocq was evidently something of a showman, and time and again these memoirs describe techniques and *modus operandi* which now, 160 years later, it is possible to find in thousands of novels written in the intervening period. His mastery of the art of disguise, and his knowledge of the lore and language of the underworld, are but two aspects of the 'great detective' which anticipated such writers of the late nineteenth century as Gaboriau and Conan Doyle, who in their turn gave rise to a tremendous upsurge of interest in the awakening field which has come to be known as detective fiction.

The Paris Sûreté had been established, but there was still in the early nineteenth century no force of professional detectives in Britain or in the USA. This has been advanced by some authorities as the reason why detective stories as such could not be written at the time, the argument being that it is not possible to write about things before they exist. Although this principle seems not to have discouraged Jules Verne or H. G. Wells, who came later, it is a fact that no professional detectives emerged in fiction until they existed in reality.

The memoirs of Vidocq quite clearly influenced the work of

Edgar Allan Poe, who is accepted as the father of the detective story. Poe (1809–49) was an American who spent his early life in Britain, and who had an abiding interest in the European scene. After producing some poetry and other literary work which took some years to attract public attention, he realised that the field of fiction was a more likely source of income, and furthermore that the short story form was capable of distinct improvement. He became literary editor of *Graham's magazine*, and during his incumbency published *The murders in the Rue Morgue*. This was a foundation stone of the genre, the first piece of fiction in which the reader is presented with a detective and a mystery which is not only integral to the work, but the reason for which the work was written at all. In contrast, Godwin's novel used a detective theme within a piece of reformist propaganda, and in Vidocq's work there was scant attention paid to intellectual analysis.

The murders in the Rue Morgue was the first pure detective story, although it is unlikely that Poe recognized it in that light. It also introduced the first great series detective of fiction, the Chevalier C. Auguste Dupin. A man 'of an excellent, indeed of an illustrious family', he is something of an intellectual recluse with powers of observation second to none, and he employed techniques of deductive reasoning never previously seen in fiction. He therefore possessed advantages which had been denied to Vidocq, as Dupin himself states: 'Vidocq . . . was a good guesser, and a persevering man. But, without educated thought, he erred continually.'

The murders in the Rue Morgue first appeared in the April 1841 issue of *Graham's magazine*. The second Dupin story, *The mystery of Marie Roget*, appeared in *Snowden's ladies companion* in the issues for November and December 1842 and February 1843. The third and last, *The purloined letter*, made its first appearance in *The gift*, an annual dated 1845 but published in the latter part of 1844 by the Philadelphia firm of Carey & Hart. Poe wrote only two more stories which may be classified in the detective canon, *The gold bug* and *Thou art the man*, neither of which featured Dupin. All three Dupin stories, together with *The gold bug*, first appeared together in the volume

Poe, Edgar A.

Tales

New York and London: Wiley & Putnam, 1845

which was edited by Evert A. Duyckincke, and all five stories appeared in

Poe, Edgar A.
The works of the late Edgar Allan Poe: with notices of his
life and genius
Three volumes
New York: J. S. Redfield, 1850
which was edited by N. P. Willis, J. R. Lowell and R. W.
Griswold. Redfield in fact published various editions of two,
three and four volumes throughout the 1850s.
   The collection published in London as
Poe, Edgar A.
Tales of mystery, imagination and humour; and poems
Simms & McIntyre, 1852
was the forerunner of numerous editions of Poe's short stories
popularly known as *Tales of mystery and imagination*. Many
modern editions are available, containing the master's studies in
murder, horror and the supernatural in addition to the exploits
of Auguste Dupin.
   At this point it is necessary to examine briefly the various
features of Poe's detective tales, for they were the models which
inspired countless others. Dupin was a man of fantastic intelligence, the first omniscient amateur detective, who gave rise to
hundreds of successors. He was a walking brain, one might
almost say a 'thinking machine' – the sobriquet chosen by
Jacques Futrelle sixty years later for his Professor Augustus S.
F. X. Van Dusen. Dupin was also a most cultured gentleman,
and again this correlation of commonsense and intellectualism –
so rare, perhaps, in twentieth-century man – was used to the full
by Poe's successors in the field. One can cite, among many, S.
S. Van Dine's creation Philo Vance, who had the attributes of
Dupin combined with a buffoonery of which Poe would almost
certainly have disapproved. Finally, there is Dupin's poor regard
for the official police, to whom he was infinitely superior. For
Dupin one could substitute Sherlock Holmes and others.
   Passing from Dupin himself, we find that the tales of his
exploits are narrated by an anonymous friend, who set the standard for Conan Doyle's Dr Watson in his awestruck admiration
of the detective, and in his desire to follow in his master's footsteps. Many great detectives from the late nineteenth century to the
1930s had their 'Watsons', chroniclers who were sometimes silly
and rarely intelligent. They never stole the great detective's thun-
der, and they originated with Dupin's nameless companion. In

the 1930s they began to be regarded as old-fashioned, but Poe had established a trend which survived for a century.

Then there are the innovations contained within each of Poe's stories. Dupin's investigation in the Rue Morgue is a case of murder in a sealed room. The 'locked room' murder mystery became a popular technique, exemplified by Gaston Leroux in *The mystery of the yellow room* and in countless tales by the twentieth-century master of that art, John Dickson Carr alias Carter Dickson.

The murder of Marie Roget, Dupin's second case, is a fictional reconstruction of an actual crime – a technique adopted by numerous writers up to the present day. It is also told largely by means of newspaper reports, proving that the conventional narrative form is not always necessary in order to retain the reader's interest, and this was proved again in, for example, Collins's *The moonstone* and Dorothy L. Sayers's *The documents in the case*. A further innovation is that Dupin solves the Roget murder purely by studying reports of the case, thus disclaiming the need to indulge in physical activity; in other words, he founded the 'armchair detective' school which was to be ably adopted, among many others, by Baroness Orczy's old man in the ABC shop and most notably by Rex Stout's immovable Nero Wolfe.

In *The purloined letter* Dupin demonstrates that the obvious solution is most likely to be overlooked. It has been done scores of times since, but rarely so effectively. Chesterton, however, made particularly clever use of the idea in several of his Father Brown stories.

The gold bug is less of a detective story as we know it, and is deprived of Dupin's presence, but the basic idea relies upon the deciphering of a code. Again, this was a device of considerable importance in the history of detective fiction, particularly to those who delighted in presenting facsimile reproductions of strange ciphers for the delectation of their readers and for contemptuous dismissal by their detectives. Consider, for example, the breaking of *The dancing men* by Sherlock Holmes, or *The Moabite cipher* which taxes R. Austin Freeman's Dr John Thorndyke – the latter being a mixture of the cipher story and the 'most obvious solution', two Poeisms in one.

Finally, *Thou art the man* reveals a murderer who has prepared a trail of misleading clues, which has become a favourite device in detective fiction, and it contains the first demonstration of rudimentary ballistic science in respect of rifling marks on bullets. The murderer is that phenomenon of so many later stories and novels, the 'least likely person'. The outstanding practitioner of this device was to be Agatha Christie, and the ultimate example probably *The murder of Roger Ackroyd*.

No apology should be necessary for devoting so much space to five short stories, the only detective stories Poe wrote. It has been demonstrated that within these stories are many – if not all – of the basic elements of pure detective fiction. Thus any edition of Poe's work may be regarded as the detective fiction writer's, or indeed reader's, *vade mecum*. If there had been no C. Auguste Dupin, would there still have been a Sherlock Holmes?

2

THE PRE-SHERLOCK ERA

Whether or not one accepts the theory that there could be no detective stories before organized detective forces existed in reality, that particular problem was solved in England in 1842. In that year the Detective Department was established in London, an extremely small number of men destined to be the forefathers of New Scotland Yard. It was therefore only a matter of time before writers turned quite naturally to works of fiction depicting the pursuit and apprehension of criminals by professional detectives.

Poe, although he founded the detective story, provided little immediate inspiration to other writers. In his native America there was no impetus whatsoever in the development of the genre, but movement was seen more clearly in France and in Britain.

The establishment of the Detective Department was reflected in a spate of fictitious reminiscences published as 'yellow backs', the most notable among many being the pseudonymous 'Waters' created by William Russell. It was published first as *Recollections of a policeman* (New York: Cornish, Lamport, 1852) and later as the better-known London edition,

Waters
Recollections of a detective police-officer
J. & C. Brown, 1856

Perhaps more important was the attention paid to the Detective Department by the novelist Charles Dickens (1812–70), who embarked upon an early example of the public relations campaign by producing articles in praise of the detectives at a time when opinion was hostile. No doubt the skulduggery of the Bow Street Runners, who had been superseded, was still fresh in the public mind, and the new force had yet to prove itself honest and impartial. Dickens's participation consisted of articles in *Household words* from July to September 1850, in which he displayed his admiration for one Inspector Field, but his patronage was similarly evident in his novel

Dickens, Charles
Bleak House . . . with illustrations by H. K. Browne
(Published in parts bound with the wrappers)
Bradbury & Evans, 1853

which was also published in New York in two volumes (Harper, 1853). Although the police of the nineteenth century were characterized in many works of fiction as barely more honest than the villains they pursued, Dickens in *Bleak House* presented a more agreeable, more human image. His 'Inspector Bucket of the Detective' is an amalgam of Field and Vidocq, and the first professional detective to appear in an English novel.

As with any novel by Dickens, *Bleak House* cannot be neatly categorized, although the author's prime message concerns the costs and delays associated with the Court of Chancery. In the case of Jarndyce and Jarndyce, the estate in question is eventually consumed by the costs of the legal action. For the connoisseur of detection, however, the interest lies in the murder of the rascally lawyer Tulkinghorn, which introduces the methods of the Detective Department. The sharp-eyed and kindly Bucket even exposes the murderer to an assembled company of suspects, an innovation which later became almost obligatory in detective novels.

There are murders and other crimes in many of Dickens's novels, but it was not until

Dickens, Charles
The mystery of Edwin Drood . . . with twelve illustrations
by S.L. Fildes, and a portrait
(Published in parts bound with the wrappers)
Chapman & Hall, 1870

that he came nearest to writing a pure detective story. In the USA this appeared as *The mystery of Edwin Drood, and some uncollected pieces* (Boston: Fields, Osgood, 1870). It was his last book, left unfinished at the time of his death. Dwarfing a host of minor Dickensian characters is the sinister John Jasper, precentor of Cloisterham Cathedral. Jasper lives a schizophrenic existence, alternating respectability with his regular visits to the opium den. His nephew Edwin Drood is betrothed to Rosa Bud, and Jasper's every machination is designed to secure Rosa for himself.

At the point where the book breaks off, two principal questions are left unanswered. Has Edwin been murdered, or has he merely disappeared? And who is Datchery, the obviously disguised figure who has arrived in Cloisterham with the apparent intention of exposing Jasper's villainy? It may be that Dickens intended Datchery as his detective, or that an official detective would have made his appearance later in the book had the author survived. The death of Charles Dickens had the effect of creating one of the most famous literary puzzles of all time. It has remained available in its incomplete form in various editions, together with numerous published endings provided by enthusiasts.

With Dickens may be linked the name of Wilkie Collins (1824–89), who today is not held in the esteem reserved for his illustrious contemporary, but who nonetheless produced some exceptionally fine work. His well-known novel,

   Collins, W. Wilkie
   The woman in white
   Three volumes
   Sampson Low, 1860

was published in New York in one volume (Harper, 1860). It is really a thriller rather than a detective novel, but still contains some of the features which later writers were to elaborate in the more intellectual field of the pure detective story. Its success was absolute, and its title – probably inspired by the lighthouse at Broadstairs in Kent – was quickly adopted by the worlds of fashion and cosmetics, providing ample proof that the cult figure is not a twentieth-century phenomenon. The woman in the novel is mentally retarded and strongly resembles her half-sister, who is an heiress. Duplicity, the starting-point for so many great stories, develops into a complicated plot with such notable characterization that Collins was for some time favourably compared with Dickens. Count Fosco is one of the few fat Italian villains of the time, whereas normally villains of melodrama were lean and hungry. The other character innovation has scarcely ever been repeated so memorably – that of introducing a heroine who is distinctly ugly. Many critics regard it as the finest sensational novel in English, and the reason is simply that Collins's command of the language was equal to his plotting ability.

The magnificent contribution which Collins made to the history of detective fiction is encapsulated in his later novel,

Collins, W. Wilkie
The moonstone
Three volumes
Tinsley, 1868

which was published in New York in one volume (Harper, 1868). T.S. Eliot described it as 'the first, the longest and the best of English detective novels'. One may pedantically query each individual facet of this definition, without in any way detracting from the quality of this masterly work. It contains so many of the elements which subsequent writers were to use – the disappearance of a diamond, murder and suicide, opium, and so on. The story is narrated by each character in turn, in some cases by the use of letters and journals, again a technique which was to be used by later writers. To solve the mystery of the moonstone's disappearance is the task of Sergeant Cuff. He is 'grizzled . . . elderly . . . face as sharp as a hatchet'. Cuff is a brilliant portrait, with his passion for roses and his throwaway lines of a type used later by A. E. W. Mason's Hanaud. His working methods, and much of the author's inspiration, were drawn from Inspector Whicher and the real-life Constance Kent case of 1860.

Although the contributions of Dickens and Collins were significant, the development of detective fiction (as stated earlier) was seen equally clearly in France. In fact the French contribution was even more positively on the lines of the classic type of intellectual puzzle, and by far the most accomplished practitioner was Emile Gaboriau (1833–73).

During his short life Gaboriau produced a comparatively large number of 'sensational' novels, and he is best remembered for his creation of a reasoning phenomenon who anticipated Sherlock Holmes by two decades. His name was Lecoq, and he first appeared in *L'affaire Lerouge* (1866), which in English translation became

Gaboriau, Emile
The widow Lerouge
Boston: James R. Osgood, 1873

and in London *The Lerouge case* (Vizetelly, 1885). In this early story Lecoq is a pupil of Père Tabaret, formerly a pawnbroker's clerk and known as 'Tirauclaire'. Tabaret, an enthusiastic amateur, runs rings round the celebrated Gévrol of the Sûreté. He particularly excels in his astonishing knack of making all manner of deductions from the briefest examination of the scene of a crime, an accomplishment which is communicated to young Lecoq and which the latter himself demonstrates in subsequent novels.

Tabaret inspects the scene of Widow Lerouge's murder, and immediately describes the assassin as 'a young man, a little above the middle height, elegantly dressed. He wore on that evening a high hat. He carried an umbrella, and smoked a trabucos with a cigar-holder'. Then, unlike some of fiction's most illustrious sleuths, he gives a full explanation of what led him to these conclusions. The tremendous popularity of Gaboriau's novels, with a readership which reputedly included Bismarck, inspired many imitators whose names were quickly forgotten. Some built and improved upon Gaboriau's techniques to establish even greater reputations for themselves, but to Gaboriau must go the credit for giving real impetus to the *roman policier* and the principles of deductive reasoning.

Lecoq takes the principal role, as its title implies, in *Monsieur Lecoq* (1869), published in translation as

Gaboriau, Emile
Monsieur Lecoq
New York: Munro, 1879

and in two volumes in London as *Lecoq the detective* (Vizetelly, 1884). It is generally accepted that Lecoq was directly inspired by Auguste Dupin, the detective created by Edgar Allan Poe, and that he also had a dash of Vidocq of the Sûreté. Nevertheless his use of logical deduction was something quite revolutionary in detective fiction, and he preceded Sherlock Holmes in his ability to construct a mental picture of a criminal by the examination of a few small clues which lesser mortals would fail even to notice.

There is little to choose between the various novels featuring Lecoq. All display his fantastic powers, which captured the public imagination on both sides of the English Channel until he was overshadowed by Sherlock Holmes. The critics' choice is probably *Le crime d'Orcival* (1867), which appeared in translation as

Gaboriau, Emile
The mystery of Orcival
New York: Holt & Williams, 1871; Vizetelly, 1884
and begins with the discovery of a woman's body by two poach-
ers. They are trespassing on the estate of the Count de Trémorel,
and it soon appears that the Count's chateau holds the key to
the mystery. A man is accused of the murder – wrongly, thinks
Lecoq – and the Count himself has disappeared. Lecoq, sucking
his inexhaustible supply of lozenges, propounds a solution and
explains exactly how each clue provides a piece of the jigsaw,
decidedly setting the pattern for hundreds of detective novelists
to come.

Two more important books published between the ages of Poe
and Conan Doyle warrant mention here. Strangely enough, one
was by a New Zealander and set in Australia, whereas the other
was American.

Among the many works of Fergus Hume (1859–1932) must be
singled out

Hume, Fergus W.
The mystery of a hansom cab: a story of Melbourne social
life
Melbourne: Kemp & Boyce, 1886; Hansom Cab Publishing
Company, 1887; New York: Munro, 1888

It seems incredible that this is probably the biggest bestseller in
the history of detective fiction, as today it is scarcely remembered. The author too is a name which will be unfamiliar to many
modern readers, in spite of the fact that he wrote well over a
hundred books. Although its literary style is less attractive than
many works of the period, it is in many respects representative of
early detective fiction, and its enormous success must give it a
place in a list of detective cornerstones. Its starting-point is
unusual – a man is found in a hansom cab in Melbourne, dead
from chloroform poisoning. Samuel Gorby, detective of
Melbourne City Police, investigates. One of the reasons for the
book's popularity in Britain is almost certainly its overseas setting, and its portrayal of Melbourne life high and low. We see the
city's leisured classes, but the detective must also follow trails
through the Chinese slum quarters. The latter is a clear indication
that Gaboriau influenced Hume.

Finally, the silence in the USA which surprisingly followed the
master works of Edgar Allan Poe was eventually broken – and

uniquely so, for it saw the entry of a woman into the field. Anna Katharine Green (1846–1935) produced one work of special distinction among her various detective novels, namely

Green, Anna Katharine
The Leavenworth case, a lawyer's story
New York: Putnam, 1878; Routledge, 1884

In spite of some stilted writing, it is an extremely important work. Ebenezer Gryce is a credible character of the period, 'a portly, comfortable personage'. We also see many of the features which were to become almost standard practice as new writers emerged, including the body in the library and a diagram of the murder scene. It set the tone for a multitude of successors, and is by no means unenjoyable in its own right.

By this time the stage was set for the emergence of a truly great detective, a major figure whose name was to become synonymous with the genre itself. And then, by contrast with the very erratic development since the initiative taken by Poe, the floodgates were to open.

3

THE GREAT DETECTIVE

It would be superfluous indeed to describe here in detail the Sherlock Holmes stories of Arthur Conan Doyle (1859–1930). Their background and plots have been more than adequately covered elsewhere. The incredible mental faculties of Holmes, his lifestyle and idiosyncrasies, and his exploits accompanied by friend and chronicler Dr John H. Watson are already known to thousands of readers. Successive generations since 1887 have followed his adventures, and it would be no exaggeration to state that 221B Baker Street is to the foreign visitor as familiar an address as 10 Downing Street.

Furthermore, the enquiring reader may be referred to Conan Doyle himself, who in *Memories and adventures* (Hodder & Stoughton, 1924; Boston: Little, Brown, 1924) not only acknowledges his debt to Gaboriau and Poe but describes how he modelled Holmes upon Dr Joseph Bell of Edinburgh.

Here, therefore, the emphasis will be bibliographical, and the earliest significant reference is the first appearance of Holmes in *A study in scarlet*, in *Beeton's Christmas annual* for 1887. The first edition in book form followed soon afterwards. The success of

Doyle, A. Conan
A study in scarlet
Ward, Lock, 1888; Philadelphia: Lippincott, 1890
resulted, strangely enough, in an American publication launching the next Holmes novel. *Lippincott's magazine*, in February 1890, began publication of *The sign of the four* but there was little delay before it was made available to British readers in book form. The

second definite article was eliminated from the title, and since publication of

Doyle, A. Conan
The sign of four
Spencer Blackett, 1890; Philadelphia: Lippincott, 1893
the title has remained in its later form.

By this time Holmes had captured the public imagination, and George Newnes of the new *Strand magazine* made the shrewd move of securing Conan Doyle's services. Doyle was commissioned to write a series of Sherlock Holmes short stories, the first of which appeared in the *Strand* of July 1891. Further stories followed, and Holmes can be truly said to have come into his own. Most devotees consider that the short stories were infinitely superior to the novels, as the particular skills of Holmes are better suited to the format; although Holmes can be a man of action when the situation demands, his gifts are primarily cerebral and his activities in the novels are supplemented by incidents, changes of scene and flashbacks which sometimes amount to little more than padding.

Following publication in the *Strand*, the first collection of short stories appeared as

Doyle, A. Conan
The adventures of Sherlock Holmes
George Newnes, 1892; New York: Harper, 1892
The public clamoured for more, and in December 1892 the *Strand* began a new series of adventures which in turn were collectively published as

Doyle, A. Conan
The memoirs of Sherlock Holmes
George Newnes, 1894; New York: Harper, 1894
but the last story in this series, *The final problem*, came to be regarded as almost a national disaster. 'It is with a heavy heart,' writes Dr Watson, 'that I take up my pen to write these last words in which I shall ever record the singular gifts by which my friend Mr Sherlock Holmes was distinguished.' The story concludes with the struggle above the Reichenbach Falls between Holmes and his arch-enemy Moriarty, when both men plunge to their death. The country – indeed the world – was stunned.

The return of Holmes was vociferously demanded, but Conan Doyle had tired of him and was unyielding. He resolved to concentrate on other literature; but by 1901 public opinion began to have its effect, and August of that year saw the serialisation in the *Strand* of *The hound of the Baskervilles*.

Doyle, A. Conan
The hound of the Baskervilles
George Newnes, 1902; New York: McClure, 1902

was but a small concession to the national appetite, for its text clearly stamps it as a posthumous adventure of Holmes. It is generally regarded as the best of the novels, and is certainly the most familiar. This fresh exploit of the great detective led to renewed demands for more, and Conan Doyle capitulated in October 1903 with the first in a new series of *Strand* short stories. Collected as

Doyle, A. Conan
The return of Sherlock Holmes
George Newnes, 1905; New York: McClure, 1905

they begin with the resurrection of Holmes by a neat piece of author's licence. The volume contains stories which, even if they lack the quality of the earliest stories, still show much of the old flair.

The novel *The valley of fear*, serialized in the *Strand* from September 1914 to May 1915, was published in volume form but

Doyle, A. Conan
The valley of fear
New York: Doran, 1914; Smith, Elder, 1915

has perhaps been less successful than the other Holmes adventures. At least it did not represent a rather dull end to a sparkling career, because it was followed by two more volumes of short stories.

Doyle, A. Conan
His last bow
John Murray, 1917; New York: Doran, 1917

contained one story that had appeared in the *Strand* as early as January 1893 (*The adventure of the cardboard box*) and others that had appeared intermittently from September 1908 to September 1917, and

Doyle, A. Conan
The case-book of Sherlock Holmes
John Murray, 1927; New York: Doran, 1927

contained stories published intermittently in the *Strand* from October 1921 to April 1927.

To remark that Sherlock Holmes has retained his popularity for a century would be an understatement. Indeed, he is a national institution. The accolade is reflected in the fact that every Holmes adventure is still in print. No discriminating reader of detective fiction can afford to be without *Sherlock Holmes: complete short stories*, containing all fifty-six of these perfect examples of the storyteller's art, which with *Sherlock Holmes: complete long stories* comprises the entire Holmes canon. These standard volumes, first published by John Murray in 1928, have remained available. Since the Conan Doyle copyright expired in 1980, various other publishers have produced comprehensive collections.

It is perhaps strange to mention here a contemporary of Arthur Conan Doyle, Robert Louis Stevenson (1850–94). He is certainly not regarded as a writer of detective stories, although a moment's consideration will show that many of his novels embodied the elements of mystery, crime and suspense. He sometimes collaborated with his stepson Lloyd Osbourne (1868–1947), as in

Stevenson, Robert Louis and **Osbourne, Lloyd**
The wrecker
Cassell, 1892; New York: Scribner, 1892

which is often considered to be a detective story, but is in reality an adventure tale set in the wide open spaces of the Pacific. As is so often the case with Stevenson's sea tales, it contains much technical and nautical detail, and the central problem of whether the *Flying Scud* was wrecked or deliberately beached is a detective problem obscured by such details and the picaresque nature of Stevenson's writing. The atmosphere of the sea and the air of mystery and romance are more significant than any scientific deductive process necessary to solve the crimes – and there are many crimes, ranging from smuggling and sabotage to murder and fraud. Its inadequacies as a detective story were of little concern to Stevenson, as witness the following much-quoted statement in the book's epilogue:

> We had long been at once attracted and repelled by that
> very modern form of the police novel or mystery story,
> which consists in beginning your yarn anywhere but at the
> beginning, and finishing it anywhere but at the end;
> attracted by its peculiar interest when done, and the peculiar
> difficulties that attend its execution; repelled by that
> appearance of insincerity and shallowness of tone, which
> seems its inevitable drawback. For the mind of the reader,
> always bent to pick up clues, receives no impression of
> reality or life, rather of an airless, elaborate mechanism;

and the book remains enthralling, but insignificant, like a game of chess, not a work of human art.

These arguments have now become familiar, used many years later by the advocates of the modern crime novel as opposed to the classic detective story. In Stevenson's case it amounted almost to heresy, hardly calculated to reach a sympathetic audience when the reading public was feasting upon a diet of Sherlock Holmes.

Such was the impact of Holmes, and of course the lucrative nature of the stories, that he was bound to inspire countless imitators rather than detractors. Not only did other authors follow Conan Doyle's lead and create 'great detectives' of their own, but some added spice to the movement by giving their creations unique characteristics which set them apart from the Holmes bandwagon. They may be described as the rivals of Sherlock Holmes, and it is regrettable that so many of them remained in the shadow of the master and are now long forgotten. Hugh Greene coined the phrase as the title of his anthology *The rivals of Sherlock Holmes* (Bodley Head, 1970; New York: Pantheon, 1970) and performed a great service by bringing some of these gems of the past to the attention of modern readers. Such was the response that *More rivals of Sherlock Holmes* (Bodley Head, 1971), *Crooked counties* (Bodley Head, 1973) and *The American rivals of Sherlock Holmes* (Bodley Head, 1976; New York: Pantheon, 1976) followed. It should be noted that in New York *More rivals . . .* was entitled *Cosmopolitan crimes* (Pantheon, 1971) and *Crooked counties* was entitled *Further rivals of Sherlock Holmes* (Pantheon, 1973).

One of the most accomplished contemporaries of Conan Doyle was Arthur Morrison (1863-1945), who is best known today for

Morrison, Arthur
Martin Hewitt, investigator
Ward, Lock, 1894; New York: Harper, 1894

in addition to his stories of London low life such as *Tales of mean streets* and *The hole in the wall*. In Martin Hewitt he created a noteworthy rival of Sherlock Holmes, and the first volume was followed by

Morrison, Arthur
Chronicles of Martin Hewitt
Ward, Lock, 1895; New York: Appleton, 1896

and

Morrison, Arthur
Adventures of Martin Hewitt
Ward, Lock, 1896

Many writers of the period deliberately set out to make their detectives as unlike Holmes as possible, and Hewitt is in many respects a commonplace chap whose idiosyncrasies do not – as sometimes happens with Holmes – obtrude upon the stories.

Hewitt, like Holmes, made his first appearance in the *Strand magazine*, and has the occasional flash of intellectual brilliance equalling that of his illustrious contemporary. All in all, however, we see Hewitt as considerably less than omniscient, and are thus able to devote more attention to Morrison's ingenious plots, his characteristic London atmosphere, and his glimpses of many aspects of Victorian life.

Conan Doyle's brother in law, E. W. Hornung (1866–1921), created a memorable character in

Hornung, E. W.
The amateur cracksman
Methuen, 1899; New York: Scribner, 1899

which in later editions appeared as *Raffles, the amateur cracksman*. A. J. Raffles was not the first gentleman crook in fiction, but together with his contemporary Arsène Lupin he remains the best known. It was unusual for British readers of the time to identify and sympathize with a central character who makes his living by means of burglary; but Raffles has his redeeming features – his sense of fair play, his mastery of the game of cricket both literally and metaphorically. Then of course there is the faithful Bunny, who takes the part of the reader on occasions and attempts to persuade Raffles to return to the straight and narrow path. Unfortunately, in the process Bunny finds himself more deeply involved in his master's burglarious activities.

Raffles is a romantic character, combining the high life of fashionable London society with the thrill of the chase brought about by his less sociable pursuits. In some of the stories he assumes the detective role, but normally it is as the antidetective that he appears, showing him as an amiable rogue rather than a complete villain. His love of country shines through the stories, which were collected in several volumes.

Raffles was not the only roguish hero of the time. There was more than a little dishonesty in the makeup of Romney Pringle, whose exploits were recorded by R. Austin Freeman (1862-1943) at the outset of his literary career. Adopting the pseudonym 'Clifford Ashdown' he produced

Ashdown, Clifford
The adventures of Romney Pringle
Ward, Lock, 1902; Philadelphia: Oswald Train, 1968
with the collaboration of J. J. Pitcairn, a prison doctor. These short stories originally appeared in *Cassell's magazine* during 1902, as did a second series in 1903 which did not appear in volume form until much later (*The further adventures of Romney Pringle*, Philadelphia: Oswald Train, 1970).

Mr Pringle is ostensibly a literary agent, and is a clean-cut character 'whose complexion . . . was of that fairness which imparts to its fortunate possessor the air of youth until long past forty; especially in a man who shaves clean, and habitually goes to bed before two in the morning.' In other words, he is in direct contrast with the drug-taking insomniac Holmes. Although, like Holmes, he is a master of disguise, Mr Pringle differs again from the sage of Baker Street in that he is no professional detective. Rather is he someone with an unfortunate knack of getting involved in other people's misfortunes, and he frequently turns them to his own pecuniary advantage. Pringle is a likeable rascal, who lives by his wits and lines his pockets at the expense of the real villains.

Freeman later dropped the Ashdown pseudonym, and was in fact not happy with his Romney Pringle stories. Using his own name he wrote

Freeman, R. Austin
The red thumb mark
Collingwood, 1907; New York: Newton, 1911
and introduced his most celebrated character, Dr John Thorndyke. A detective novel without a murder is a comparatively rare phenomenon, but several examples have found places as cornerstones in the history of the genre. This is one of them, and the absence of a corpse makes it no less enthralling. Diamonds are stolen from a safe, and a thumbprint in blood is found nearby. Moreover, the thumbprint is identified and a man is charged. But Dr Thorndyke, probably the most famous medico-scientific detective in fiction, thrives on lost causes. Such an open-and-shut case, with the new technique of fingerprinting on the side of the prosecution, is just the sort of challenge Thorndyke relishes. He is assisted by Polton and Jervis, subsequently his companions in numerous cases, in tackling the major question which remains

unanswered until the final stages of the trial – is it possible to forge a thumbprint?

Dr Thorndyke became particularly effective in the short story form, most of which were collected in

Freeman, R. Austin
The famous cases of Dr Thorndyke
Hodder & Stoughton, 1929

and, in the USA, *The Dr Thorndyke omnibus* (New York: Dodd, Mead, 1932). The stories often turn on small points and clues which are unravelled by Thorndyke's razor-sharp brain and his medical, forensic or scientific skills. Some are straightforward whodunits, while others are inverted stories, with Thorndyke exposing a criminal already known to the reader.

The creator of the Scarlet Pimpernel, Baroness Orczy (1865-1947), also produced some very acceptable detective fiction, and in

Orczy, Baroness
The case of Miss Elliott
T. Fisher Unwin, 1905

she presented a character who, physically at least, derived nothing whatsoever from Sherlock Holmes. The old man in the corner is birdlike, with watery eyes, spectacles, and bony fingers tying knots in pieces of string. He is always to be found in his seat in the ABC tea shop. Thus he is one of the first 'armchair detectives' of fiction, in that he solves his cases by pure process of thought and scarcely ever moves from his seat. The stories are narrated by a young journalist, Polly Burton, who sits entranced as her acquaintance sifts the newspapers for crimes and arrives at their solutions in little more than the time taken to consume his inevitable cheesecake. The stories are skilfully contrived, eminently readable, and contain little extraneous matter.

The case of Miss Elliott was the first volume of Old Man stories to be published, although some had appeared earlier in *The royal magazine* and were collected subsequently as

Orczy, Baroness
The old man in the corner . . . Illustrated by H. M. Brock
Greening, 1909

which was published in New York as *The man in the corner* (Dodd, Mead, 1909).

Another original detective created by Baroness Orczy is Patrick Mulligan. 'Fat and rosy and comfortable as an Irish pig', Mulligan is a lawyer who in

Orczy, Baroness
Skin o' my tooth: his memoirs, by his confidential clerk
Hodder & Stoughton, 1928; New York: Doubleday, Doran,
1928

uses his exceptional gifts of acumen and intuition to extricate his clients from the various messes into which they have tumbled. His sobriquet is believed by his clerk, Mullins, to have been bestowed by one such client who was acquitted by the skin of his teeth, and in this volume Mullins narrates twelve of his chief's celebrated cases. Although not a well-known book today, the stories are neatly plotted and enjoyable.

Robert Barr (1850–1912) was a prolific writer whose best work in the detective field was

Barr, Robert
The triumphs of Eugène Valmont
Hurst & Blackett, 1906; New York: Appleton, 1906

It has been suggested that Valmont, a French detective operating in London, was the model for Agatha Christie's Belgian maestro Hercule Poirot, and whether or not this is true they are decidedly of a type. Valmont is depicted as vain, pompous, and of course comic, and the official policeman, as personified by Spenser Hale, is a fallible being qualified to be no more than Valmont's confidant. It may be that Barr was merely setting out to be humorous, but equally he might have deliberately intended to satirize Anglo-French differences. Even if deep study of these stories is less than profitable, they provide sound plots of considerable ingenuity. Some of them, particularly *The absent-minded coterie*, are *tours de force* which have found their place in detective anthologies.

Among the victims of the *Titanic* disaster was a man of thirty-seven named Jacques Futrelle (1875–1912), an American whose life was cut short at a time when he was regarded as one of detective fiction's white hopes. His fame was founded, and remains firmly based, upon his sheer ingenuity and his creation of one of the most original characters in the field. Professor Augustus S. F. X. Van Dusen appeared in

Futrelle, Jacques
The thinking machine
New York: Dodd, Mead, 1907; Chapman & Hall, 1907

These stories demonstrate the tremendous brainpower of this man whose academic brilliance – he has degrees from half the world's universities – is matched by an enviable intellect. Logic, he insists, will solve any problem. In *The problem of cell 13* he wagers that he will escape from a closely guarded prison merely by using his mind, and in subsequent stories he cuts through the evidence in various criminal cases by the application of sheer logic.

Futrelle, Jacques
The thinking machine on the case
New York: Appleton, 1908

was the second volume, called *The professor on the case* for the British edition and published as Nelson's Library no. 62 (Nelson, 1909). In it we are reminded of how he received his nickname, when he defeats a Russian chess master after merely learning the rudiments of the game. 'You are a brain – a machine – a thinking machine', says the Russian. The professor's grotesque appearance, with his enormous head invariably wearing a 'number eight hat', makes him a memorable character physically, but his brain is the main feature of these stories. He is faced with some of the most unusual cases to be devised by any author. One can instance *The superfluous finger*, which opens with a visit to an eminent surgeon by a beautiful woman. 'The forefinger,' she explains calmly. 'I should like to have it amputated at the first joint, please.' And so another case occupies the professor's mind.

The rivals of Sherlock Holmes were created predominantly by British writers, but the Gallic equivalent of Hornung's Raffles was the brainchild of Maurice Leblanc (1864–1941). In the volume of stories called

Leblanc, Maurice
The seven of hearts . . . Translated by A. Teixera de
Mattos, with illustrations by Cyrus Cuneo
Cassell, 1908

which is also entitled *The exploits of Arsène Lupin* (New York: Harper, 1907; Cassell, 1909), the hero is shown in roughly the same light as Raffles. He is a thief, but basically a decent enough fellow. He also champions the underdog and ladies in distress, and spends a considerable amount of time running rings around the English detective Holmlock Shears (note the family likeness). Although in later books Lupin often assumes the role of amateur detective, it is in the earlier stories as the gentleman burglar, the master of disguise, that he is at his most entertaining. To enlist the reader's sympathy and association, he bites the biter or exercises his villainy on the more obnoxious members of society, providing an enduring form of sheer escapism.

A compatriot and contemporary of Maurice Leblanc, although writing in a different vein, Gaston Leroux (1868–1927) was a journalist whose occupation enabled him to acquire considerable experience of courtroom procedure. He made good use of this, and the drama generated during a murder trial, in the one detective novel for which he is remembered.

Leroux, Gaston
The mystery of the yellow room
Daily Mail, 1908; New York: Brentano, 1908
contained devices which have been used by scores of subsequent writers, namely the 'locked room' murder and the 'least likely person' exposed in the final pages. Most authorities claim that Leroux was greatly influenced by an earlier novel, *The big bow mystery* by Israel Zangwill (Henry, 1892; Chicago: Rand McNally, 1895), although the deductive element in which the reader can participate is much more evident in Leroux's work. As a locked room puzzle it was admired by John Dickson Carr, himself the absolute master of the technique.

The detective Joseph Rouletabille is a young and precocious journalist, whose name has been assured of a place in the annals of crime fiction by his performance in this one case. In contrast with many books of the period, *The mystery of the yellow room* remains highly readable, if one overlooks the emphasis on coincidence and the many examples of improbability. Neither of these traits can be ruled totally out of court in the classic detective novel, as opposed to the realistic crime story.

One can not get further from Sherlock Holmes than Father Brown, the classic character created by G. K. Chesterton (1874–1936). He made his first appearance in

Chesterton, G. K.
The innocence of Father Brown
Cassell, 1911; New York: John Lane, 1911
and is still very much with us today, the little priest from Essex with 'face as round as a Norfolk dumpling' and 'eyes as empty as the North Sea'. The sheer cleverness of these small masterpieces of detection is enhanced by Chesterton's brilliant use of words, his characterization, and his thesis that the commonplace can be startling because it is so often overlooked. As examples of the latter, *The invisible man* and *The queer feet* have deservedly become classics of the genre. If some of the stories are sermons, they are still the most enjoyable sermons ever delivered.

Following his initial success, Father Brown reappeared in *The wisdom of Father Brown* (Cassell, 1914; New York: John Lane, 1915), *The incredulity of Father Brown* (Cassell, 1926; New York: Dodd, Mead, 1926), *The secret of Father Brown* (Cassell, 1927; New York: Harper, 1927) and *The scandal of Father Brown* (Cassell, 1935; New York: Dodd, Mead, 1935). The first four volumes were collected together in

Chesterton, G. K.
The Father Brown stories
Cassell, 1929

Later editions of this contain all five Father Brown volumes, as does *The Father Brown omnibus* (New York: Dodd, Mead, 1935).

All too often writers have descended to sheer gimmickry in order to make their detectives stand out from the others. Ernest Bramah (1868–1942) had a brilliant idea rather than a gimmick. The detective in

Bramah, Ernest
Max Carrados
Methuen, 1914; Westport, Connecticut: Hyperion, 1975

is blind, but his blindness has heightened his other senses, and thus it is an integral factor in the stories which Bramah contrived. This puts the detective on a somewhat different level from the reader and is perhaps a little unfair, but the stories are nonetheless enjoyable. The three volumes of Carrados cases, in which he is accompanied by an unusually sensible assistant called Louis Carlyle, comprise a mixture of crimes from robbery to murder, kidnapping and sabotage. All the stories are worth reading, being competently written with a lightness of touch as well as meticulously plotted. The two subsequent volumes,

Bramah, Ernest
The eyes of Max Carrados
Grant Richards, 1923; New York: Doran, 1924

and

Bramah, Ernest
Max Carrados mysteries
Hodder & Stoughton, 1927; Baltimore: Penguin, 1964

each contain examples of the sort of thing which has placed Bramah among the greats of detective fiction.

The history of crime fiction is bestrewn with the names of authors who, once popular, are now completely forgotten. Many of them deserved this fate, and a reappraisal of their work today will serve only to make their original popularity unaccountable. There are mixed opinions regarding Arthur B. Reeve (1880–1936), who sprang to fame with his tales of Craig Kennedy and particularly

Reeve, Arthur B.
The silent bullet
New York: Dodd, Mead, 1912

which appeared in London as *The black hand* (Eveleigh Nash, 1912). His large following is undeniable, and some may find it incredible. It was assisted by his activities in the field of silent movies, for which he wrote melodramatic serials with titles such as *The exploits of Elaine*. His name must appear in any representative list of detective fiction, however, as the creator of one of the earliest scientific detectives. White-coated Craig Kennedy alternates between the laboratory and the field of action, in a series of adventures which reflect Reeve's passable narrative ability and a whole succession of ingenious scientific devices. Many of the latter were novel in their day, but soon became either commonplace or else discredited figments of the writer's imagination. Perhaps this is the principal reason why Reeve, at one time the foremost American crime writer, sank later into oblivion.

And finally, although he did not appear until 1918, one must not fail to include Uncle Abner as a prominent rival of Sherlock Holmes. One of the few American exponents at this time, Melville Davisson Post (1871-1930) made his supreme contribution with

Post, Melville Davisson
Uncle Abner, master of mysteries
New York: Appleton, 1918; Tom Stacey, 1972

There is something of the Old Testament prophet in Abner, the West Virginia squire whose exposure of evildoers is recounted in stories which have been described as the best since Poe. These tales appeared in magazines before publication in book form, and were roughly contemporaneous with Chesterton's Father Brown. Uncle Abner, accompanied by his nephew and Squire Randolph, encounter evil in many forms. Abner has the capacity to see it in men's souls, and woe betide them when he does.

These are not simply stories of a ranting, hellfire and damnation character. The points which bring a murderer to justice or to meet his maker are often small, but they are devilishly ingenious in the hands of Abner. The fertile imagination of Melville Davisson Post, together with his mastery of the short story format, combine to make Uncle Abner unforgettable.

4

THE TRADITIONAL TWENTIES

The development of detective fiction tends to be categorized by its historians into neatly defined periods. Howard Haycraft in *Murder for pleasure* described the period from Sherlock Holmes to the first world war as 'the romantic era', and 1918 to 1930 as 'the golden age'. Everything following that, to Haycraft writing in 1941, was modern. Julian Symons in *Bloody murder*, thirty years later, could identify a new perspective by placing the rivals of Holmes in the 'first golden age' and labelling a 'second golden age' as that embracing the 1920s and 1930s. Various authors began to break away from the traditional pattern in the 1930s, both in terms of form (Francis Iles *et al.*) and of content (Hammett and the hard-boiled school). They are still, in Julian Symons's treatment of the subject, within the 'second golden age', and the moderns date from the second world war.

No-one has denied, however, that considerable overlaps occurred between these various eras. In the golden 1930s – golden at least as far as crime fiction was concerned – there were omniscient sleuths of the Holmes variety and authors who in style were years ahead of their time. Today, when the cosy detective story has been smothered by a superfluity of sex and violence, there remain some highly active writers of the classic school.

One thing is certain. In the confused history of crime fiction, the 1920s were almost completely traditional.

Edgar Wallace (1875–1932) was very much a writer of the

1920s, although his first crime novel appeared much earlier. When first published

Wallace, Edgar

The four just men

Tallis Press, 1905; Boston: Small, Maynard, 1920

was incomplete. The solution to the 'locked room' murder mystery only appeared after 1905, whereas the first edition contained a tear-out form offering £500 in prizes to the most accurate solutions furnished by readers. It was a clever idea, but was not in the event to Wallace's financial benefit.

The four just men, as by now is well known, are idealists who murder in cases where the law is unable to act, and where despots and tyrants would otherwise go free. Thus they have the reader's sympathy from the beginning. This, the incredible Edgar Wallace's debut in the field in which he was to become a household name, culminates in the seemingly impossible murder of the Foreign Secretary behind closed doors, with half the Metropolitan Police keeping watch.

What was the secret of Wallace's popularity? Perhaps one of his best-known works,

Wallace, Edgar

The crimson circle

Hodder & Stoughton, 1922; New York: Doubleday,

Doran, 1929

provides the answer. He was a craftsman storyteller, completely without literary pretensions, who gave an easy read untaxing of the intellect. Many of his books followed set patterns, and were thrillers rather than detective stories. There is, however, rather more of the detective element in this case, where we follow the police on the track of a master criminal and multiple murderer. His subordinates obey him without question, or die; his victims pay with their money or their lives. He seems unassailable – but Inspector Parr and the 'psychometrical' Derrick Yale know his identity, and all is revealed in the final few pages.

So many detectives and heroic characters dash through the pages of Wallace's work, most of them faceless and wooden, that his memorable Mr Reeder comes as a welcome surprise. In

Wallace, Edgar

The mind of Mr J. G. Reeder

Hodder & Stoughton, 1925

which was published in New York as *The murder book of J. G.*

Reeder (Doubleday, Doran, 1929), we are introduced to this unassuming man who works for the Public Prosecutor. He is a gem of a character, Victorian in appearance and manners, with his side-whiskers and pince-nez and his umbrella which is never unfurled. He also has his catchphrase, 'I have a criminal mind', and the stories demonstrate his skill at recognizing evil when it is at hand. One can go so far as to state that this collection of eight stories, polished and neatly plotted, represents Wallace's supreme contribution to the field of detection as opposed to action thrillers.

Another writer popular during the 1920s, who like Wallace began much earlier, was Mary Roberts Rinehart (1876–1958). Her books spanned several decades. In

Rinehart, Mary Roberts
The circular staircase
Indianapolis: Bobbs-Merrill, 1908; Cassell, 1909

a middle-aged spinster rents a furnished house for the summer, its imposing proportions and eerie atmosphere dominated by a rather mysterious circular staircase. It is not long before our heroine is plagued by uninvited nocturnal visitors, one of whom is murdered. From this point on, the narrator plunges headlong into the adventure in true Rinehart tradition. Although it retains a quality of readability, this book also demonstrates such faults as the excessive use of coincidence and the withholding of important clues from the official detective.

'Had I but known how important this was, four lives could have been saved' is the sort of statement which occurs frequently in her works and in those of her imitators. In fact they became known as the 'Had I but known' school. But, in spite of the scorn of the critics, there is no pretentiousness about Mary Roberts Rinehart and her melodramas; one must admit she tells a good story, meticulously plotted, and moreover it is all great fun. From 1930 she produced her best and more complex work, beginning with

Rinehart, Mary Roberts
The door
New York: Farrar & Rinehart, 1930; Hodder & Stoughton, 1930

This is a satisfying mystery, far more than a simple 'HIBK' tale of danger and suspense. Its well-drawn cast of characters, relatives and dependants of Miss Elizabeth Jane Bell, encounter numerous crimes, including three murders.

A work which is almost as familiar today as in the 1920s is

Bentley, E. C.
Trent's last case
Nelson, 1913
which was published in New York as *The woman in black* (Century, 1913). Strangely enough, Bentley (1875-1956) wrote no detective fiction in the 1920s, and this particular novel was originally intended, as its title implies, to be the only appearance of Philip Trent.

The murder of tycoon Sigsbee Manderson is the sort of event which provides ample newspaper copy, although it is soon obvious that not everyone mourns his passing. Bentley deliberately set out to write a detective novel with a difference, breaking with tradition in several respects by revealing some of the genre's weaknesses. His use of humour, his love interest and, to cap it all, the detective proving all too fallible, are features contrary to the conventions of detective fiction accepted at the time. And Philip Trent, artist and journalist, is less than a great detective in the Holmes tradition. Possibly to Bentley's surprise, he had written what turned out to be a bestseller. He later revived Trent, but with little of the flair shown in the original.

E. C. Bentley's master work was in the flavour of the 1920s, although written earlier; and the same can be said of the novels of A. E. W. Mason (1865-1948). His famous book,

Mason, A. E. W.
At the Villa Rose
Hodder & Stoughton, 1910; New York: Scribner, 1910
concerns the murder of a wealthy widow at Aix-les-Bains, and introduces one of the indisputably great fictional detectives, Inspector Hanaud of the Paris Sûreté. Like Holmes he has his Watson, the elderly Mr Ricardo, whose knowledge of food and wine is matched only by his inability to fathom the various clues as he follows the detective around. It is a period piece, and displays the classic form as Hanaud skilfully picks his way through pieces of evidence and false trails. One of his more irritating habits is his failure to explain the significance of the clues as he finds them, so we are left in the dark until he finally springs the solution. After the revelation of the murderer's identity there are several chapters of flashback showing how the crime was planned and committed, which modern readers might find somewhat flat.

The second Hanaud novel

Mason, A. E. W.
The house of the arrow
Hodder & Stoughton, 1924; New York: Doran, 1924
was published fourteen years after the first, and many critics have judged it to be better. It shows Mason to be a serious novelist who is interested in communicating the fine gradations of the human character, more than merely presenting a puzzle and its solution. Solicitor Jim Frobisher receives a letter from a rich woman's brother-in-law, demanding an advance on her will. The woman dies and her niece is arrested. Back to the south, to Dijon this time, hurries Inspector Hanaud to investigate the mystery. The big man is likened to a St Bernard dog, but he is nevertheless one of the sharpest policemen in fiction, and his cases are always triumphs of deductive reasoning.

The world of crime fiction has produced several writers who, for various reasons, may be described as remarkable. One such is J. S. Fletcher (1863–1935), whose fame dates from

Fletcher, J. S.
The Middle Temple murder
Ward, Lock, 1919; New York: Knopf, 1919
It was praised by President Woodrow Wilson, and established a vogue for Fletcher's books in the USA as well as in his native England. From the moment journalist Frank Spargo is involved in the discovery of a body in Middle Temple Lane, the pace is faster than most detective novels of the period and the atmosphere of London is well conveyed. Although he carefully depicted the English country scene with a love of the open spaces befitting a Yorkshireman, it is for his London novels that Fletcher is remembered. A case in point is

Fletcher, J. S.
The Charing Cross mystery
Herbert Jenkins, 1923; New York: Putnam, 1923
When Hetherwick, a young barrister, catches the last train at Sloane Square, he is unaware that within a few minutes he will be playing detective. At St James's Park two men board the train, and by the time it reaches Charing Cross one of them has died. It is a nicely contrived mystery, with the feel of London.

Fletcher has been described as remarkable because for a period he was one of the best-known and most prolific authors in the field on both sides of the Atlantic. Yet he is virtually unknown today. He exercised a great influence on the popularization of detective fiction, his main faults being his descent into melodrama on occasions and his frequently poor characterization. Nevertheless, he inspired others, who in turn were more accomplished; and for that at least he should be remembered.

Dr Reginald Fortune is another character who is not as familiar to present-day readers as he perhaps ought to be. It is a strange verdict on the twenty or so books in which he appeared, and which made H. C. Bailey (1878–1961) one of the top crime writers of the 1920s and 1930s. Admittedly Fortune – plumply cherubic, facetious, drawling – can be intensely irritating at times, but he nevertheless brings to the stories a freshness and a nice intuitiveness that few of the great detectives can match. H. C. Bailey was at his best in the short story form, the first volume in the series being

Bailey, H. C.
Call Mr Fortune
Methuen, 1920; New York: Dutton, 1921
which was followed by other collections of comparable standard.

An important landmark in the history of detective fiction,

Crofts, Freeman Wills
The cask
Collins, 1920; New York: Seltzer, 1924
was the first work of an author who established a reputation for solid, plodding, logical detection and an almost fanatical attention to detail. Freeman Wills Crofts (1879–1957) specialized in the unbreakable alibi, often based upon railway timetables. In his most famous book, the cask of the title is being unloaded after a voyage from Rouen to London. It should contain statuary, but instead contains gold sovereigns and a woman's hand. Not only that, but it disappears before the police arrive. The clues tell a story which alternates between France and England, and we follow two detectives – Inspector Burnley and George La Touche – on their painstaking paths through an unusually long story before the last piece of the puzzle fits into place.

The unsensational detective work typically displayed by Crofts might not be to every reader's liking. None of his plots can be described as racy or fast-moving, but

Crofts, Freeman Wills
The pit-prop syndicate
Collins, 1922; New York: Seltzer, 1925
combines the elements of the thriller and the detective novel

rather well. The activities of the syndicate, ostensibly shipping pit-props from France to England, are stumbled upon by two amateur detectives. Beyond suspecting that dirty work is afoot they know little else, but are determined to investigate. Murder follows, and the professional detective Inspector Willis takes over.

Crofts, Freeman Wills
Inspector French's greatest case
Collins, 1924; New York: Seltzer, 1925
marked the first appearance of the Scotland Yard man who was to become an institution. It opens with the discovery of a corpse near the rifled safe of a diamond merchant in London's Hatton Garden. French gets to work in a way which, for many years and many novels to follow, he was to make very much his own; meticulous, skilful, as neatly dovetailed as the railway timetables which were so often his stock-in-trade. Call them what you will, the French stories are undeniably the product of a brilliantly logical mind. One receives the impression that the work of a Scotland Yard man is singularly unexciting at times, and this somehow endows all the works of Crofts with the stamp of authenticity. Pedantic it may be, but the reader works side by side with French until the break comes and the loose ends are neatly tied up.

The 'inverted' technique was also used from time to time by Crofts. In his collection of twenty-three short stories entitled

Crofts, Freeman Wills
Murderers make mistakes
Hodder & Stoughton, 1947
there are twelve in which the criminal's actions are first described, and then French reveals how he learned the truth.

Milne, A. A.
The Red House mystery
Methuen, 1922; New York: Dutton, 1922
may be described as typical of the period rather than outstandingly accomplished, although it has subsequently appeared in many editions. A. A. Milne (1882–1956) attempts to be conventional – the country house party, the murder of the black sheep of the family, the amateur detective and his rather silly confidant. The ultimate revelation of the murderer hardly comes as a surprise, although the book has its clever touches. One can only define it as the 'Here's a murder, what fun!' school and in a

way wish that the author had stuck to Winnie the Pooh, but it is often quoted as a cornerstone of 1920s detective fiction.

Quick to follow in the footsteps of Freeman Wills Crofts was G. D. H. Cole (1889–1959), renowned as a Fabian economist. As a diversion Cole turned to detective fiction and produced

Cole, G. D. H.
The Brooklyn murders
Collins, 1923; New York: Seltzer, 1924

The last will and testament of theatre impresario Sir Vernon Brooklyn is the starting-point, and three deaths are clearly linked with the ultimate disposal of his fortune. The case is handled by Superintendent Wilson of Scotland Yard, who was to feature in many subsequent novels. Known as 'The Professor' in allusion to his scholarly habits and his pre-eminently intellectualist way of reasoning out the solutions to his cases, Wilson is an investigator of the Inspector French school. He does not appear, however, to get out of his room at the Yard to the same extent as most policemen in fiction; he prefers instead to let Inspector Blaikie do the legwork and much of the questioning of suspects, while Wilson himself sits and exercises his intellectual faculties upon all the reports which Blaikie provides. Following Wilson's debut, G. D. H. Cole embarked upon a succession of detective novels in collaboration with his wife Margaret (1893–1980), and probably the best of these is

Cole, G. D. H. and **Margaret**
The murder at Crome House
Collins, 1927; New York: Macmillan, 1927

The criticism levelled at the Coles is that, particularly by modern standards, their novels are dull. It is true that many passages consist of routine interviews with suspects, and that Superintendent Wilson then thoroughly sifts all the evidence and proceeds systematically towards discrediting the guilty party's alibi. Nevertheless, it must be appreciated that this type of detective fiction was a popular form in the 1920s and 1930s, and that the examples produced by the Coles – together of course with those of Crofts – were among the best of an extremely large bunch. They are well written, they hold the reader's interest for most of the time, and the detective puzzles are on occasions ingenious. Although the later output of the Coles became somewhat slapdash, the earlier stories are well worth reading.

The Crome House case is in fact a non-Wilson novel, with

rather more pace than other works by the Coles. Somewhat light-heartedly, it follows the adventures of university lecturer James Flint, an amateur detective who becomes involved in the murder of Sir Harry Wye. Sir Harry, described as a first-class old rip, follows tradition by being murdered in his library. The absence of a detective of the omniscient variety, together with the complications of the plot, are factors which make this novel stand out from others by the Cole partnership.

Another follower of Crofts, meticulous in plotting but often providing more action than his contemporaries, was Alister McAllister (1877–1943) writing as 'Lynn Brock'. His detective, Colonel Warwick Gore, pursued ingenious criminals in complex mysteries against well-drawn backgrounds, often with touches of the esoteric and the bizarre. Gore himself may be criticized for his verbosity and his occasional tendency to behave like the archetypal ex-military bore; but Brock was generally better at character presentation than other practitioners of the Crofts school, just as he was better at drawing a picture of the social scene and providing credible settings. Of special merit is

Brock, Lynn
Colonel Gore's third case: The kink
Collins, 1927; New York: Harper, 1927

which involves the theft of some letters and develops into a story of hereditary depravity, pornography and bizarre orgies. There is a murder mystery, but the book remains specially interesting for the fact that Brock was prepared to be sexually explicit for his time. It might seem tame by today's standards, but it was most adventurous on the part of a writer who refused to be tied completely by the conventions of the genre in the 1920s.

Unconventional in another way was the American authoress Frances Noyes Hart (1890–1943), who set her *tour de force*,

Hart, Frances Noyes
The Bellamy trial
New York: Doubleday, Doran, 1927; Heinemann, 1928

entirely within a courtroom. It is a day-by-day study of a murder trial, and widely regarded as one of the finest of its kind. The atmosphere is authentic and tense, never routine or monotonous, and it builds to an exciting climax. On trial are two Long Island socialites, Stephen Bellamy and Susan Ives, charged with the murder of Stephen's wife. The evidence appears to be against them, but in the hands of a good writer there is always room for doubt. Particularly effective is the manner in which the trial is presented through two contrasting journalists, a young woman on her first story and a more hard-bitten colleague.

Major Cecil Street (1884–1964) was a competent writer who produced, under the pseudonyms 'John Rhode' and 'Miles Burton', a succession of straightforward detective novels spanning three decades.

Rhode, John
The Paddington mystery
Bles, 1925

is listed here as a good introduction to his detective Dr Lancelot Priestley, together with the other characters who were to become regular stalwarts in Rhode's long list of conventional tales. Priestley is a mathematician, and employs pure scientific analysis rather than any flair for the intuitional approach. These novels might be considered humdrum, but they are dependable and solid, and few writers can claim to equal Rhode/Burton in the variations of ingenious murder methods he contrived over the years. Of his other works, the mass murder case

Rhode, John
The murders in Praed Street
Bles, 1928; New York: Dodd, Mead, 1928

can be singled out as one which deserves to survive.

Among the multitude of detective characters created in the 1920s and 1930s, some were sufficiently original for their names to be remembered over fifty years later. Others went further, becoming cult figures of timeless popularity. One such is Charlie Chan of the Honolulu Police, whose principal adventures were collected in

Biggers, Earl Derr
Celebrated cases of Charlie Chan
Indianapolis: Bobbs-Merrill, 1933; Cassell, 1933

One of the main reasons for Charlie's success is probably that at the time of his conception in the 1920s it was customary for fictional Chinese to be the villains, and new ground was broken when Earl Derr Biggers (1884–1933) introduced a Chinese detective. He was subsequently portrayed on radio and television, and in a host of movies and comics. The original stories themselves, rather contrived and looking a little like period pieces today, will nonetheless remain significant. They represented an important era in American crime fiction, and brought to a wide public the urbane Charlie and his mannerisms. The compendium volume, essential in any collection, comprises *The house without a key* (Indianapolis: Bobbs-Merrill, 1925; Harrap, 1926); *The Chinese parrot* (Indianapolis: Bobbs-Merrill, 1926; Harrap, 1927); *Behind that curtain* (Indianapolis: Bobbs-Merrill, 1928; Harrap, 1928); *The black camel* (Indianapolis: Bobbs-Merrill, 1929; Cassell, 1930); and *Charlie Chan carries on* (Indianapolis: Bobbs-Merrill, 1930; Cassell, 1931).

Van Dine, S. S.
The Benson murder case
New York: Scribner, 1926; Benn, 1926

was the first in a series of twelve novels featuring Philo Vance, one of the most famous amateur detectives of the 1920s. The author, alias art critic Willard Huntington Wright (1888–1939), set out to present problems in detection in which he followed a code of rules, every detail being carefully fitted into its place like a jigsaw puzzle. The Benson case concerns the murder of a wealthy New York stockbroker and *bon viveur*. The suspects are restricted in number, and Philo Vance smoothly proceeds to a very satisfactory solution. Vance himself, a dilettante with a penchant for intellectual one-upmanship and a pseudo-English manner of speaking, can be intensely irritating. Equally affected at times is the author's excessive use of footnotes to amplify the artistic or literary allusions to which Vance is so partial. Perhaps these helped to give the novels their special flavour. In any case they quickly became the best-known American detective fiction since Poe, and comparatively few writers have since been put in that category.

The second Philo Vance novel,

Van Dine, S. S.
The canary murder case
New York: Scribner, 1927; Benn, 1927

fully established the author's reputation and broke publishing records in the field of detective fiction. The canary of the title is Margaret Odell, star of Broadway, who gained the name after appearing in a follies ballet in a canary costume. Her scintillating rise to fame is cut short suddenly when she is strangled, in circumstances which bring Philo Vance into the case. He is, as usual, accompanied by John F.-X. Markham, District Attorney of New York, who is not the brightest of confidants but nonetheless habitually gets the kudos for solving the Vance cases. This novel shows the Van Dine style and ingenuity beginning to develop, and is a good example of 1920s detection.

There is little to choose between one Van Dine novel and another, except that his last two or three were markedly inferior. Possibly the best are

Van Dine, S. S.
The Greene murder case
New York: Scribner, 1928; Benn, 1928
in which Vance investigates several murders which occur in one ill-fated family, and

Van Dine, S. S.
The Bishop murder case
New York: Scribner, 1929; Cassell, 1929
with its terrifying series of murders connected with the old nursery rhyme, *Who killed Cock Robin?*

An underrated writer of the period was C.H.B. Kitchin (1895–1967), who wrote

Kitchin, C. H. B.
Death of my aunt
L. and V. Woolf, 1929; New York: Harcourt, Brace, 1930
Stockbroker Malcolm Warren is the obvious person to advise his moneyed aunt about her financial affairs, and he visits her for just that purpose. When she is poisoned, and it seems that the solution to the mystery is within the family circle, Malcolm finds himself playing the amateur detective. Although Kitchin was no innovator in the field, his books have a cosiness, a slightly light-hearted flavour, a thorough Englishness which critics have admired. What is more, his ideas were channelled into very few books, in contrast with many writers of the time who produced a flood of potboilers.

The Roger Sheringham novels by Anthony Berkeley (1893–1971) are urbanely witty and wickedly satirical. In

Berkeley, Anthony
The poisoned chocolates case
Collins, 1929; New York: Doubleday, Doran, 1929
we are presented with a mystery in a unique form. The six members of the Crimes Circle are gathered together to consider the murder of Mrs Joan Bendix, as recounted by Chief Inspector Moresby of Scotland Yard. Then, one by one, they give their solutions to the mystery. To devise six solutions in one detective novel, and to demolish them in turn, requires an unusual mind. A

rereading of Anthony Berkeley today will convince anyone that the history of crime fiction owes him a debt as a masterly practitioner and an innovator. It will also be seen in Chapter 9 that, as 'Francis Iles', he also paved the way for the modern crime novel.

One of Berkeley's most entertaining books is

Berkeley, Anthony
Trial and error
Hodder & Stoughton, 1937; New York: Doubleday,
Doran, 1937

which is specially memorable for its delightful central character Mr Lawrence Todhunter. Mr Todhunter's doctor gives him only a few months to live, and he decides to occupy his time by planning and carrying out the murder of someone whose death would be a distinct gain to the world. He decides to shoot Jean Norwood, a celebrated and bitchy actress, as his final contribution to society. It is after the murder is committed that complications begin to arise, as another man is arrested and the police refuse to accept Mr Todhunter's confession. There must be very few detective novels in which the central character has to prove his own guilt, and Berkeley also provides a most unpredictable ending.

Some of the writers flourishing in the 1920s were still producing new work in the 1930s and 1940s, or even later. But one, Agatha Christie, began in 1920 and wrote at least one book each year for six decades. Mrs Christie is featured in the next chapter with three other 'queens of crime', forming a quartet which dominated the genre.

5

QUEENS OF CRIME

This chapter recognizes the distinction of four writers by pin-pointing some of their best books, segregating them from their contemporaries. No apology is made for this, as each writer created detective fiction of the very highest standard, and none fits neatly into period divisions.

The creator of Lord Peter Wimsey, Dorothy L. Sayers (1893–1957) displayed less interest in the detective story *per se* than in developing a trend towards the novel of manners. Her most unusual detective novel was

Sayers, Dorothy L. and **Eustace, Robert**

The documents in the case

Benn, 1930; New York: Brewer, Warren, 1930

which is told entirely by means of letters, telegrams, statements and newspaper reports, all being reproduced in a most effective manner. It is still, perhaps surprisingly, an enthralling detective story. It is also a classic in the field of medical mysteries, thanks presumably to joint author Robert Eustace, who collaborated with many authors over a lengthy period on plots involving forensic medicine.

The skill of Dorothy L. Sayers was evident in her short stories as clearly as in her novels. Indeed, the volumes of short stories could be decidedly more to the taste of some readers, as her novels have been criticized for the way in which the detective element sometimes takes second place to Lord Peter's family affairs. No extraneous material is to be found in the clever cases collected under the title

Sayers, Dorothy L.
Hangman's holiday
Gollancz, 1933; New York: Harcourt, Brace, 1933
We also get a change from Lord Peter, as most of the stories feature the humorous Mr Montague Egg, wine salesman and amateur detective. Without Lord Peter, a totally different Miss Sayers emerges. There are also two little masterpieces without a central detective, which in style may be compared with the work of Roy Vickers and Cyril Hare.

The investigations of Lord Peter Wimsey, however, are the basis of Dorothy L. Sayers' reputation. Of these, special mention must be made of

Sayers, Dorothy L.
Murder must advertise
Gollancz, 1933; New York: Harcourt, Brace, 1933
for its perfect blend of murder mystery, cocaine-trafficking among bored young people, and the affectations of the advertising world. At Pym's Publicity, a man is killed in a headlong fall down a flight of stairs. Bredon, alias Lord Peter Wimsey, is brought in to replace him, and conducts his investigation against a background made authentic by the author's own working experience in advertising.

It is rare to find a detective novel with a specialized setting where neither the puzzle nor the credibility of the background suffers. Dorothy L. Sayers did it again, and some feel even more credibly, in

Sayers, Dorothy L.
The nine tailors
Gollancz, 1934; New York: Harcourt, Brace, 1934
This classic of death among the change-ringers of an East Anglian village provides details of bellringing which are clearly the result of patient research, and the villagers of Fenchurch St Paul are depicted with loving care. These salt-of-the-earth characters have been pursuing the same activities year in and year out, and nothing untoward ever happens until the day a savagely mutilated corpse is found in the graveyard. Lord Peter finds that campanology is of greater assistance to him than criminology, but he fortunately has a smattering of both.

Most detective novels rely upon murder as the mainspring of the plot, particularly those written when readers felt the thrill of the chase keenly because the criminal was risking the supreme penalty. It was something of a gamble on the part of Dorothy L. Sayers, therefore, when at the peak of her career she produced the bloodless

Sayers, Dorothy L.
Gaudy night
Gollancz, 1935; New York: Harcourt, Brace, 1936
In fact it became another classic. Harriet Vane, mystery novelist, returns to her old Oxford college and becomes involved in an unpleasant outbreak of poison pen letters. Although she sets out to investigate the affair herself, she soon enlists the aid of Lord Peter Wimsey, who earlier secured Harriet's acquittal in the murder case entitled *Strong poison* (Gollancz, 1930; New York: Brewer, Warren, 1930).

The university setting is skilfully portrayed, and the detective puzzle succeeds admirably in spite of the absence of corpses; but some writers have criticized the author for deliberately attempting to transform the detective novel into something it was never intended to be. Certainly in this case there is much that is entertaining in the book, and the detective element is by no means the be-all and end-all, but it was not until

Sayers, Dorothy L.
Busman's honeymoon: a love story with detective
interruptions
Gollancz, 1937; New York: Harcourt, Brace, 1937
that she made her intention plain. Lord Peter and Harriet marry, and after much society chitchat they set off on their honeymoon. It transpires that the house in which they arrive has been conveyed to Lord Peter complete with a dead body, and this provides the detective interruptions which give further evidence of Miss Sayers's plotting ability.

Possibly her skill as a detective novelist made her readers expect too much of her, and inclined some to dislike the romanticizing to which she was prone. It has even been suggested that she became too personally involved with her creation, Lord Peter; and there is little doubt of her disappointment at the critics' failure to accept the need to communicate more in a detective novel than a clever puzzle and its solution. In the twenty years between *Busman's honeymoon* and her death, no new Lord Peter Wimsey novels were produced.

In contrast, Agatha Christie (1890–1976) made no noticeable attempt to do other than tell a good story, to baffle her readers with ingenuity and sleight-of-hand. She used every trick of the trade – or so it always seemed until her next novel appeared. Other writers wrote more erudite detective stories or employed greater skill in characterization, but none sustained a comparably high standard in the conjuror's art throughout more than fifty years.

Agatha Christie's first detective novel was

Christie, Agatha
The mysterious affair at Styles
New York: John Lane, 1920; Bodley Head, 1921

which, although not her most accomplished, is significant in that it introduced Hercule Poirot. The dapper Belgian with the tidy mind, who solves cases by exercising his 'little grey cells', is arguably the best-known fictional sleuth since Sherlock Holmes. He makes his first appearance in an Essex village, where old Mrs Inglethorp dies from strychnine poisoning. In the tradition which Agatha Christie was to make her own, the field of suspects is restricted without diminishing the element of surprise when the murderer is finally unmasked.

Generally regarded as the author's *tour de force,*

Christie, Agatha
The murder of Roger Ackroyd
Collins, 1926; New York: Dodd, Mead, 1926

holds a unique position in the history of detective fiction. This is because of its highly original use of a technique which transforms it from a run-of-the-mill whodunit to something special. Although subsequently copied by many writers, the technique has never again been so adroitly achieved. Agatha Christie was accused of cheating by several critics, but others, including Dorothy L. Sayers, came to her defence. It would be churlish to reveal who killed Roger Ackroyd while the special satisfaction of reading this book has yet to be experienced by new generations of enthusiasts. But from the moment Hercule Poirot comes out of temporary retirement in the village of Kings Abbot to investigate this case of blackmail and murder, any reader who fails to question the meaning of everything Mrs Christie says will only have himself to blame.

Another most ingenious plot from the pen of Agatha Christie is

Christie, Agatha
Murder on the Orient Express
Collins, 1934

which was published in New York as *Murder in the Calais coach* (Dodd, Mead, 1934). On this particular journey there is a motley assortment of passengers, including Hercule Poirot and a child-murderer. When the snowbound train comes to a halt, the child-murderer is found dead in his berth, stabbed with most unusual ferocity. Which of the passengers could have been guilty of such a crime, Poirot asks, and could it be that they have something in common?

Mrs Ascher at Andover . . . Betty Barnard at Bexhill . . . Sir Carmichael Clarke at Churston . . . One by one

Christie, Agatha
The ABC murders
Collins, 1936; New York: Dodd, Mead, 1936

are committed and an *ABC railway guide* is left by each victim. Surely this is the work of a maniac? But the killer's first mistake is to challenge Hercule Poirot, whose ability as a detective is matched only by his supreme vanity. Accompanied by the rather silly Captain Hastings, as in most of his early cases, Poirot is in brilliant form. The solution is logical yet unexpected.

Not all of Agatha Christie's books feature Hercule Poirot. Her other principal detective, the elderly Miss Jane Marple, appears in many cases. On the whole, however, it is Poirot who appears in her most memorable novels. There are also some with no central detective character, perhaps the best known of these being

Christie, Agatha
Ten little niggers
Collins, 1939

which was published in New York as *And then there were none* (Dodd, Mead, 1940). Subsequently adapted for stage and screen without matching the book's accomplishment, this story starts conventionally enough when ten unconnected people are invited to an island by a host who apparently fails to materialize. Then they are murdered one by one, and it becomes gradually clear that the mysterious host is in fact among them.

In another novel without a series detective,

Christie, Agatha
The pale horse
Collins, 1961; New York: Dodd, Mead, 1962

the question posed is whether or not it is possible to commit murder by remote control, not by any mechanical device but by something like telepathy. This is the implication of a list of seemingly random names found on the dead body of a murdered priest, the common factor being that they all died suddenly. The pace and excitement of this novel, combined with its sting in the tail, are sufficient to demonstrate that one does not need to go back to the 1920s and 1930s for examples of the Christie genius. This one is among her best.

Toward the end of Agatha Christie's career, readers were reminded of the early days of Hercule Poirot and his confidant Hastings by a collection of short stories,

Christie, Agatha
Poirot's early cases
Collins, 1974

Published in New York as *Hercule Poirot's early cases* (Dodd, Mead, 1974), this contains eighteen excellent examples of the little Belgian at work. 'Pure chance,' begins the first story, 'led my friend Hercule Poirot . . . to be connected with the Styles case.' And so her readers were brought full circle.

The later Christie novels are generally regarded as patchy in quality, with few displaying her former flair and the best of them being little more than the repetition of conjuring tricks that had been successful the first time around. Even the two long-awaited books placed in cold storage decades earlier – *Curtain* (Collins, 1975; New York: Dodd, Mead, 1975) and *Sleeping murder* (Collins, 1976; New York: Dodd, Mead, 1976) – were disappointing final cases for Poirot and Miss Marple respectively. Fortunately,

Christie, Agatha
Miss Marple's final cases
Collins, 1979

provided for British readers an unexpected bonus. Published three years after the author's death, this collection contains short stories from the vintage Christie years which originally appeared only in British magazines and American volumes.

In Margery Allingham (1904–66) there was something more akin to Sayers than to Christie. Her fame dates from the publication of

Allingham, Margery
Death of a ghost
Heinemann, 1934; New York: Doubleday, Doran, 1934

in which, unlike her earlier novels, the mystery puzzle is set against a background which is authentically conveyed, and in which impressions of the social scene flow from the Allingham pen in a manner which was to make her mark. In contrast with Agatha Christie, the whodunit element is not necessarily always the most important aspect, although Miss Allingham was still a superbly competent practitioner. She may have lacked the Christie sleight-of-hand, but this was more than balanced by her exquisite character-drawing and her devastating thumbnail portraits.

In *Death of a ghost*, the unlikely murder scene is the fashionable annual exhibition of the work of John Sebastian Lafcadio RA, organized by his widow and by art dealer Max Fustian. A distinguished gathering of art enthusiasts and poseurs, finely drawn by the penetrating Miss Allingham, are on the spot when Tommy Dacre is stabbed. Inspector Stanislaus Oates is fortunate that Mr Campion is on hand also. Albert Campion, 'a lank, pale faced young man with sleek fair hair and hornrimmed spectacles . . . well bred and a trifle absentminded', is the mainstay of Margery Allingham's detective novels. He bears certain resemblances to Lord Peter Wimsey and to Ngaio Marsh's Roderick Alleyn, at least in respect of his dilettantism and aristocratic connections.

Another of Albert Campion's well-known cases,
Allingham, Margery
Dancers in mourning
Heinemann, 1937; New York: Doubleday, Doran, 1937
finds him investigating a series of vicious practical jokes which have been plaguing dancer Jimmy Sutane. At Sutane's country house it is clear that murderous intent lurks beneath the facade of theatrical camaraderie which his guests display, and death occurs in an atmosphere of tension which Miss Allingham conveys faultlessly.

Her perception and insight, particularly in matters psychological, are much in evidence in the collection of short stories,
Allingham, Margery
Mr Campion and others
Heinemann, 1939
and in the slightly different collection *Mr Campion: criminologist* (New York: Doubleday, Doran, 1937). Albert Campion has a large circle of acquaintants, many of whom seem only too eager to involve him in their problems. Be they questions of blackmail, robbery or worse, the combination of Campion and Stanislaus Oates of Scotland Yard is one which

meets with considerable success. The stories are clever, eminently readable, and with that touch of social satire which gives them spice.

Probably the most unusual Allingham novel, and arguably her best in some respects, is

Allingham, Margery
The tiger in the smoke
Chatto & Windus, 1952; New York: Doubleday, 1952

A truly outstanding work, and somewhat outside her style of earlier years, this shows Margery Allingham's almost uncanny ability to create atmosphere. Here it is the atmosphere of London, the 'smoke' of the title. Whether the characters are sinister or agreeable, from a group of buskers to a canon, the author's artistry in characterization is yet again demonstrated. Basically it is a novel of suspense rather than a detective story, a fast-moving journey as we pursue the trail of Jack Havoc – the tiger – following his escape from prison. Many of the regular Allingham characters are involved, including Albert Campion, his man Lugg, and Stanislaus Oates – the latter having progressed from Inspector to Assistant Commissioner since *Death of a ghost*. It may be felt that Campion is superfluous on this occasion, and that this exciting and strangely moving novel can stand on its own.

The last in this quartet of queens of crime, Ngaio Marsh (1899–1982), has a long list of books to her credit. Like Miss Allingham, she displays far more than the ability to devise a cunning puzzle. Her detective, Superintendent Roderick Alleyn, is one of the acknowledged greats of crime fiction. One of the classics of the genre is

Marsh, Ngaio
Artists in crime
Bles, 1938; New York: Furman, 1938

in which Alleyn investigates the murder of a model at the home of Agatha Troy RA. Miss Troy's art students are a motley gathering, and somewhere among their interpersonal relationships lies the motive for murder. This competent novel, with the artistic background well presented, also introduces Alleyn to his future wife. The romance and marriage of Alleyn and Agatha Troy span Ngaio Marsh's novels, just as Dorothy L. Sayers combined crime with the romantic affairs of Lord Peter and Harriet Vane.

There is no disagreement among the critics concerning the excellence of

Marsh, Ngaio
Overture to death
Collins, 1939; New York: Furman, 1939

It is Saturday night in the parish hall at Winton St Giles, and the audience is about to enjoy a play. Miss Idris Campanula takes her seat at the piano to perform the overture, Rachmaninoff's prelude in C sharp minor. It begins with the familiar Pom Pom POM, and then Miss Campanula's foot comes down on the soft pedal. There is a report from a revolver which someone has carefully arranged in the piano, and Miss Campanula has a bullet hole in her head. The mind behind this elaborate murder severely tests the intellectual capabilities of Roderick Alleyn.

In the case of

Marsh, Ngaio
Death of a peer
Boston: Little, Brown, 1940

which was published in London as *Surfeit of Lampreys* (Collins, 1941), the principal claim to fame is its impeccably etched characterization. It is a good example of a detective novel which is also a creditable piece of literature. The Lamprey family will be remembered by many readers long after they have forgotten details of the crime itself – the stabbing of the Marquis of Wutherwood and Rune in a lift.

Another of Miss Marsh's notable features is her ability to make the setting complementary to the plot; and several of her novels demonstrate to perfection how settings can be far more than just a backcloth against which a murder mystery is enacted. Although specially admired for her stories set in the world of the theatre, one of her most original is

Marsh, Ngaio
Died in the wool
Collins, 1945; Boston: Little, Brown, 1945

which uses a sheep station in her native New Zealand as an unusual locale for one of Alleyn's most absorbing cases. The corpse of Florence Rubrick, a Member of Parliament who has been missing for some weeks, is found in a bale of wool at a textile manufactory. Alleyn, not accompanied this time by his usual retine from Scotland Yard, confines the mystery to Mount Moon sheep station and to Mrs Rubrick's circle of family and friends. The problem is aggravated by the fact that the murder is already more than a year old when Alleyn comes on the scene.

Eccentric and earthy characters abound in the books of Ngaio Marsh, perhaps never more so than in

Marsh, Ngaio
Death of a fool
Boston: Little, Brown, 1956

which was published in London as *Off with his head* (Collins, 1957). The village of Mardian is the setting for the annual ritual of the Dance of the Five Sons. The weird costumes and the complex dances around the ruins of Mardian Castle provide concealment for a murderer to commit a macabre crime. Alleyn has to enter into the spirit of things and to take the ceremony as seriously as do the villagers, so that his reconstruction can expose the killer.

The later novels of Ngaio Marsh are all competent and puzzling, with little deterioration in her ability to explore interesting characters and to devise an ingenious mystery. It is nevertheless fair to say that the essential Ngaio Marsh is to be found in her early and middle years.

6
DETECTION OF THE GOLDEN AGE

During the 1930s and 1940s, many of the most famous writers of classic detective fiction emerged or reached their peak. Some of them continued to write for many years afterwards. Although in the 1930s various attempts were made to break away, traditional detective stories were produced in considerable numbers. Ample scope for innovation existed, leading to a refreshing variety rather than the demise of any particular form.

Neither the psychological crime novel nor the hard-boiled and laconic private eye story succeeded in putting the cosy puzzle out of business, either then or now, although these became important areas of crime fiction which will be separately covered later in this book. Here we shall remain with the pure detective story and pinpoint some of the key writers of the 1930s and 1940s, a golden age which saw a wide range of highly absorbing detective fiction on both sides of the Atlantic. There was a fascinating mixture of approaches, including locked room mysteries, the donnish school, and more exponents of the maligned 'Had I but known' technique.

During the 1920s, Ronald A. Knox (1888–1957) formulated rules governing the art of the detective story, on the grounds that there must be a fair game played between the author and the reader. These rules appeared in a preface to *The best detective stories of the year 1928* (Faber & Gwyer, 1929), edited by Knox and H. Harrington, which was published in New York as *The best English detective stories of 1928* (Liveright, 1929). They were later reproduced, with a commentary, in the essay entitled

'Detective stories' in Knox's *Literary distractions* (London and New York: Sheed & Ward, 1958).

Many writers adhered to the Knox rules, but even those who bent them a little were creating work with its own peculiar fascination. One such author, Philip MacDonald (1899–1981), could at times demonstrate the features of classic detective fiction, then sometimes cross into the field of the macabre, and on other occasions produce plots little short of farce. Although born in London and writing with an English flavour, he went quite early in his career to the USA and was responsible for many Hollywood scripts. His first novel featuring Anthony Gethryn was published as early as 1924, and

MacDonald, Philip
The rasp
Collins, 1924; New York: Dial Press, 1925
is still regarded as a classic of the genre.

MacDonald could write well, as befits a member of a literary family; his father was novelist and playwright Ronald MacDonald, and his grandfather was the Scottish poet and novelist George MacDonald. He was responsible for some superb variations on certain techniques of detective fiction and, although not primarily an innovator, he devised improvements and added new twists which stamped almost every MacDonald novel as very much his own.

In *The rasp* he basically uses the well worn theme of 'body in the study of a country residence'. But this is only the beginning, and MacDonald adds his own special dashes of humour, touches of the macabre, and Gethryn working inexorably to a surprise climax in true golden age tradition.

Following the publication of *The rasp*, MacDonald went from strength to strength. He specialized in snappy titles, of which

MacDonald, Philip
The noose
Collins, 1930; New York: Dial Press, 1930
was the very first Crime Club selection and highly praised by Arnold Bennett. Its basic idea, with the detective working against time to clear a condemned man and find the real murderer, has been done many times since but rarely so effectively.

MacDonald, Philip
Murder gone mad
Collins, 1931; New York: Doubleday, Doran, 1931
was selected by John Dickson Carr for a list of ten best detective

novels. It shows MacDonald's penchant for the bizarre in full flight, as an unhinged killer known as The Butcher carries out a daring series of atrocities in a small town and sends taunting messages to the police. It is a solo investigation for Superintendent Arnold Pike, who appears also in many of Anthony Gethryn's cases. Here Pike masterminds a meticulous and positively machine-like enquiry in which the whole town is suspect, and gradually narrows it down to the killer. Detective stories with multiple murders are apt to become monotonous, losing the reader's interest by their very artificiality, but MacDonald could create the sort of atmosphere which guaranteed the reader's full attention. Moreover he repeated the exercise under the pseudonym 'Martin Porlock', when he produced

Porlock, Martin
X v Rex
Collins, 1933

which was published in New York as *Mystery of the dead police* by Philip MacDonald (Doubleday, Doran, 1933). Later editions in Britain appeared under MacDonald's own name. It begins when an unknown murderer kills a police sergeant at his station desk. This is quickly followed by the strangling of a constable and the stabbing of another. It soon becomes apparent that the mysterious X is a maniac whose crimes are likely to extend indefinitely, and the case creates a national problem of Cabinet proportions.

The talents of Philip MacDonald are to be seen in many short stories in addition to his excellent novels. The collection entitled

MacDonald, Philip
The man out of the rain, and other stories
New York: Doubleday, 1955; Herbert Jenkins, 1957

reveals his many facets – his mastery of suspense, the knockout climax, the combination of humour and horror, and his overall technique as a superior craftsman in the art of storytelling. There are six stories here, the style of which is reminiscent of the author's association with such giants of the film industry as Alfred Hitchcock.

MacDonald's output thinned during the 1940s and 1950s, presumably as his film work increased, but much later he produced what must rank as one of his most intriguing books,

MacDonald, Philip
The list of Adrian Messenger
New York: Doubleday, 1959; Herbert Jenkins, 1960

Major Messenger writes the names of ten men on a slip of paper and gives it to a friend at Scotland Yard. A ruthless killer is the common factor, and Anthony Gethryn finds this one of his most complex cases. Incidentally, Gethryn was detecting throughout some thirty-five years and, rather like his creator, he has been somewhat underrated. It would be a pity if MacDonald's ingenuity and sense of fun were allowed to fall into obscurity.

MacDonald's novels spanned a long period. Another of whom this can be said, but whose best work appeared in the 1930s, was Sir Henry Aubrey-Fletcher (1887–1969). A soldier and civic dignitary, Sir Henry wrote

Wade, Henry
The Duke of York's steps
Constable, 1929; New York: Payson & Clarke, 1929

under the pseudonym which was to become well known. It is a neat mystery concerning the murder of Sir Garth Fratten, killed by a projectile on the famous steps in London, which provides Detective Inspector Poole with a host of suspects and an unusual murder method to unravel.

In his short stories,

Wade, Henry
Policeman's lot
Constable, 1933

Wade demonstrated that his work had a quality shared by few, namely that he could write puzzle stories which also depicted the life and work of police officers with admirable realism. His policemen were not superhuman, and indeed were often of comparatively lowly rank. Detective Inspector Poole of Scotland Yard is seen here in top form, as he persistently unearths the facts and alights upon those minute matters of detail which murderers overlook. For good measure the volume also contains six brilliant stories of the inverted variety, using techniques which were later to be effectively deployed in the work of such masters as Roy Vickers and Cyril Hare.

A further collection of short stories,

Wade, Henry
Here comes the copper
Constable, 1938

follows the career of a policeman called John Bragg. From the beat in Chelsea, he proceeds to Downshire and then returns to London as a detective constable in the CID. Each story bears Wade's authentic stamp, showing the rough and the smooth of a copper's life. They are also excellent examples of the detective short story, well plotted and in some cases relying upon small points of an ingenious nature which serve to trap villains.

For many years from the mid-1920s, John Leslie Palmer (1885–1944) and Hilary St George Saunders (1898–1951) produced novels of detection and espionage under the pseudonym 'Francis Beeding'. It is regrettable that their detective novels in particular are now remembered only by the most ardent enthusiast, as they were skilful, exciting and well-characterized examples of the classic tradition. Special mention must be made of

Beeding, Francis
Death walks in Eastrepps
Hodder & Stoughton, 1931; New York: Mystery League, 1931

which was described by the discerning Vincent Starrett as 'one of the ten greatest detective novels'. It concerns a series of brutal murders in a quiet English seaside village, and is notable for its mounting suspense as well as for its mystery puzzle. Few readers are likely to spot the guilty party among the well-drawn cast of characters, or to be disappointed by the atmosphere of panic as the hunt for the apparently motiveless killer develops.

A few years later on the scene than Freeman Wills Crofts, although very much of his school, scientist Alfred Walter Stewart (1880–1947) wrote, as 'J. J. Connington', a series of mysteries featuring Sir Clinton Driffield and Squire Wendover. His professional knowledge was frequently put to ingenious use, particularly on medical matters. In numerous cases set in the county of which Wendover is a prominent landowner and Driffield is Chief Constable, the two men share equal honours as detectives in collaboration. Of these largely forgotten stories,

Connington, J. J.
The sweepstake murders
Hodder & Stoughton, 1931; Boston: Little, Brown, 1932

is particularly commendable. When several men agree to share a Derby sweepstake ticket, their syndicate stands to win a quarter of a million pounds. Then strange accidents begin to occur, each making the survivors richer. A very readable example of the sometimes dull school of the period, there is ample solid detection enhanced by technical details presented in an authoritative yet lively fashion, including photographic trickery and the identification of typewriting.

If Wade, Beeding and Connington are no longer household names, that surely can not be said of John Dickson Carr (1906–77). He wrote under his own name and as 'Carter Dickson', and no other writer has devised more variations on the locked room mystery. Most of them have a horrific or quasi-supernatural atmosphere, which generally turns out to have been fabricated by the murderer.

Carr, John Dickson
The three coffins
New York: Harper, 1935

which was published in London as *The hollow man* (Hamish Hamilton, 1935), is a good example of this and presents 'impossible' crimes which only the true connoisseur will come within a mile of unravelling. Another nice touch is that one chapter provides the Chestertonian Dr Gideon Fell with an opportunity to discourse upon the various methods by which locked room murders may be committed. Mr Carr was generous in revealing these secrets, but his subsequent career was to show that he had dozens of alternative solutions in mind.

Another typical example of his work is

Dickson, Carter
The Plague Court murders
New York: Morrow, 1934; Heinemann, 1935

which presents a combination of the supernatural and the seemingly impossible murder. In a room which apparently no living creature can have entered, a fake spiritualist is brutally killed. As with all locked room mysteries, the identity of the killer is only part of the puzzle and the deductive skill of the reader is challenged even more by the question of how it was done. The massive and eccentric Sir Henry Merrivale solves it, and the author plays scrupulously fair.

Carr, John Dickson
The burning court
New York: Harper, 1937; Hamish Hamilton, 1937

is less typical, with the supernatural as a key element in a story which many enthusiasts regard as one of Carr's finest. It does not feature one of his regular series detectives, but is instead narrated by a publisher who has the closest personal involvement in the case. Set in Pennsylvania, it begins with the narrator discovering a photograph of his wife which proves to be that of a notorious poisoner who was executed in 1861. Then a man is poisoned, and his body disappears from a sealed, granite-lined crypt.

To return to Sir Henry Merrivale and the Dickson pseudonym, perhaps the most polished example of his ability to bamboozle the reader is

Dickson, Carter
The Judas window
New York: Morrow, 1938; Heinemann, 1938

Here Sir Henry's role as a barrister is more than usually evident, as he defends a man on a murder charge. Jimmy Answell was the only other person in the locked and shuttered room at the time of banker Avery Hume's murder, and his fingerprints were found on the lethal arrow. Yet it is betraying no secret to reveal that Answell is innocent, and that Hume was killed by a third party in Answell's presence. The murder method, staggering in its simplicity, truly provides a locked room mystery par excellence.

Many writers of detective fiction have admired the skill and ingenuity of John Dickson Carr. Some have attempted to emulate him, turning their hands to the locked room puzzle and usually achieving little success. It is nevertheless worth drawing attention to a little-known American, Henning Nelms, who adopted the pseudonym 'Hake Talbot'. He was reputed to be a devotee of G. K. Chesterton and Melville Davisson Post, some of whose short stories involve 'impossible crimes'. Talbot created as his detective a nomadic gambler named Rogan Kincaid, and his second novel,

Talbot, Hake
Rim of the pit
New York: Simon & Schuster, 1944; Tom Stacey, 1972

may be described as a superlative mystery in the Carr tradition. It tells of ten people who assemble in an isolated hunting lodge deep in a Canadian forest to invoke the spirit of Grimaud Desanat, to whom the property once belonged. When the seance begins, terrifying things happen. Rogan Kincaid is faced with a murder which defies explanation, a crime which no human being could have committed. Snow lies around the lodge pure and white, and the killer's footprints on the roof disappear into thin air.

To turn to less spectacular crimes, the detective novels of Georgette Heyer (1902–74) have been obscured by the popularity of her numerous historical romances, and her name is scarcely ever mentioned as one of the more competent crime writers. This is a pity, for she produced a dozen neat puzzles in the classic form, mostly during the 1930s. One of her best,

Heyer, Georgette
Death in the stocks
Longmans, Green, 1935

was published in New York under the title *Merely murder* (Doubleday, Doran, 1935). The village stocks at Ashleigh Green are a well-known feature, but Constable Dickenson sees them in use for the first time when he discovers the body of Arnold Vereker. Mr Vereker, a weekend visitor to a local cottage, is not short of people who stand to profit by his death. There are many possible motives, which it is the lot of Superintendent Hannasyde to disentangle.

Not all classics of the 1930s were of the intellectual variety. The novels of Ethel Lina White (1887–1944) were cast in the mould of Mary Roberts Rinehart, with the reader invited to associate with a helpless woman in danger. A title which succeeds admirably in this intention is

White, Ethel Lina
The wheel spins
Collins, 1936; New York: Harper, 1936

Its effectiveness stems from the fact that anyone might easily have the same experience on a train as heroine Iris Carr. This very ordinariness of the situation, with small everyday events gradually assuming sinister significance, is the very stuff of which Hitchcock films were made – indeed, this novel was adapted for the screen as *The lady vanishes*, and later editions of the book bear this better-known title. The story of how Iris Carr met the chatty governess Miss Froy on a train is brim-full of menace, particularly when Miss Froy disappears and her fellow travellers all deny that she ever existed. Poor tortured Iris begins to feel that she must have imagined her conversation with the harmless little lady, but various small pieces of evidence indicate otherwise.

There can be no greater difference in style and content than that between the works of Ethel Lina White and two other crime writers, 'Michael Innes' and 'Nicholas Blake', whose careers began simultaneously with the publication of *The wheel spins*.

J. I. M. Stewart (b. 1906), academic and novelist, has produced a considerable number of detective novels and thrillers since the 1930s under the pseudonym 'Michael Innes'. It is on his first few titles that his reputation is securely based. Together with 'Nicholas Blake' and 'Edmund Crispin', he brought a new literacy and intellectualism to a field which had become increasingly humdrum. Too many writers were relying upon the dull formula whereby the detective systematically interviews all the suspects and then minutely sifts the points of the various alibis; other writers were setting out deliberately to produce light-hearted works of the 'What fun, here's a body' variety. Innes played a large part in pulling detective fiction out of the rut, but it must not be assumed that his work was in any way pretentious. He intended to write detective novels, not novels 'with detective interruptions' like Dorothy L. Sayers.

Let anyone who feels that the employment of good English is wasted in the field of crime fiction pay careful attention to Mr Innes's early works, where literary craftsmanship and the ability to devise ingenious plots are equally apparent. His first was

Innes, Michael
Death at the President's lodging
Gollancz, 1936

which was published in New York as *Seven suspects* (Dodd, Mead, 1937). It was described in *The Times literary supplement* as 'the most important contribution to detective literature that has appeared for some time'. This debut by Inspector John Appleby, who later became Commissioner of the Metropolitan Police and was knighted, concerns the murder of the President of St Anthony's College. Only the Fellows have keys to his lodging, and so Appleby appears to have a neatly confined group of suspects. Moreover, the detective is by no means faced with a wall of silence, as scandals and passions incline the Fellows toward self-protection and to produce evidence against their colleagues. The acclaim given to this first book was exceeded on the publication of his second, intriguingly entitled

Innes, Michael
Hamlet, revenge!
Gollancz, 1937; New York: Dodd, Mead, 1937

in which Appleby investigates the murder of the Lord Chancellor at the Duke of Horton's country seat, Scamnum Court. A private production of *Hamlet* sets the scene, and it is during the performance that the murder is committed. Appleby is, as usual, urbane and replete with literary allusions – his penchant for swapping quotations has followed him throughout his career, giving him an erudition which few readers should find as irritating as the pseudo-intellectual chitchat of Philo Vance or

Lord Peter Wimsey. Possibly it is because Appleby is unobtrusive, so unaggressively normal, that he has survived the passage of time.

Michael Innes, with only two books published, was received by *The Times literary supplement* as 'in a class by himself among writers of detective fiction'; but any guide to the best in the field must also include his third,

Innes, Michael
Lament for a maker
Gollancz, 1938; New York: Dodd, Mead, 1938
This is generally recognized as his supreme achievement. Scotland is the setting and Appleby is again investigating a murder, although he does not make his appearance until some considerable way through the book. The unusual feature is that each part is narrated by one of the principal characters, and the style varies from one to another. Innes succeeds beautifully in conveying the feel of Scotland through his characters. In particular the prose of Ewan Bell, shoemaker of Kinkeig and elder of the Kirk, has a richness very few contemporary writers can convey.

To date Michael Innes has produced over forty crime novels and several volumes of short stories. While many of them have been of a high standard, including some espionage thrillers which are outside the scope of this book, there are critics who feel that the superlative quality of his earliest work was not maintained. The most frequent complaint about his books of recent years is that they are too farcical, with a strained humour rather than the urbane wit of his early novels. Although his many admirers might disapprove of the apparent dismissal of his considerable body of work from the 1940s onwards, this book therefore restricts itself to his first three novels. To those at least it awards the highest praise.

'Nicholas Blake' was another who brought a new literacy and a donnish flavour to the detective novel. He was Poet Laureate C. Day Lewis (1904–72). The quality of his books, maintained over many years, was further evidence of the fact that literary credentials of the highest standing were not wasted in the fields of straight detection, the thriller and the spy story, for he produced excellent examples of all these forms. It was the classic whodunit, however, to which he paid most attention. His first was

Blake, Nicholas
A question of proof
Collins, 1935; New York: Harper, 1935
and it received considerable critical acclaim, among the enthusiasts

being Dorothy L. Sayers and Sir Hugh Walpole. Of the multitude of murder mysteries which have been set in boys' schools,
high honours should go to this debut by Nicholas Blake. An
unpopular boy named Wemyss is found strangled at Sudeley
Hall preparatory school, and it is likely that one of the staff is the
murderer. Unlike Michael Innes, Blake places his mysteries in the
hands of an amateur detective, and the appearance of Nigel
Strangeways at Sudeley Hall was a cornerstone in crime fiction,
introducing a character who was to hold a significant position on
the roll of honour. From the outset he is portrayed as a rebel,
having left university after answering his mods papers in limer-
icks because 'the spectacle of so many quite decent youths being
got at and ruined for life was too much for him'. Physically he is
described as 'like one of the less successful busts of T. E.
Lawrence', and he is a man of many fads. His considerable problems at Sudeley Hall culminate in a second murder, but the
main difficulty is proving the identity of the murderer even when
he is sure of it.

Although *A question of proof* is not Blake's outstanding
achievement, it heralded a career of major proportions. Another
of his earliest novels,

Blake, Nicholas
The beast must die
Collins, 1938; New York: Harper, 1938

is regarded by many as his most accomplished book. A mixture
of detection and psychological suspense, it may be compared
with the work of Francis Iles and yet still ranks as an exercise in
deduction. 'I am going to kill a man. I don't know his name, I
don't know where he lives, I have no idea what he looks like.'
These are the opening words of a book which should be required
reading for every enthusiast.

Devotees of detective fiction will have their own particular
favourites among the novels featuring Nigel Strangeways.

Blake, Nicholas
Minute for murder
Collins, 1947; New York: Harper, 1948

is one of special ingenuity, set in the Ministry of Morale during
wartime. A cyanide capsule, taken from a captured Nazi chief,
disappears but is soon put to use. An attractive secretary is poisoned in front of seven witnesses, and fortunately Strangeways is
one of them. The difficulty of establishing a motive, and the

unearthing of office and extramural relationships, are problems which he has to take in his stride in this highly competent piece of classic detective fiction.

On occasions Blake produced work outside the whodunit or thriller format, and demonstrated what a really superlative novelist he was.

Blake, Nicholas
A tangled web
Collins, 1956; New York: Harper, 1956
is not typical of his work, but it was one of his own favourites and is by any standards an excellent book. Based on an Edwardian *cause célèbre*, it concerns the love of a simple girl for a young cat-burglar with the charm of Raffles. The murder of a policeman puts their love to the test, and the author gives a powerful picture of the investigating officers determined to run their quarry to ground. A story of poignant love and of despicable betrayal, it is also beautifully written.

The postwar novels of Nicholas Blake were of generally high standard, but special mention must be made of

Blake, Nicholas
The private wound
Collins, 1968; New York: Harper & Row, 1968
which was his last work. It is at once a love story, a fragment of autobiography, an examination of the divisions in Ireland, and a murder mystery. The storyteller, Dominic Eyre, tells how as a young novelist in 1939 he rented an isolated cottage in Ireland and had an affair with the wife of the local landowner, a man who once fought famously against the Black and Tans. The narrative develops into a story of murder and investigation, but it is primarily effective as a study of the central characters and a haunting mystery set against a beautiful and lovingly evoked background.

Slightly later on the scene, but very much associated with the breakthrough started by Innes and Blake, was 'Edmund Crispin'. Under his own name, Bruce Montgomery (1921–78), he was a successful composer particularly known for his film music. The pseudonym was employed for nine craftsmanlike detective novels and many short stories; and the Crispin name also occurred regularly as one of the foremost reviewers of detective fiction, and as a crime and science fiction anthologist. In his first novel,

Crispin, Edmund
The case of the gilded fly
Gollancz, 1944
which appeared in Philadelphia as *Obsequies at Oxford*
(Lippincott, 1945), we are introduced to Gervase Fen, Professor
of English Language and Literature in the University of Oxford.
Fen is a character who tends always to be around when murder is
committed, and on this occasion the obnoxious Yseut Haskell is
done to death in one of the Oxford colleges. The action alternates
between the University and the Oxford Repertory Theatre, as
befits the Crispin forte of the academic and the literary. Inter-
spersing the action with his own brand of pungent comment, Fen
concludes a highly entertaining novel with a theatrical exposure
of the murderer.

In his second novel,
Crispin, Edmund
Holy disorders
Gollancz, 1945; Philadelphia: Lippincott, 1946
the setting is a cathedral in the English West Country, and the
theme of church music abounds. When the organist unaccountably goes mad, Gervase Fen summons the composer Geoffrey
Vintner to replace him. Things go from bad to worse for Vintner,
with the minor inconvenience of having to transport a large but-
terfly net that Fen has ordered, to the major inconvenience of
three attempts on his life during the journey. At this point it is
clearly going to be a further feast for Crispin enthusiasts, and
indeed it surpasses his first novel for murder and mystery spiced
with intelligent hilarity.

One of Crispin's strong points is his ability to bring satirical
wit to the detective novel. He displays a sense of fun which might
occasionally be facetious, and he reminds us that it is all a story
which should not be confused with real life, but he never quite
descends to low farce. A special example of his comic approach is
Crispin, Edmund
The moving toyshop
Gollancz, 1946; Philadelphia: Lippincott, 1946
which is his most highly regarded book. Again set in Oxford,
it provides poet Richard Cadogan with a unlikely problem.
Cadogan discovers a strangled corpse in a toyshop at midnight,
but when he returns with the police the shop has disappeared.
Although this immediately types him as a madman, Cadogan

and his friend Gervase Fen set out in hilarious pursuit. Perhaps on reflection this *is* farce, but intelligent farce for all that.

Edmund Crispin's short stories, many of them miniature masterpieces originally published in the London *Evening standard*, were collected in the two volumes *Beware of the trains* (Gollancz, 1953; New York: Walker, 1962) and *Fen country* (Gollancz, 1979; New York: Walker, 1980).

Another writer of elegance and distinction was Gordon Clark (1900–58), who combined a career as a detective novelist with a busy legal practice which culminated in his appointment as a county court judge. Using the pseudonym 'Cyril Hare', he wrote a handful of excellent mystery novels and some superb short stories, his best-known book being

Hare, Cyril
Tragedy at law
Faber & Faber, 1942; New York: Harcourt, Brace, 1943

This stands out for its realistic portrayal of a judge on circuit rather than for its puzzle plot, and is indeed accepted as a classic among detective novels with a legal setting. It may be compared with some of the best work of Dorothy L. Sayers for its combination of detection, manners, and authentic background details. Barrister Francis Pettigrew is the investigator, and it would be churlish to reveal details of the plot, since even the victim's identity is not easily foreseeable. Suffice it to say that it is a satisfying novel which will remain a detective fiction cornerstone.

In respect of pure detection, Hare's masterpiece is

Hare, Cyril
When the wind blows
Faber & Faber, 1949

which was published in Boston as *The wind blows death* (Little, Brown, 1950). Francis Pettigrew is again the detective, investigating the death of a celebrated violinist who is scheduled to perform with a local music society. Hare's interest in music is much in evidence, as is his wit and his delicious power of character observation. All are skilfully wrapped into an absorbing mystery package.

Cyril Hare also wrote many short stories, and

Best detective stories of Cyril Hare: chosen with an introduction by Michael Gilbert
Faber & Faber, 1959; New York: Walker, 1961

is an excellent collection. Many of the stories are very short, consisting of four pages or so, and revolve around the one small point which gives a murderer away. There are comparatively few masters of the crime short story; it is a difficult art, avoided by many writers, in spite of the fact that, recalling Poe, it was the original form of the genre. Cyril Hare's stories are among the best.

Gladys Mitchell (1901–83) produced many detective novels from 1929 onwards featuring the eccentric and reptilian figure of Dame Beatrice Lestrange Bradley, psychiatric adviser to the Home Office. They are whodunits written with great verve, liberally larded with literary allusions, and most competently plotted. Some of the works of her first two decades were particularly impressive, a good example being

Mitchell, Gladys
When last I died
Joseph, 1941; New York: Knopf, 1942

Here Mrs Bradley, long before becoming a Dame, investigates murder against a background of an allegedly haunted house and an institution for delinquent boys. Another institutional setting is to be found, and is most authentically depicted, in

Mitchell, Gladys
Tom Brown's body
Joseph, 1949

Set in a boys' public school, as so many good detective stories seem to be, it concerns the murder of an unpopular junior master. It is clear that boys and masters know considerably more than they are prepared to admit, and it is fortunate indeed that Mrs Bradley is staying at this time in the village. From researching into witchcraft, as is her wont, she takes time off to investigate.

The versatility of Gladys Mitchell was very evident. Throughout more than sixty books she was unfailingly original, sometimes rebelliously experimental, and never resorted to a standard formula. While there were common factors – Mrs Bradley appeared in all books, and most had elements of satire and black humour – she could always be relied upon for interesting ideas. Sherlock Holmes enthusiasts, and indeed many others, regard

Mitchell, Gladys
Watson's choice
Joseph, 1955; New York: McKay, 1976

as one of her finest works. It features a party game that ends in murder, and uses the Holmes canon most effectively.

It may be that her later years produced works which lacked some of the freshness and sparkle for which she had been admired, but still this octogenarian could teach younger writers a thing or two. Still she could intrigue and entertain with her blend of eccentricity, the macabre and the literary. In

Mitchell, Gladys
Lovers, make moan
Joseph, 1981

the mystery stems from an amateur dramatic society's open-air production of *A midsummer night's dream*, in which the suicide by stabbing of Pyramus is all too real.

Robert Furneaux Jordan (1905–78), an architect writing mystery novels as 'Robert Player', was for many years an enigma. Having produced in 1945 a book which was well received for its ingenuity and originality, he wrote no more crime fiction for a quarter of a century. That first book,

Player, Robert
The ingenious Mr Stone
Gollancz, 1945; New York: Rinehart, 1946

was described by the publisher as the best first detective story which had come their way since the first Michael Innes. It uses several narrators, each telling what they know of the death by strychnine of a Devon headmistress while she is lecturing in London. Each account gives a clear picture of the character of the storyteller, as well as of the people whose actions are being described. Some wry comments, particularly relating to the girls' school run by the ill-fated headmistress, enliven the narratives still further. As to the significant role played by the ingenious Mr Stone himself, that is a treat for new readers still to discover.

Twenty-five years later saw the publication of

Player, Robert
The homicidal colonel
Gollancz, 1970

which, together with several more, provided ample evidence that the author had not lost his touch for outrageous crimes, original settings and an unconventionally lighthearted approach to the serious subject of death. It is the tale of a seemingly doomed family with suspicious deaths occurring over many years, switching from one tragedy to another and between locations as diverse as England, Ireland and the USA. Told with great relish, it was aptly described on publication as a zany Gothic extravaganza. In addition, it proved Player to be a great springer of surprises upon the reader, a skill which was borne out in subsequent novels.

Clifford Witting, an underrated writer working from the 1930s in the field of classic detection, was sometimes adventurous in his construction and proved himself a master of the unexpected. Very few works of this British author were published in the United States, but his

Witting, Clifford
Measure for murder
Hodder & Stoughton, 1941; New York: Garland, 1976

was perspicaciously revived by Jacques Barzun and Wendell Hertig Taylor as one of their *Fifty classics of crime fiction 1900–1950*, published by Garland. This is an excellent mystery, and a triumph of construction. In the prologue, a corpse is discovered in the Lulverton Little Theatre and the weapon is known to be a property sword. The first half of the book consists of a flashback describing life and relationships in the amateur dramatic society, narrated by one of its members. It is not until the mid-point that the murder victim's identity is revealed, which itself comes as a surprise. An investigation then follows by Inspector Harry Charlton, Witting's series detective, and everything falls neatly into place in what is undoubtedly one of the finest theatrical whodunits ever written.

From the 1930s until her death, Lucy Malleson (1899–1973) entertained countless readers with her stories of Arthur Crook, the unmannerly lawyer who treads a narrow path between legal practice and the opposite. Using the deceptive pseudonym 'Anthony Gilbert', she wrote almost fifty novels featuring Crook, who began to mellow in the later novels and is seen to his best advantage in the titles from the 1950s onwards. In

Gilbert, Anthony
Is she dead too?
Collins, 1955

which was published in New York as *A question of murder* (Random House, 1955), Crook sets out to find a housekeeper who has dangerous evidence in her possession. Her employer has killed twice already, and is eager to find her before Crook does.

Damsels in distress were Crook's stock in trade. The damsel in

Gilbert, Anthony
Murder's a waiting game
Collins, 1972; New York: Random House, 1972

has been accused of the murder of her husband and cleared. Now, after ten years, a blackmailer is threatening to produce new evidence.

Turning to the 1930s in the USA, the first really major name which occurs is that of 'Ellery Queen'. A list of the great names in mystery fiction must inevitably include this one, the pseudonym of cousins Frederic Dannay (1905–82) and Manfred B. Lee (1905–71). Their first half-dozen novels were written to a standard format, with titles on series lines and a 'Challenge to the reader' at the point at which all clues are in the reader's possession. The detection is of the classic English variety, although this is not to detract from the superb plotting skill and a crafty inventiveness that few writers have equalled.

Ellery Queen is the amateur detective hero of the series, aiding and abetting his father, Inspector Richard Queen. As with many classic detective novels, the early output of Ellery Queen puts puzzle before character analysis, and Ellery himself can only be described as a figure of somewhat annoying mannerisms only redeemed by his superb powers of deduction. He first appeared in

Queen, Ellery
The Roman hat mystery
New York: Stokes, 1929; Gollancz, 1929
and solved the case of a member of the audience poisoned at the Roman Theater off Broadway.

Queen, Ellery
The Greek coffin mystery
New York: Stokes, 1932; Gollancz, 1932
begins with the death of Georg Khalkis, prominent blind art dealer and connoisseur. The search for his will leads to the exhumation of his body, and the discovery of a strangled corpse sharing Khalkis's coffin. Once Ellery has applied his 'famous analytico-deductive method', the solution with its revelation of the murderer is stunning.

The activities of Ellery Queen were as celebrated in the short form as in the full-length novel.

Queen, Ellery
The adventures of Ellery Queen
New York: Stokes, 1934; Gollancz, 1935
is one noteworthy collection consisting of eleven investigations, which display the perfect blend of puzzle and pace with just a

touch of horror. Detective short stories by Queen, according to John Dickson Carr, are 'in a class by themselves'.

Mention has already been made of the lack of characterization in the early Queen novels, but it must be emphasized that a change of style occurred later. From the 1940s onwards, it may be said that the Queen novels became more serious in tone and Ellery himself lost his silly mannerisms and priggishness. This is not to say that the novels became less entertaining: indeed, the later period saw some of the most interesting and ingenious work. A clear example of the transformation,

Queen, Ellery
Calamity town
Boston: Little, Brown, 1942; Gollancz, 1942

is regarded by many as the best in the series. It finds Ellery in Wrightsville, a small New England town, using the alias Ellery Smith and trying to write a book in peaceful seclusion. Readers at the time doubtless expected murder to occur, and so it does. What must have surprised them, particularly if they had been fans of the earlier Queen, is the careful exploration of personalities and attitudes in the town, the analysis of relationships between the characters, and the awakening of the formerly sexless Ellery. It led to more books which became known as the 'Wrightsville novels'.

While the plots of Dannay and Lee in the 1950s and 1960s were variable in quality, they consistently maintained their successful new mixture of detection and naturalism. In addition they used an abundance of clever devices, together with cunning double or treble twists. It may be fairly said that very few of the Ellery Queen titles published since 1942 are likely to disappoint the aficionado.

The 1930s saw the emergence also of another great 'character' detective, Mr Moto. John P. Marquand (1893–1960) introduced him in a series of novels which may be categorized as secret service tales rather than pure detection, but which include more than a few detective elements. The Japanese Mr Moto is akin to his Chinese counterpart Charlie Chan, created by Earl Derr Biggers a few years earlier. Moto is, of course, inscrutable and razor-witted. The novels, set in the mystic Far East, are full of political intrigue and murder. Mr Moto, small and chunky, has a tendency to murmur 'so sorry' and other stock phrases while completely pulling the wool over the villains' eyes.

John P. Marquand originally wrote the Moto stories for the *Saturday evening post* after spending some time in the Orient. The omnibus volume
Marquand, John P.
Mr Moto's three aces
Boston: Little , Brown, 1956
contains *Thank you, Mr Moto* (Boston: Little, Brown, 1936; Herbert Jenkins, 1937), *Think fast, Mr Moto* (Boston: Little , Brown, 1937; Hale, 1938) and *Mr Moto is so sorry* (Boston: Little, Brown, 1938; Hale, 1939).

The early novels of Mignon G. Eberhart (b. 1899) were examples of the 'Had I but known' school founded by Mary Roberts Rinehart, with hospital and nursing home settings her particular forte, although she later explored into the field of the psychological suspense novel. In spite of her association with the Rinehart school, Mrs Eberhart produced some excellent stories blending detection with terror. One of her most popular and memorable characters is Susan Dare, who appears in
Eberhart, Mignon G.
The cases of Susan Dare
New York: Doubleday, Doran, 1934; Bodley Head, 1935
Susan is a typical young heroine, charming and somewhat emotional, and displays understandable horror at being caught up in situations involving murder in menacing locations. She is a writer of mystery stories who, together with gallant young reporter Jim Byrne, has a knack of getting drawn into murder cases at the drop of a hat. The six stories in this collection contain some nice ingenious touches, and are a pleasant mix of whodunit and hair-raiser.

As Mignon G. Eberhart's career developed, she became known for a skilful and balanced combination of mystery, romance and Gothic suspense. She also manages invariably to convey the feel and colour of her settings, which are sometimes exotic, and exploits the background to project the right degree of pervading evil. One could cite many examples from the 1930s through the 1980s, but an early instance of Eberhart at her best is
Eberhart, Mignon G.
Fair warning
New York: Doubleday, Doran, 1936; Collins, 1936
From the moment that the first murder is committed with a garden knife in the eeriest of circumstances, to the climax of a

deadly plot when the killer is exposed, the uneasy atmosphere of death and its warnings is never lost. Love and fear, faith and treachery, murder and detection are brilliantly fused.

A character who was to become an institution, Perry Mason, made his debut in the 1930s and proved to be one of the most popular figures in detective fiction. Erle Stanley Gardner (1889–1970) produced the books very much to a pattern, and with surprising rapidity. Their plots were entertaining, their characters cardboard, and in short they were nothing more than an enjoyable read. Gardner's legal experience, together with his work for the pulp magazines, provided him with vast experience when he launched this series of courtroom puzzles. Over eighty titles appeared, in which defence attorney Mason uses all his wily skills and chicanery, invariably pulling off the acquittal of his client and the exposure of the murderer in the final pages.

Gardner, Erle Stanley
The case of the sulky girl
New York: Morrow, 1933; Harrap, 1934
is a very early example, concerning a beautiful girl who is worried about her father's will. When the trustee has his head beaten in, her problems are only just beginning.

In another early case,
Gardner, Erle Stanley
The case of the sleepwalker's niece
New York: Morrow, 1936; Cassell, 1936
the problem Mason ponders is whether or not a man who walks in his sleep is criminally responsible for his actions while so doing. Peter Kent certainly appears to have committed murder, as the bloodstained knife is found under his pillow. His inability to answer questions, together with the fact that his pretty blonde niece is championing his cause, are guaranteed to attract Perry Mason's interest.

From the characters of Erle Stanley Gardner, who are little more than ciphers, it is a far cry to the work of Rex Stout (1886–1975) and his larger-than-life creation Nero Wolfe. Gourmet, beer drinker and orchid fancier, the massive Wolfe made his first appearance in
Stout, Rex
Fer-de-lance
New York: Farrar & Rinehart, 1934; Cassell, 1935
and became a dominant figure on the crime fiction scene for

forty years. An armchair detective in the literal sense, Wolfe moves as rarely as possible from his study out of deference both to his immense weight and to his superior intellect. Naturally he interviews suspects and searches for clues, but he does so principally through his young legman Archie Goodwin, who incidentally is one of the most active and catalytic 'Watsons' in the history of the genre. There were many Nero Wolfe novels but, apart from being the first, *Fer-de-lance* is also a good example of detection at its purest, as Wolfe exercises his ego and his infallibility upon the case of the professor who drops dead while playing golf.

As with any long series, the Nero Wolfe stories are variable. Nevertheless Rex Stout proved himself capable of producing mysteries of the highest order to the very end of his career, as witness

Stout, Rex
The father hunt
New York: Viking Press, 1968; Collins, 1969
in which a young woman asks Archie Goodwin to find the father whose identity is unknown to her. When Wolfe learns that her mother was murdered and that her family history encompasses the highest social and financial circles, he knows that the case will interest him. In fact, it turns out to be among the best Rex Stout devised. To cap it all, however, Stout floored even his most ardent admirers with

Stout, Rex
A family affair
New York: Viking Press, 1975; Collins, 1976
Detectives may be tempted into a case by the fee offered or by their sympathy for an underdog client. Here Wolfe is motivated by the sheer audacity of the unknown adversary who has the gall to plant a bomb in Wolfe's own home, killing the gourmet's favourite waiter from his beloved restaurant. Stout shows a Nero Wolfe more determined than ever in his last case, with a final revelation which is astounding.

An American writer reputedly admired by Agatha Christie was Elizabeth Daly (1878–1967). Her stories of amateur detective Henry Gamadge, New York bibliophile, were in the Christie tradition of civilized murder unsullied by mean streets or sordid sentiments. She wrote well, and cleverly arranged for Gamadge to encounter murder while pursuing his passion for

antiquarian volumes, manuscripts, inks and autographs. In an
early case,

Daly, Elizabeth
Murders in volume 2
New York: Farrar & Rinehart, 1941; Eyre & Spottiswoode,
1943

a rich old man falls under the influence of a beautiful girl, whom
he believes to be the reincarnation of his family's nineteenth-
century governess. When the original governess disappeared, so
too did the second volume of a set of Byron's poetry. Gamadge's
interest is attracted by the fact that the volume has now returned,
giving verisimilitude to the girl's claim. On the other hand, it
could all be a plot to secure the family fortune, and two murders
indicate that Gamadge is competing with villainy of this world
rather than with the supernatural.

Daly, Elizabeth
Arrow pointing nowhere
New York: Farrar & Rinehart, 1944; Hammond,
Hammond, 1946

is another well plotted mystery, which begins when Gamadge
becomes intrigued by the puzzle of the mailman's crumpled enve-
lopes. Such small beginnings lead him to the rich and secretive
Fenway family, two murders and a suicide.

For sheer originality, however, mention must be made of
Patricia McGerr (b. 1917). Her earliest contributions to the genre
provided some genuinely new techniques, and her first novel

McGerr, Patricia
Pick your victim
New York: Doubleday, 1946; Collins, 1947

was recognized as a *tour de force*. The boredom of a group of
Marines in the Aleutians is broken when they exercise their minds
on a murder committed in Washington at the Society for the
Uplift of Domestic Service. The basis of their puzzle is a torn
newspaper clipping which informs them of the murderer's name,
but not the identity of the victim. Such a variation, which was
aptly described as the 'whodunin?', she made very much her own
in other early novels, before exhausting the vein and turning to
more conventional detection and espionage.

Comic detective novels are difficult to produce, but Elliot
Paul (1891–1958) was highly successful with the satirical, bor-
dering on the zany, stories featuring Homer Evans. Homer is a

tall, broad-shouldered playboy with a seemingly inexhaustible range of talents. In his first case,

Paul, Elliot
The mysterious Mickey Finn
New York: Modern Age, 1939; Penguin, 1953
he is in search of a disappearing millionaire in a romp in the Parisian artists' quarter. The author's introduction sets the tone, including an apology for the absence of corpses in the first few pages but warning that 'the casualties are going to be fairly heavy before we get through'.

Another expert at combining detection with farce was Phoebe Atwood Taylor (1909–76). Her novel,

Taylor, Phoebe Atwood
The Cape Cod mystery
Indianapolis: Bobbs-Merrill, 1931
introduced homespun detective Asey Mayo, and was particularly praised in its time for its lighthearted detection and nicely conveyed Cape Cod dialect. Some two dozen Asey Mayo mysteries followed, but arguably her best books were written under the pseudonym 'Alice Tilton'. They feature a most unusual detective named Leonidas Witherall, a gently unassuming academic who also happens to bear a striking physical resemblance to William Shakespeare. In the first, bearing the unlikely title

Tilton, Alice
Beginning with a bash
Collins, 1937; New York: Norton, 1972
the musty calm of Peters's secondhand bookstore is shattered when Professor North is killed by a blow to the skull. Luckily 'Bill Shakespeare' is on hand, and he pursues a characteristically mirthful course to the solution. Paradoxically, the Witherall stories are a very English brand of detection by an American writer.

Humour of the English variety came from Caryl Brahms (1901–82) and S. J. Simon (1904–48) in their novels featuring Inspector Adam Quill, most notably

Brahms, Caryl and **Simon, S. J.**
A bullet in the ballet
Joseph, 1937; New York: Doubleday, Doran, 1938
The authors' theatrical knowledge and satirical bent are put to good effect in this case of three murdered Petroushkas, and Quill encounters many larger-than-life characters in what James

74

Sandoe described as 'a burlesque for balletomanes'.

Not just lighthearted but sometimes downright crazy are the novels of American Georgiana Ann Randolph (1908-57), who used the pseudonym 'Craig Rice'. Another exponent of the zany school of detection, she featured street photographers cum detectives Bingo Riggs and Handsome Kusak in prime examples of knockabout comedy murder. But it is

Rice, Craig
Trial by fury
New York: Simon & Schuster, 1941; Hammond,
Hammond, 1950

on which her excellent reputation is founded. Jackson County, with its first murders for thirty-two years, is a small community with some fascinating characters. Young marrieds Jake and Helene Justus, together with tippling Chicago lawyer J. J. Malone, dig beneath the surface respectability in their search for the killer. Toughness and humour combined, without the forced wackiness of her later novels, place this in the forefront of Craig Rice's work.

Perhaps vying for recognition as her best novel is her semi-autobiographical mystery story

Rice, Craig
Home sweet homicide
New York: Simon & Schuster, 1944

which concerns a crime writer distracted by the murder of her neighbour, a mystery which is solved by her three children.

The field of crime fiction is rich in curiosities and individual works which are difficult to classify. One such, now acknowledged as a classic, is

Heard, H. F.
A taste for honey
New York: Vanguard Press, 1941; Cassell, 1942

Heard (1889-1971) was the author of numerous works on sociology and religion, normally using the forename Gerald. In fact, the British edition of *A taste for honey* quotes Gerald Heard as the author. There is a touch of whimsy about it which is still delightful today. It tells of Sydney Silchester, a solitary man with a passion for honey, who obtains his supply from the village beekeepers Mr and Mrs Heregrove. When the lady's body is discovered, black and swollen from stings, Silchester looks elsewhere for his honey and meets an elderly man who harbours grave suspicions about Heregrove and his bees. The mystery man is quite obviously Sherlock Holmes in retirement, but is never mentioned by the name.

Turning from Britain and the USA to Australia, a popular writer of the period and for many years afterward was Arthur Upfield (1888–1964). Born in England, he spent most of his life in Australia, and produced some thirty atmospheric novels featuring half-caste Detective Inspector Napoleon Bonaparte. 'Bony' is the pride of the Queensland Police, a most original detective endowed with skills and powers which stem from Upfield's detailed knowledge of that fascinating land and its peoples. An expert tracker who has inherited his aboriginal mother's ability to read 'the book of the bush', Bony's prowess as an investigator is also enhanced by the good education he received after leaving an orphanage. In

Upfield, Arthur

Mr Jelly's business

Sydney: Angus & Robertson, 1937; John Hamilton, 1938 which was published in New York as *Murder down under* (Doubleday, 1943), Bony breaks his vacation in Western Australia and goes undercover in the small wheat town of Burracoppin, where farmer George Loftus has disappeared and there is suspicion of murder. Gradually he begins to learn more of the local community and becomes specially interested in the genial farmer and criminologist Mr Jelly, whose secret is the business which takes him away from the town on mysterious journeys.

A later novel,

Upfield, Arthur

Man of two tribes

Heinemann, 1956; New York: Doubleday, 1956 sees Bony searching for Myra Thomas, acquitted of murder and missing from a train somewhere in the vast desolation of Nullarbor Plain in South Australia. Assisted by two camels and a dog, Bony is the only policeman able to cope with such country. He is more successful than he anticipated, finding not only a murderess but five murderers. In a story of survival and strange mystery, Upfield excels also in his vivid scenic descriptions when he takes the reader to intriguing locations with names such as Bumblefoot Hole and Nightmare Gutter.

There remains the question of European writers. Strange to tell, considering that Gaboriau was one of the founding fathers of the genre, Continental detective novels at the time were few and far between. At the very least, they failed to achieve international recognition. In the 1930s to 1950s there was really only one major figure translated into English, Georges Simenon, who was born in Belgium and moved to France as a young man.

Georges Simenon (b. 1903) rivals Edgar Wallace in terms of sheer quantity, but here the comparison ends. A large proportion of his stories feature the solid, pipe-smoking Inspector (later Commissaire) Maigret. In conception the early stories were influenced by the *romans policiers* of Emile Gaboriau, and the painstaking thoroughness of the first Maigret cases owed something also to Freeman Wills Crofts; but, as his career progressed, Simenon developed a unique style amounting to genius.

The stories are normally of novelette length, with little time wasted on elaborate descriptive passages. Instead the reader is treated to impressions, even atmospheres, as sensed by Maigret himself, and they are the more realistic for this – if Paris has a distinctive smell, Maigret communicates it to us.

Unlike many fictional detectives, Maigret is no superman. He was allegedly based upon Inspector Guillaume, the greatest French detective of his day and a close friend of Simenon. He has a capacity for pity in no small degree. His methods are sometimes plodding, his humour is often cynical, and his success is frequently achieved by the possession of an innate sense of evil. He knows the frailties of human nature, and the criminal's compulsive desire to unburden his soul means that Maigret need only bide his time. We see him therefore as a patient man, so much so that two Maigret books appeared with the same translated title. We are here concerned with

Simenon, Georges
The patience of Maigret
Routledge, 1939; New York: Harcourt, Brace, 1940
rather than the 1966 book of the same title. The former contains two novelettes, *A battle of nerves* and *A face for a clue*, which are a perfect introduction to the early Maigret and have a flavour which some of the later stories did not quite achieve.

In *A battle of nerves*, Maigret persuades the authorities to allow a man to escape from prison, a course of action made even more unusual by the fact that the man is awaiting execution for murder. Maigret now believes in his innocence, and only by gaining freedom can the man lead him to the truth. *A face for a clue* finds Maigret in the port of Concarneau, where the shooting of a respected local citizen is but the first in a series of strange and violent events. At the heart of the mystery is a yellow dog with no apparent master, who appears at the scene of each new misfortune.

Highly praised by André Gide, Stefan Zweig, François Mauriac and Maurice Leblanc, among many others, it was inevitable that Simenon should be translated into English and become a firm favourite. The publisher George Routledge announced that volumes, each containing two stories, would be published quarterly. Many such volumes followed *The patience of Maigret*, and even with a later change of publisher the popular two-story format continued. A feast for the Maigret enthusiast, however, is the collection of five published in London as

Simenon, Georges
A Maigret omnibus
Hamish Hamilton, 1962

and in New York as *Five times Maigret* (Harcourt, Brace, 1964). Of particular merit in this collection are *Maigret in Montmartre* and *Maigret's mistake*. For the purist, it should perhaps be mentioned here that these two stories had earlier been published together in London as *Maigret right and wrong* (Hamish Hamilton, 1954), and that *Maigret in Montmartre* had been separately published in New York as *Inspector Maigret and the strangled stripper* (Doubleday, 1954).

Maigret in Montmartre concerns a striptease girl at Picratt's, a small nightclub, who overhears two men planning to murder a countess. She tells the police, but is herself killed soon afterwards. A second murder, followed by a breathtaking chase, occurs before Maigret can solve the mystery. In *Maigret's mistake* the body of a *demi-mondaine* is found in a luxury apartment house in a wealthy section of Paris. Why was she living there? A distinguished doctor, his wife, and a musician reputed to be the dead girl's lover are three of the suspects who must be questioned by Maigret. The case proves to be one of his most perplexing.

On occasions the Maigret stories were published separately rather than in two-story volumes. One of the best of these was

Simenon, Georges
My friend Maigret
Hamish Hamilton, 1956

which appeared in New York as *The methods of Maigret*

(Doubleday, 1957). The brutal murder of an old tramp who claimed to know Maigret brings the detective from his usual haunts to the Mediterranean island of Porquerolles. He is accompanied by an Inspector from Scotland Yard who wants to study his methods, but the Yard man finds that Maigret prefers intuition to textbook detection. This particular story is specially fine as a mixture of good characterization and humour; but the tone darkens into a study of young criminals with more than a passing resemblance to the notorious Leopold and Loeb.

7

MID-CENTURY DETECTION

It is impossible to place all the crime writers covered by this book into neat chronological divisions. This chapter, for example, purports to deal with writers of the 1950s and 1960s. While it may be suggested that this period represented their heyday, such treatment must not be allowed to obscure the fact that a dozen or more of the writers concerned began their careers as early as the 1930s, or that many of them continued to produce excellent books long after the 1960s. Indeed several are still writing today, with remarkable vigour and adaptability sustained over at least five decades.

A case in point is Michael Gilbert (b. 1912), who from his first book in 1947 has developed into one of Britain's most reliable practitioners in the field. His work has always been typified by good writing, a neat eye for characterization, and liberal helpings of humour. He has covered a wide range from the classic detective form to novels of suspense, action and espionage, using a variety of settings. In

Gilbert, Michael
Smallbone deceased
Hodder & Stoughton, 1950; New York: Harper, 1950
the corpse is found in a solicitor's office, of an impeccable authenticity no doubt attributable to the author's own legal background. It is found, moreover, in a hermetically sealed deed-box, and to discover the murderer among the mixed bag of eccentrics concerned with the firm presents a daunting prospect for Inspector Hazlerigg and Henry Bohun.

Gilbert, Michael
Death in captivity
Hodder & Stoughton, 1952
which was published in New York as *The danger within* (Harper, 1952), is another of Gilbert's novels which has carved a special niche for itself. A combination of murder mystery and escape story, it is a skilful portrayal of men within a tense environment. The atmosphere of an Italian prisoner-of-war camp is well conveyed.

One of Gilbert's most unusual novels of the 1960s is
Gilbert, Michael
The crack in the teacup
Hodder & Stoughton, 1966; New York: Harper & Row, 1966
which is as readable and witty as all his work, but concentrates upon local government corruption in a resort on the South Coast of England rather than upon violence and murder. The principal character is a young solicitor, which again gives Gilbert ample scope to bring his own professional expertise into play. Cynical and thought-provoking, it is one of his best works.

Even as recently as 1983, in
Gilbert, Michael
The black seraphim
Hodder & Stoughton, 1983; New York: Harper & Row, 1984
Gilbert was in good form. It is a story of clashes and intrigues at Melchester Cathedral, a perfect mixture of matters ecclesiastical and scientific. The characters are superbly drawn, the setting and atmosphere almost Trollopian. When suspicious death occurs, it falls to a young pathologist on sabbatical to tie up the loose ends.

John Michael Evelyn (b. 1916), who as 'Michael Underwood' has produced many sound mystery novels since the mid-1950s, served for twenty-five years in the office of the Director of Public Prosecutions. This has meant that details of police procedure and legal practice have always been presented by him in an authoritative and interesting manner, and he has often displayed the insight into forensic quirks and loopholes which give his stories added bite and sometimes provide the basic plot ideas. Some of his most recent work has been particularly good, and for this reason
Underwood, Michael
The juror
Macmillan, 1975; New York: St Martin's Press, 1975
is featured here as one of many highly competent examples. It

centres on the trial of racketeer Bernie Mostyn at the Old Bailey, and the threats received by some members of the jury. When one of them is found dead in a North London park, the police keep an open mind rather than accept the obvious explanation that it is the work of gangland. In a briskly moving whodunit with some nice character cameos, an attractive team of investigators gradually collects the clues from among the jurors and beyond.

Another firm favourite, Leopold Horace Ognall (1908–79), produced work of a high standard over many years, particularly when writing as 'Harry Carmichael'. They may be categorized as suspense novels, although there is a strong detective element. Carmichael's principal characters are John Piper, an insurance assessor, and reporter Quinn of the *Morning post*. They specialize in finding themselves unwittingly in situations involving murder, and many of the books show how they extricate themselves and expose the guilty party. For example, in

Carmichael, Harry
Remote control
Collins, 1970; New York: McCall, 1971

Quinn has a drink in a pub with a man called Hugh Melville, and later a man is run down and killed by Melville's car. When Mrs Melville is found dead and murder is suspected, Quinn finds the police are looking a little too determinedly in his direction. That is when Piper lends a hand.

The relationship between the self-assured Piper and the flippant but insecure Quinn is what gives Harry Carmichael's mysteries their special flavour. The two men complement each other, and find themselves jointly enmeshed in elaborate plots which seem to defy logical solution, until all falls neatly into place. The later titles are by far the best. In

Carmichael, Harry
Candles for the dead
Collins, 1973; New York: Saturday Review Press, 1976

Quinn senses a promising story when a traveller has a strange experience at Heathrow airport on his return from Sweden, involving photographic negatives hidden in a child's birthday cake. As always, the pace quickly becomes hotter, with an apparently motiveless killing and an attack on Quinn leading to the swapping of theories by Piper and Quinn in an atmosphere of mounting suspense.

Roderic Jeffries (b. 1926) has an excellent knowledge of the law and of police methods, and his novels show a welcome degree of ingenuity. In recent years he has turned to detective puzzles set in Mallorca and featuring Enrique Alvarez, but his courtroom and police mysteries of the 1960s are still memorable for their technical detail and clever construction. In

Jeffries, Roderic
Evidence of the accused
Collins, 1961; New York: British Book Centre, 1963
two men are consecutively tried for the murder of a rich socialite, and each confesses while the other is on trial. This is only the starting-point of the many complications in a most absorbing story.

Jeffries has also produced police procedural novels as 'Jeffrey Ashford', which are mentioned in Chapter 10. Not entirely in this subgenre, but rather a refreshing variation of the whodunit with a police background, is

Jeffries, Roderic
A traitor's crime
Collins, 1968
It is brought home to John Keelton, Chief Constable of Flecton Cross, that one of his detectives is 'bent'. But which one? An investigation begins, and provides an unusual mystery.

The novels of Laurence Meynell (b. 1899) often concern people who get progressively deeper into desperate situations. Sometimes this arises from their own weakness, and sometimes because they deliberately set out to commit crimes. Several have featured worldly private detective Hooky Hefferman, a character created in 1952 and retained spasmodically to the present day. Meynell began writing crime fiction in the 1920s, but his best work is to be seen in the non-series novels of the 1970s such as

Meynell, Laurence
A little matter of arson
Macmillan, 1972
which shows two detectives investigating a case of arson in an English South Coast town, each with a different suspect in mind. Quite different is

Meynell, Laurence
The fatal flaw
Macmillan, 1973; New York: Stein & Day, 1978

in which two young members of the Chelsea set plan to carry out the perfect crime and then – like so many others – find they cannot stop.

The career of mystery novelist Morna Doris Brown (b. 1907), writing as 'Elizabeth Ferrars', dates from the 1940s. Civilized and entertaining, at times thought-provoking, her list of titles is considerable. In the 1970s she displayed an ability to keep up with the times, a determination to produce work which was not a mere hollow echo of the mystery fiction of earlier decades. In

Ferrars, Elizabeth
The small world of murder
Collins, 1973; New York: Doubleday, 1973

Nicola Hemslow accepts the Foleys' invitation to spend Christmas with them. The atmosphere is unlikely to be particularly happy, as their daughter has vanished from her pram outside a shop, but Nicola hardly expects them to start accusing each other of murderous intent.

A noteworthy feature of Elizabeth Ferrars is her skill at taking the reader into the lives of ordinary people who are going about the daily round, whether domestic or professional, and then transforming the situation at one fell swoop by the intrusion of sudden death. Thus in

Ferrars, Elizabeth
Hanged man's house
Collins, 1974; New York: Doubleday, 1974

the turning-point is when Dr Charles Gair, Director of the Martindale Research Station, is found dead at his home, together with the mummified corpse of a man missing for over a year. Superintendent Dunn has to probe deeply into the lives and characters of those personally and professionally involved, and to peel away the outer layers obscuring guilty secrets. In complete contrast,

Ferrars, Elizabeth
Alive and dead
Collins, 1974; New York: Doubleday, 1975

concerns the National Guild for the Welfare of Unmarried Mothers and the problems befalling adviser Martha Crayle. She has to cope with a new client who is pregnant but married, and who insists that her husband, believed killed in a plane crash, is still alive. This leads Martha into a complex web of intrigue involving two murders, and her amateur detection brings personal danger and a shock denouement.

Another authoress of the 1940s, whose name remains very well regarded in the field today, is Christianna Brand (b. 1907). Her limited output has displayed considerable plotting ability and ingenuity, combined with a lovely sense of the absurd which results in a refreshing unwillingness to take her murders and her characters too seriously. A true classic of the genre is

Brand, Christianna
Green for danger
New York: Dodd, Mead, 1944; Bodley Head, 1945

which is one of several featuring the shabbily dressed Inspector Cockrill of the Kent police, an endearing and enduring figure who combines perkiness with pathos and eccentricity with a finely tuned analytical mind. Here he encounters what must be one of the cleverest murders ever devised, when a patient is killed on the operating table with seven witnesses present. Set in a military hospital, it provides a brilliant evocation of the atmosphere of the second world war in England. Readers who have not yet experienced this picture of Heron's Park Hospital waiting for the next bomb to drop are promised a treat, and for many it will arouse nostalgia.

Among the non-Cockrill novels is one which specially demonstrates Christianna Brand's versatility, and her power to inspire emotions deeper than those raised by the routine whodunit.

Brand, Christianna
Cat and mouse
Joseph, 1950; New York: Knopf, 1950

is a melodrama, perhaps even a Gothic tale, with a perfect setting amid the mountains of Wales. A women's magazine 'agony aunt' finds herself in a frightening situation when she tries to trace a girl who has been writing to her. The classic scenario of a woman in danger and a handsome man with an air of tragic mystery has rarely been more effectively presented, and this has the added bonus of a puzzle element which should satisfy readers of all tastes.

Then there is Joan Fleming (1908–80), another consistently good crime novelist over a long period. In

Fleming, Joan
You can't believe your eyes
Collins, 1957; New York: Washburn, 1957

she was fairly traditional in tone, demonstrating that four witnesses to a mysterious death each saw something different – even the witness who is understood to be blind. She later received considerable acclaim and a Crime Writers' Association award for

Fleming, Joan
When I grow rich
Collins, 1962; New York: Washburn, 1962

in which she introduced the Turkish philosopher Nuri Izkirlak. The plot, with English teenager Jenny Bolton drawn into the world of opium smuggling, is suspenseful and enthralling. The characters, particularly her philosopher protagonist and the mysterious Madame Miasma, are finely drawn and memorable. The setting, conveying the exotic atmosphere of Istanbul combined with the bizarre attraction of its very squalor, shows Joan Fleming at her best. In its exploration of the contrasts between cultures, beliefs and moral codes, particularly in placing the young English girl within the different world of Nuri Izkirlak and his friends and enemies, it demonstrates clearly how a mystery plot can be enhanced by a writer of exceptional ability.

Within her English settings, Joan Fleming was again determined to combine crime with other important themes and to present her own social commentaries. For example, her smart doctor in

Fleming, Joan
Kill or cure
Collins, 1968; New York: Washburn, 1968

has his stamping-ground in the 'gin-and-tonic or Jag-belt south of London', and the money flows freely enough for abortions to be arranged smoothly and confidentially. Comes a death, however, and Jeremy finds himself being blackmailed.

Unlike so many women writers in the field, Joan Fleming did not confine herself to tales of the high life or even of the middle classes. The antihero of

Fleming, Joan
Young man, I think you're dying
Collins, 1970; New York: Putnam, 1970

is a young and successful criminal. Nevertheless, this self-made man, known only as W. Sledge, can in no way be regarded as an acceptable member of society. His latent psychopathic tendencies make it only a matter of time before his actions lead to his own destruction. Sledge, perhaps appropriately for one so named, slides inexorably down the slippery slope to murder and its consequences. It is fitting that this chilling portrait of London's youth underworld earned Miss Fleming a further award from the Crime Writers' Association.

There are many authors whose books displayed a transformation from detection to the modern crime novel. Dr Doris Bell Collier Ball (b. 1897), for example, has been writing for some fifty years as 'Josephine Bell'. From her series of detective novels featuring Dr David Wintringham, which began in the 1930s, she turned to stories with an atmosphere of the 1960s and 1970s. This can be clearly seen in

Bell, Josephine
A hydra with six heads
Hodder & Stoughton, 1970; New York: Stein & Day, 1977
when the newly qualified Dr Cartwright is accused of the rape of an unattractive patient. The same thing happened to the doctor for whom he is locum, and who has since been found dead. Cartwright becomes involved in a complex web of corruption, and the plot demonstrates Josephine Bell's success in retaining the twists and surprises of conventional detective fiction without its prewar cosiness.

There is more than crime in

Bell, Josephine
Such a nice client
Hodder & Stoughton, 1977
which was published in New York as *Stroke of death* (Walker, 1977). She uses the peril of an elderly man to show that the social services can sometimes be simplistic and complacent. From the day of her first appointment as old Mr Lawrence's physiotherapist, Lucy Summers suspects that he is being starved to death by his daughter-in-law. The social services department, however, considers Mrs Lawrence 'such a nice client'. While the bureaucracy grinds on, the evil situation escalates; and then Mr Lawrence is drowned, when his wheelchair rolls into the sea.

Of the unusual English mysteries devised by Constance Lindsay Taylor (b. 1907) as 'Guy Cullingford', still the best is

Cullingford, Guy
Post mortem
Hammond, Hammond, 1953; Philadelphia: Lippincott, 1953
in which author Gilbert Worth is shot while asleep at his desk, and his ghost becomes the detective.

Evelyn Berckman (1900–78) began with fairly straightforward mysteries, although of high quality. A good example from her more complex middle period is

Berckman, Evelyn
A simple case of ill-will
Eyre & Spottiswoode, 1964; New York: Dodd, Mead, 1965
where bridge club quarrels lead to the mysterious death of a member. Miss Berckman later diversified in style and subject matter, with novels in the suspense and supernatural categories of which a particularly interesting example is featured in Chapter 11.

The early novels of Mary Kelly (b. 1927) were praised for their industrial settings as well as for their puzzles, and they are still in many ways better than her later explorations of character and concentration upon suspense. In

Kelly, Mary
The spoilt kill
Joseph, 1961; New York: British Book Centre, 1961
a private detective called Nicholson is engaged to investigate industrial espionage at Shentall's pottery works in Stoke-on-Trent, and the case takes a dramatic turn when a body is found in a tank of liquid clay. Mary Kelly shows great skill in conveying the feel of the English pottery city, and she provides memorable insights into the characters involved. Her investigator is not merely there to play a part, but is a totally involved and complex participant in the drama.

Other original detectives and unusual settings were devised by John and Felicity Coulson (both b. 1906), who wrote competent detective novels in the classic form using the pseudonym 'John and Emery Bonett'. An early book of considerable merit was

Bonett, John and **Emery**
A banner for Pegasus
Joseph, 1951
which appeared in New York as *Not in the script* (Doubleday, 1951). Set in the English West Country village of Steeple Tottering, it paints a witty picture of a small community invaded by movie-makers, and spices it with a neat murder mystery. It was comprehensively described by Barzun and Taylor as 'the best example of the motion-picture-company theme, superimposed on the city-slicker-invasion-of-peaceful-village motif'.

Later mysteries by the Coulsons were set in Spain, and feature the courteous and unassuming Inspector Borges. One of the best,

Bonett, John and **Emery**

This side murder?

Joseph, 1967

was published in New York as *Murder on the Costa Brava* (Walker, 1968). It concerns the murder of the unpopular Gilbert Tarsier, a newspaper columnist who is a distinct embarrassment to the guests at the luxury hotel in Cala Cristina. A tissue of lies, evasions and self-protection has to be pierced by Borges before he reaches the solution. One of the novel features – a complete recipe for *paella Catalana* – adds a brilliant touch of authenticity.

Remaining in Spain, mention must be made of Delano Ames (b. 1906), who turned from light and somewhat inconsequential mysteries featuring Jane and Dagobert Brown to create a really solid character, Juan Llorca of the *Guardia Civil* in the fishing village of Madrigal. In

Ames, Delano

The man in the tricorn hat

Methuen, 1960; Chicago: Regnery, 1966

major problems are imported to the peaceful setting with the arrival of a Texan oil millionaire, his sexy niece, an English blackmailer and a temptingly beautiful painter. Murder is done against the noisy and colourful background of the local festival, and Juan's investigation has just the right mixture of excitement and humour supplemented by his own amorous leanings. Specially worthwhile is the picture of Juan's relations with his colleagues and superiors, and the clear delineation of Madrigal citizens according to their social status. It is that comparatively rare item, a whodunit where one does not mind whodunit.

It is difficult to assign Val Gielgud (1900–81) to a specific period in the history of the genre. He began writing crime fiction in the 1930s, and proved over many years to be a competent purveyor of the old fashioned mystery as well as those which move with the times. Many of his later novels feature Gregory Pellew, formerly of Scotland Yard, who joins with Viscount Humphrey Clymping to found the detective agency Prinvest London. One of the best is

Gielgud, Val

A necessary end

Collins, 1969

in which Pellew and Clymping, together with Clymping's wife Kate and his mother Lady Hannington, are among the passengers on board the freighter *Daisy Belle*. This formidable team need to put their skills and wiles to the test when a savage murder is committed, which provides classic detection at its best with a closed circle of suspects. The book is enhanced by credible characterization, and by Gielgud's ability to present an authentic shipboard atmosphere as the freighter makes her way down the western seaboard of America amid mounting tension.

Like Gielgud a public figure in England, Beverley Nichols (1898–1983) had been a popular writer for over thirty years before producing his first detective novel,

Nichols, Beverley
No man's street
Hutchinson, 1954; New York: Dutton, 1954

His investigator is Horatio Green, a retired detective who still has a nose for a mystery; indeed he makes frequent use of his finely tuned nostrils, his 'olfactory sense'. Mild-mannered and plump, Mr Green is no obviously charismatic figure, but his performance is nonetheless equal to that of those great detectives of striking physical presence. He appears in only five novels, which were admired by Somerset Maugham yet remain unaccountably forgotten today. This is totally undeserved, since they go well beyond stylishness and ingenuity and each novel introduces a completely original idea, plot device or twist. *No man's street*, for instance, is set in the world of music and concerns the murder of a critic. That may be said of other detective novels, but the unique feature in this case is that the plot hinges upon the very anonymity of the Chelsea street in which the victim lives.

Although J. F. Straker (b. 1904) has written a succession of typically English detective stories and thrillers, his masterpiece remains his first novel,

Straker, J. F.
Postman's knock
Harrap, 1954

in which he introduced Detective Inspector Pitt. This well-balanced story observes the residents of one road, where a postman has mysteriously vanished. At first it is suspected that he has absconded with the mail, it being just before Christmas, but there then emerges the possibility of kidnapping or something even more serious. Grange Road is normally a peaceful and law-abiding area, but do some or all of the residents have something to hide?

The considerable talent of Kenneth Giles (1922–72) produced several good series of mysteries in only six years before his death, a prolific period including titles under his own name and the pseudonyms 'Charles Drummond' and 'Edmund McGirr'. Those by Giles feature an intelligent young Scotland Yard man called Harry James, who rises to the rank of Chief Inspector as the series progresses. In

Giles, Kenneth
Death and Mr Prettyman
Gollancz, 1967; New York: Walker, 1969

there is a Dickensian fog seeping into every London nook, and Dickensian characters abound. There is Mr Greasing, a publisher of pornographic books, and there is the lawyer Prettyman who is found with a knife in his back. It is the twelfth such stabbing within a few weeks, always with a black-handled knife. Thought of a latter day Jack the Ripper must be modified, however, as this time all victims are male and evidence suggests that the murderer is a woman. It presents Harry James with a fascinating case, and the reader with more than a few surprises.

Sergeant Reed of Scotland Yard is the series character of 'Charles Drummond', and in

Drummond, Charles
A death at the bar
Gollancz, 1972; New York: Walker, 1973

he investigates the murder of a London publican, Harry Alwyn, found at the Admiral Byng with his head bashed in by a bottle. Reed is a complex character with his own ideas about justice, as the conclusion of this case shows.

Journalist and writer on diverse subjects, Dudley Barker (1910–80) turned to detective fiction in 1960 and produced a dozen readable and well-plotted examples as 'Lionel Black', many in comfortable English settings and several featuring crime reporter Kate Theobald. A typical locale is the village of Linchester in

Black, Lionel
Death has green fingers
Collins, 1971; New York: Walker, 1971

which was published in New York as by 'Anthony Matthews'. Linchester gardeners have the competitive spirit when it comes to breeding new varieties of rose, but it appears to have gone too far when one of the enthusiasts is found with a pruning knife in his throat.

One of the great losses to classical detective fiction was the death of Dominic Devine (1920–80), who from 1961 wrote some of the finest examples of the genre in Britain. His hallmarks were impeccable characterization, an easy flow of words, and his credible settings in Northern England and Scotland. The first six were published under the name 'D. M. Devine', before he began using his forename. One of the best is

Devine, D. M.
The fifth cord
Collins, 1967; New York: Walker, 1967

which is set in the northern town of Kenburgh, where a young journalist is seeking the perpetrator of the sensational 'cord murders'. The action moves to Scotland in

Devine, Dominic
Illegal tender
Collins, 1970; New York: Walker, 1970

where a junior clerk, who suspects fraud in the town council, is murdered before she can reveal what she knows to the police. The plot involves corruption, jealousies, and illicit activities both professional and domestic. When a second murder occurs at the staff dance, Inspector Hemmings is not satisfied with the obvious solution.

Devine, Dominic
Three green bottles
Collins, 1972; New York: Doubleday, 1972

opens with a strangled schoolgirl on the golf links, and an unstable young doctor found dead at the foot of a cliff. To the police it seems clear that the case is closed, but the doctor's brother is determined to bring the true facts to light. There is a small circle of characters, and the story is told through their interwoven narratives. Like any other of Devine's books, it is compulsively readable and the killer is not easy to spot.

Dominic Devine used no series characters, as his situations and settings would have made it unrealistic to do so. In contrast, Sara Bowen-Judd (1922–85), writing as 'Sara Woods', was responsible for a very long series of detective novels from the early 1960s. Her world of London solicitors' offices, barristers' chambers and lawcourts became well known and popular with readers, as did her regular characters – lawyer Antony Maitland, his wife Jenny, and his eminent uncle Sir Nicholas Harding QC. Together they tackled a wide variety of cases, some of them most ingenious and well planned, and usually they were faced with the task of clearing an innocent client. This is all somewhat reminiscent of Gardner's Perry Mason stories, but the differences are more significant than the similarities.

Woods, Sara
Bloody instructions
Collins, 1962; New York: Harper & Row, 1962

showed the members of the Maitland *ménage* to be clever in the courtroom arts and brilliant at fusing detection with forensic procedures, so as to pull the metaphorical rabbit from the hat in a neat denouement. There is little of the legal chicanery of Mason, however, and much that is essentially English and gentlemanly. In this first case, an elderly solicitor is stabbed in his office near Sir Nicholas Harding's chambers, and Antony Maitland is a principal witness who is likely even to be regarded as a suspect. It is an excellent novel which was followed by a fine series, and there is the perfect combination of authenticity in legal matters, mounting suspense and a good standard of writing.

In the detective novels of Barbara Alison Neville (b. 1925), the regular policeman Superintendent Burnivel appears. Writing as 'Edward Candy', and using her medical and academic background most effectively in slightly esoteric settings, Mrs Neville has produced very few such novels and maintained a high standard. Her witty and literate prose, combined with a genuinely puzzling mystery, was first seen in

Candy, Edward
Which doctor
Gollancz, 1953; New York: Rinehart, 1954

in which a delegate is murdered on the eve of a paediatric conference. A likely witness, a patient at the nearby children's hospital, then disappears.

Candy is adept at conveying the passions and rivalries which can exist in closed professional situations, and in

Candy, Edward
Words for murder perhaps
Gollancz, 1971

they occur in the world of literature rather than medicine. A lecturer in the extramural department at Bantwich University receives a telephone call from his ex-wife to say that her husband is missing, and the only clue is a postcard containing two lines of verse. Thus begins a series of murders, seemingly connected only by elegies from English literature.

Highly intelligent and absorbing, Candy's books are in parts deliciously tongue-in-cheek and in these respects bear comparison with those of Edmund Crispin. So too do the contributions of V. C. Clinton-Baddeley (1900–70), who was arguably the finest reviver of the don-detective tradition. His beautifully constructed stories brought us the nostalgic septuagenarian Dr R. V. Davie of St Nicholas College, Cambridge. Again, it is a tragedy that Clinton-Baddeley wrote only five detective novels late in life; but they are among the cream of the field in the late 1960s. His characters are skilful pen portraits, his dialogue a delight. In

Clinton-Baddeley, V. C.
Only a matter of time
Gollancz, 1969; New York: Morrow, 1970

Dr Davie visits the King's Lacy music festival, a very English affair, and encounters a host of eccentrics in the worlds of the arts, antiques and local light industry. Two murders provide a beguiling puzzle, but the principal pleasures for the reader lie in the charming writing and the fads and foibles of King's Lacy folk.

There are similar pleasures in

Clinton-Baddeley, V. C.
No case for the police
Gollancz, 1970; New York: Morrow, 1970

when Dr Davie returns to his boyhood haunts in South Devon. He nostalgically recalls his escapades with the friend who later achieved eminence as an explorer, and whose death has brought Davie back to the village. Soon there is another death requiring his attention, and the whole is another helping of Clinton-Baddeley magic.

While on the subject of idiosyncratic detectives, one must not forget two really accomplished exponents of the humorous crime novel, Joyce Porter and Colin Watson.

In Chief Inspector Wilfred Dover, Joyce Porter (b. 1924) created the most unspeakable character in modern detective fiction. Obese, idle and boorish, with his efficiency as a police officer constantly open to question, it is almost surprising that we can find him amusing. But Miss Porter has a deftly humorous way with words, and Dover muddling through is a marvellous piece of farce. His first appearance, in

Porter, Joyce
Dover one
Cape, 1964; New York: Scribner, 1964
sees Dover crashing his disagreeable way through a case
involving the nasty murder of a servant girl on a country estate. It
was followed by several others, but the joke began to wear a little
thin. Miss Porter was equal to the occasion, and set readers
laughing again with a new character, the Hon. Constance
Morrison-Burke. In
Porter, Joyce
A meddler and her murder
Weidenfeld & Nicolson, 1972; New York: McKay, 1973
an Irish au pair is murdered near the Hon Con's residence, and
that worthy lady tramples forth on another case. She is aggres-
sively upper-crust, with a hide like a rhinoceros and a tendency to
bully the lower classes. In the 'Hon. Con.' novels, Joyce Porter
combines first-class detection with black comedy.

Colin Watson (1920–83), on the other hand, built his comedy
around a whole town rather than a central character. Behind the
faultless facade of Flaxborough there lurk many feelings which
are far from exemplary, and the principal citizens display more
than a trace of hypocrisy. Watson pricks such hypocrisy unmer-
cifully, and provides many belly laughs in the process. In his
obituary in *The Times* of London, his books were described as
'Donald McGill postcards set down in print'.

Colin Watson caricatures while managing to walk the thin line
between comedy and farce. He presents detective problems to be
solved, but does not intend them to be taken too seriously.
Among his regulars, etched so admirably, are Chief Constable
Chubb and the get-there-in-the-end Inspector Purbright. The
Flaxborough novels can be thoroughly recommended, and the
best introduction to them is the omnibus volume
Watson, Colin
The Flaxborough chronicle
Eyre & Spottiswoode, 1969
which includes an introduction by Julian Symons and consists of
Coffin, scarcely used (Eyre & Spottiswoode, 1958; New York:
Putnam, 1967); *Bump in the night* (Eyre & Spottiswoode, 1960;
New York: Walker, 1962); and *Hopjoy was here* (Eyre & Spot-
tiswoode, 1962; New York: Walker, 1963). Between the covers
of this collection can be found the citizen who is apparently

electrocuted by scaling a pylon while munching marshmallow, some explosive vandalism perpetrated upon pompous monuments, and an unusually hilarious acid-bath murder.

One of Colin Watson's best novels,

Watson, Colin
Lonelyheart 4122
Eyre & Spottiswoode, 1967; New York: Putnam, 1967

sees Inspector Purbright grappling with the fact that several Flaxborough ladies have disappeared. The only common factor, apart from their wealth, is their matrimonial availability. This leads Purbright to a marriage bureau called Handclasp House, and to some murderous skulduggery in true Watson vein. It also leads to his involvement with a genteel confidence lady, Miss Lucilla Edith Cavell Teatime.

No consideration of American detective fiction would be complete without Hugh C. Wheeler (b. 1912), who with Richard W. Webb collaborated under the pseudonyms 'Patrick Quentin', 'Q. Patrick' and 'Jonathan Stagge'. Under the Quentin banner from 1936 they wrote a satisfying series of mysteries featuring Broadway theatrical personalities Peter and Iris Duluth. After Webb left the partnership in 1952, Wheeler continued to produce fine mysteries for many years, a superb example being

Quentin, Patrick
The man with two wives
New York: Simon & Schuster, 1955; Gollancz, 1955

This is a strangely compelling mixture of whodunit and psychological thriller, presenting a dramatic situation with frightening credibility. Bill Harding meets his ex-wife Angelica again, and finds she has become emotionally involved with a nasty piece of work called Jaimie Lumb. While Harding's second wife is out of town, Angelica visits him in the small hours – at the precise time, it seems, that Jaimie is being murdered. Can Harding give her an alibi, and risk his second marriage? To make matters worse, his rich father-in-law wants him to provide an alibi for someone else. The whole complex story is narrated by the unfortunate Harding, totally innocent himself and yet caught like a fly in a web until the final startling revelation.

This technique of presenting an innocent central character who becomes increasingly stuck in the mire proved to be a great favourite with Wheeler in his solo novels. Often the detection is in the hands of Lieutenant Timothy Trant of New York, who is at first a thorn in the side of the suffering protagonist but always comes up with the right solution in the end.

To return to the collaboration of Wheeler and Webb, they also produced many short stories which have come to be regarded as classics of suspense. The superlative collection

Quentin, Patrick
The ordeal of Mrs Snow and other stories
Gollancz, 1961; New York: Random House, 1962
presents the best of these early stories, blending the mysterious with the bizarre and including several spine-chilling portraits of childhood evil.

An extremely prolific novelist since the mid-1930s, Aaron Marc Stein (b. 1906) has written many books under his own name as well as series by 'Hampton Stone' and 'George Bagby'. The Hampton Stone books featuring New York's Assistant District Attorney Jeremiah Gibson are particularly good, with great ingenuity and plots that are enhanced by a lively style of writing. It is also noteworthy that in

Stone, Hampton
The murder that wouldn't stay solved
New York: Simon & Schuster, 1951
Gibson has to deal with a hotel murder which arises from a homosexual relationship. This was at the time an unusual theme for a mystery novel, and could well account for the fact that it was not published in Britain. No such risky themes normally appeared in his series featuring Inspector Schmidt of the Manhattan Homicide Bureau, although the conventional detection could at times be spiced with social comment. For example, in

Bagby, George
The body in the basket
New York: Doubleday, 1954; Macdonald, 1956
'Schmitty' and his Watson-narrator Bagby are in what is (for them) an unusual setting, trying to relax on vacation in Madrid. Instead they wrestle with complications including a disappearing American girl, a criminous shoeshine boy, and an unexpected delivery to Bagby's hotel room – a basket containing the body of a man wearing the uniform of the *Guardia Civil*. The book is pervaded with the menace of the Spanish authorities, especially with Schmitty outside his jurisdiction, although liberally larded with humour. There is a neat puzzle to be solved, without the usual distraction of Schmitty constantly complaining about his aching feet.

97

A Grand Master of the Mystery Writers of America and the author of over 100 crime novels, Aaron Marc Stein has never achieved in Britain the recognition he deserves for solid and reliable standards maintained over half a century. Much the same may be said of Judson Philips (b. 1903), writing also as 'Hugh Pentecost'. Creator of many series detectives and intriguing puzzles, perhaps his best-known creation as Pentecost is the manager of New York's prestigious Hotel Beaumont, Pierre Chambrun. Also as Pentecost, he produced some interesting cases featuring a giant red-bearded artist of Greenwich Village called John Jericho, the first of which,

Pentecost, Hugh
Sniper
New York: Dodd, Mead, 1965; Boardman, 1966
concerns the murder of the head of a preparatory school in New England.

Another Pentecost sleuth, arguably his most interesting, is Uncle George Crowder. He is a man living with his conscience in secluded retirement, the setting being the wooded Connecticut country around Lakewood. Formerly a county prosecutor, he spends his time in open-air pursuits and is haunted by the fact that he once sent an innocent man to the electric chair. His sanctuary is enlivened by his young nephew Joey Trimble, who describes him as 'my dear Uncle Sherlock' and involves him in local mysteries. Crowder appeared mainly in short stories and novelettes, and most of them were later collected as

Pentecost, Hugh
Around dark corners
New York: Dodd, Mead, 1970
Writing under his own name, Judson Philips has again used several series detectives. The best known is Peter Styles, a one-legged crusading journalist whose assignments for *Newsday* magazine seem continually to bring him face to face with violent crime. Suspenseful and fast-moving, the Styles novels involve less detection than the various series by Pentecost. One of the most gripping is

Philips, Judson
Hot summer killing
New York: Dodd, Mead, 1968; Gollancz, 1969
which concerns a threat by alleged black militants to blow up Grand Central Station during the rush hour. Such a threat is well

used by Philips, by showing the steps taken to avert a tragedy and inflicting mounting tension upon the reader.

Slightly later on the scene than Stein and Philips but in many respects in the same mould, Harold Q. Masur (b. 1909) contented himself with one series detective, attorney Scott Jordan. Rather like Gardner's Perry Mason, his cases involve him in detection in pursuit of his client's defence, but Masur relies more upon points of law than the contrived devices of Gardner. In a very good example,

Masur, Harold Q.
Make a killing
New York: Random House, 1964; Boardman, 1964
Jordan encounters mayhem arising from a battle for control of a motion picture studio. The world of the movies, with the gloves off, is well presented by a writer who is able to keep the reader guessing in a most entertaining manner.

Contemporary with Masur as a mystery novelist, although he began in the 1930s with pulp novelettes, Fredric Brown (1906–72) remains best known for his cases of Ed and Am Hunter, a teen-ager and his uncle who appeared in some well-written stories. The first,

Brown, Fredric
The fabulous clipjoint
New York: Dutton, 1947; Boardman, 1949
received an award from the Mystery Writers of America as the best first crime novel of its year. It establishes this original detective duo by describing how Ambrose, a carnival pitchman, goes to Chicago to help his young nephew solve a vicious murder in their own family. Even the title is well conceived, the fabulous clipjoint being Chicago itself.

Born in Ireland but resident in America for many years, Leonard Wibberley (1915–83) turned to mystery novels as 'Leonard Holton' and introduced as his detective the Catholic priest Father Joseph Bredder. To Father Bredder the seamier streets of Los Angeles provide the mysteries which other fictional detectives find in the city's more glamorous environs, and his spiritual mission makes him a more credible character than the amateur sleuth who finds detection little more than a parlour game. It is not for self-gratification or personal pleasure that Father Bredder probes into a mystery, but to clear the innocent and expose the guilty to a more supreme and more forgiving court than is to be found on earth. This does not mean that he is a soft touch, and indeed his experience as an amateur boxer and a Marine sergeant have given him the toughness and confidence to face up to villains from the slums as well as those from the more affluent classes. A strong religious theme is the basis of

Holton, Leonard
The saint maker
New York: Dodd, Mead, 1959; Hale, 1960

in which a killer is selecting victims while they are in a state of grace, having received absolution from their sins, in the belief that in dying they will go to Heaven unsullied by this world. Father Bredder's involvement in the case arises from particularly dramatic and bizarre circumstances, when the head of a victim is left in his church before a statue of John the Baptist.

Turning to one of America's more interesting women novelists in the genre, Mary McMullen (b. 1920), it is of note that her mother was the veteran mystery writer Helen Reilly (1891–1962), while her sister, Ursula Curtiss, is featured elsewhere in this book. Mary McMullen produced her first book in 1951 and did not resume her writing until 1974, since when she has produced many competent mysteries and suspense novels. Nevertheless the first,

McMullen, Mary
Stranglehold
New York: Harper, 1951

which was published in London as *Death of Miss X* (Collins, 1952) remains for many readers her best. Set in a New York advertising agency, it tells how newly appointed copywriter Eve Fitzsimmons discovers a nude corpse in the boardroom, strangled with a tartan tie. The Mystery Writers of America judged it to be the best first crime novel of its year, acclaim which was well merited not only for its mystery puzzle but also for its tense atmosphere, characterization and carefully observed background.

Finally, having covered major contributors from Britain and the USA, it is worth turning attention again to Australia. S. H. Courtier (1904–74) was in the mould of Arthur Upfield, spelling a powerful atmosphere with his settings and characters in spite of the fact that he had no strong central detective with the persona of Upfield's Napoleon Bonaparte. His feeling for the Australian peoples and their traditions makes his novels particularly impressive, and this, together with his original plots, makes it unaccountable that he has been neglected by historians of the genre. A good example of his work is

Courtier, S. H.
Death in Dream Time
Hammond, Hammond, 1959

which opens with Jock Corless being summoned to the wilds of Queensland to help his cousin Laurie Moore. Laurie is involved in Alchera, the Dream Time Land, a park consisting of a fantastic series of dioramas depicting the beliefs and initiation ceremonies of the Aranda tribesmen. Laurie is murdered before the two can meet, and this signals the arrival of the incredibly ugly Inspector 'Digger' Haig of Brisbane. In a timespan of less than twenty-four hours, Courtier not only takes the reader along with the investigation, which involves more murders, but also brings the dioramas to life in sequence. The book achieves a brooding and often chilling atmosphere, combining ancient rites and the supernatural with the murder mystery.

'Digger' Haig appeared in several of Courtier's novels, but there are others with no series character. In

Courtier, S. H.
Murder's burning
Hammond, Hammond, 1967; New York: Random House, 1968

a fire patrol officer investigates the death of his friend in a fire that devastated a small town. Again Courtier shows himself to be a master of locale, and his descriptive passages bring Paladin Valley to life most effectively.

Another regrettably underrated Australian, 'Margot Neville', was the pseudonym used by Margot Goyder (b. 1903) and Anne Neville Joske (b. 1893) of Melbourne. From the 1940s to the 1960s they wrote a series of detective novels of a uniformly high standard, but very different from those of their compatriots Upfield and Courtier. The background is Sydney or its suburbs, the characters and the situations sophisticated and modern. The detectives, Inspector Grogan and Sergeant Manning, are of the persistent and highly efficient school rather than quaint or bizarre characters. Suspects invariably form a closed circle, members of a middle-class family and their friends and neighbours. Their loves, hates and fears are skilfully revealed, and the plots are in all cases twisting and clever. The tone was set from the beginning with

Neville, Margot
Lena hates men
New York: Mystery House, 1943
which was published in London as *Murder in Rockwater* (Bles, 1944). It was followed by some twenty examples of the literate and intelligent detective novel. All of them rival the best in the genre produced by Britain and the USA. Compulsive readers of whodunits often find it easy to spot the murderers, having become accustomed to the wiles and devices used by authors to conceal them; but Margot Neville usually manages to spring a complete surprise.

Neville, Margot
Murder of the well-beloved
Bles, 1953; New York: Doubleday, 1953
is one of many ingenious stories, tightly plotted and with skilfully drawn characters, one of whom proves to be a totally unexpected murderer.

8

THE HARD-BOILED SCHOOL

Rebellion against the quiet gentility of the classic detective story took various forms. One of these resulted in a whole new movement known as 'the hard-boiled school', which is still a major force today.

It is an American movement, and its characters were tough, laconic, and infinitely more world-weary than the usual run of fictional detectives. They used guns and physical force more than intellectual reasoning, but this is not to say that the novels consisted only of action-packed incident. The best of them dig into the various forms of corruption in both high and low places, and secure the reader's interest and sympathy by demonstrating that a situation is rarely all black or all white. This view is normally through the eyes of a hard detective who, although capable of fighting fire with fire, is often also something of a philosopher.

The trends of detective fiction in the 1920s and 1930s were roundly rejected. The tendency to over-elaborate was resisted, and the hard-boiled school made little or no use of footnotes, diagrams, lists of characters, challenges to the reader, and the varied impedimenta of the English school. The crossword puzzle brigade, with their strict rules of the game, held no relevance for this gritty school which emerged in the USA from the early 1930s.

'When in doubt have a man come through a door with a gun in his hand' was Raymond Chandler's tongue-in-cheek answer to plotting difficulties. To this may be attributed the pace of Chandler's novels and those of his fellows, but there is much more than this in the best of the hard-boiled school. The work of Hammett, Chandler and others frequently retain the old whodunit element, with a degree of characterization and social commentary found in too few mystery novels of the classical form.

Dashiell Hammett (1894–1961) was the undisputed father of the school. It would be wrong to regard his work as sheer sensationalism, or even to categorize his stories purely as hard-boiled. Although his detectives display a toughness and cynicism which was revolutionary in the history of the genre, they are also capable of compassion and have an inherent honesty; very few of Hammett's imitators have been able to produce characters with quite the same strength of personality. It is Hammett's dialogue which is particularly memorable, and he has been seriously compared with both Faulkner and Hemingway in this respect.

Hammett's early stories and novellas mainly appeared in the legendary pulp magazine *Black mask*. The best of them featured an anonymous narrator from the Continental Detective Agency, decribed only as 'fat and forty' and known as the Continental Op. These tales had the authentic tang derived from Hammett's own experience with the famous Pinkerton Agency, but arguably his reputation today rests on his five full length novels, most notably *The Maltese falcon* and *The glass key*. In

Hammett, Dashiell
The Maltese falcon
New York and London: Knopf, 1930

Sam Spade, the prototype of the private eye which has never been bettered by subsequent authors, wisecracks his way in pursuit of the person who killed his partner. There can be few readers or movie enthusiasts who do not know that the root of all the evil is a priceless black falcon statuette. But the book, on rereading, still impresses with its pace, its crisp dialogue, and the sting in the tail. If this is Hammett's most famous book, it is generally accepted that

Hammett, Dashiell
The glass key
New York and London: Knopf, 1931

is his best. It represented his full development as a novelist, not just as a crime writer but an explorer of human relationships. The most important is that between Ned Beaumont, the intelligent 'fixer' working in the ruthless milieu of political chicanery, and his boss Paul Madvig.

It is more than the story of Beaumont's search for the killer of a

New York senator's son. The world of gambling, of gangsters and of politics is all here, in a manner which suggests most vividly that guilt and innocence are relative terms and there is often a thin dividing line. What a pity it is that Hammett is judged too frequently as a crime writer, a pulp writer even, when voices in the wilderness have compared him with some of the finest American novelists.

A comprehensive collection of crime fiction should contain all of Hammett's novels, together with the best of the Continental Op stories and novellas. Fortunately this cornucopia is provided by three omnibus volumes: *The Dashiell Hammett omnibus* (Cassell, 1950), *The big knockover* (New York: Random House, 1966) and *The Continental Op* (New York: Random House, 1974; Macmillan, 1975). *The big knockover* was published in London as *The Dashiell Hammett story omnibus* (Cassell, 1966).

A contemporary of Hammett, James M. Cain (1892–1977) produced a novel with an intriguing title,

Cain, James M.
The postman always rings twice
New York: Knopf, 1934; Cape, 1934

which is a comparatively slight volume with a well-worn theme – the wife and lover who plan to eliminate the husband. It has been done before and since, but this particular book stands out for its economy of words, and the rough justice of its denouement which makes the reader's sympathy difficult to place. It is a portrait of two amateur murderers enmeshed in a situation where they cannot escape from each other, prisoners alternately of love and of the consequences of their act.

Raymond Chandler (1888–1959) ranks with Hammett as the exemplar of the hard-boiled school. Although his work might seem as American as his birth, Chandler was brought up and educated in England. His experience of life was considerable, as he passed through many occupations before becoming a contributor to pulp magazines. To his writing he brought a worldly manner and a degree of shrewd observation, which justified his own contention that a plot should not be regarded as more important than the actual writing. He set out to write well, and he succeeded admirably. His way with words, his characterization and his exceptional gift for dialogue improved markedly as his output increased. The seven novels featuring Philip Marlowe, the private investigator who could cut someone down to size with a wisecrack, are of course the basis of Chandler's fine reputation in the field.

Marlowe is a good guy, but not embarrassingly so; an honourable man, who abhors cruelty and corruption. To use Chandler's own words, Marlowe has to walk down mean streets without himself being mean. He encounters richly assorted characters, nice, neurotic and nasty. The Marlowe cases are whodunits, but their atmosphere is the complete antithesis of that of the vicarage murder or the body in the library. Their principal players are of flesh and blood, which is one reason why Chandler succeeded where so many of his imitators failed.

While Chandler's later novels have their admirers, it is the early works which to the aficionado represent the quintessential Marlowe. Collected as

Chandler, Raymond
The Raymond Chandler omnibus
Hamish Hamilton, 1953; New York: Knopf, 1964
they are *The big sleep* (New York: Knopf, 1939; Hamish Hamilton, 1939); *Farewell, my lovely* (New York: Knopf, 1940; Hamish Hamilton, 1940); *The high window* (New York: Knopf, 1942; Hamish Hamilton, 1943); and *The lady in the lake* (New York: Knopf, 1943; Hamish Hamilton, 1944).

Although regarded as a follower of Hammett and very much a representative of the hard-boiled school, Jonathan Latimer (1906–83) demonstrated a degree of lightheartedness, sometimes combined with more sexual explicitness than other writers of the period displayed. There is very little situation comedy in his novels, but the dialogue is laced with humour. In

Latimer, Jonathan
The lady in the morgue
New York: Doubleday, Doran, 1936; Methuen, 1937
private detective Bill Crane, although less physical than some of Hammett's creations, is still a master of the wisecrack. This is no mean tribute to Jonathan Latimer's skill; so many later writers tried their hands at it, and either failed miserably or descended to the level of unintentional pastiche. On this occasion Crane is faced with the puzzle of a corpse which is stolen from the morgue, and the murder of an attendant. The action is fast and furious.

'From the way her buttocks looked under the black silk dress, I knew she'd be good in bed.' These opening words by private investigator Karl Craven give a foretaste of what some critics regard as Latimer's best novel,

Latimer, Jonathan
Solomon's vineyard
Methuen, 1941

which was later published in New York as *The fifth grave* (Popular Library, 1950). It is an advance on *The lady in the morgue* with less humour, more violence, and considerably more sex, including a masochistic broad. Latimer also brings to this story a theme previously used by Hammett – who killed the detective's partner? – and a novel idea connecting gangsters with a rather questionable religious sect.

Another follower in the wake of Hammett was Cornell Woolrich (1903–68), who wrote also as 'William Irish'.

Woolrich, Cornell
The bride wore black
New York: Simon & Schuster, 1940; Hale, 1942

is a taut tale of an unknown woman who enters the lives of four men, strikes, and then vanishes. Who is this beautiful murderess, and what is her motive? A fifth man is next on the list, and the reader is left in doubt until the final pages as to whether the killer will succeed again. It builds to an exciting climax. Woolrich's technique was based upon subordinating everything to what he called the 'line of suspense'. Irrespective of one's acceptance or otherwise of the technical term, it certainly worked. It can be seen again under his *alter ego* in

Irish, William
Phantom lady
Philadelphia: Lippincott, 1942; Hale, 1945

which shows a young man, Scott Henderson, in a predicament. At the time his wife is being strangled with his necktie, he is wining and dining a mysterious lady. So mysterious is she, in fact, that no-one else can remember having seen her or can vouch for her existence – which is distinctly awkward for Scott, who is convicted of murder and sentenced to the electric chair. The dialogue crackles, and the pace moves fast towards the day of execution.

In spite of various excellent examples, many of the writers who followed Hammett and Chandler in style are little known today. Take, for example, 'Wade Miller', a pseudonym adopted by two ex-sergeants of the USAF when they collaborated to write crime novels. Bob Wade (b. 1920) and Bill Miller (1920–61) wrote some twenty books under this name and others as 'Whit Masterson', the first of which,

Miller, Wade
Deadly weapon
New York: Farrar, Straus & Rinehart, 1946; Sampson Low, 1947

received great acclaim. It contains several well-drawn characters, notably the detective Walter James, stripper Shasta Lynn, and a dry cop named Austin Clapp. The plot has the pace and violence of Hammett, without his inherent commentary upon the corruption which he sees around. It also has a sensational climax, and among a mass of similar books it calls out for greater recognition.

Several titles by Wade Miller featured the world-weary San Diego private eye Max Thursday. In

Miller, Wade
Uneasy street
New York: Farrar, Straus & Rinehart, 1948; Sampson Low, 1949

Max takes on an apparently straightforward assignment to deliver an antique music-box to a Count von Raschke. This is but a prelude to murder, and he has to expose a clever killer in order to clear himself of Inspector Austin Clapp's suspicion. It is a fast-moving, readable and ingenious story, providing further evidence of Wade Miller's distinction in the field of the private eye novel.

Similarly unknown today is Paul William Ryan (1906–47), who wrote a handful of books as 'Robert Finnegan' and displayed a very real talent. With a sure touch he painted backgrounds of low and high life, and permeated his stories with the atmosphere of the immediate post war years. In

Finnegan, Robert
The bandaged nude
New York: Simon & Schuster, 1946; Boardman, 1949

journalist Dan Banion feels this atmosphere even within himself, as he drifts around after his discharge from the army. In the people he meets, he 'could see it in their eyes and sense it in their conversation. Restlessness. Dissatisfaction. An uncertainty about the world and about themselves. The war had left everybody on edge.' In a San Francisco bar, Dan learns of the painting of a bandaged nude, and soon afterwards the artist is found dead in a lorry load of spaghetti. There is much wisecracking dialogue worthy of Raymond Chandler, some irresistible dry humour, and plenty of twists and turns before the killer is revealed.

Turning from private eyes and amateur detectives, another manifestation of the hard-boiled novel was the tale of gangster warfare. One of the most prominent early names in this field was W. R. Burnett (1899–1982), who broke new ground in

Burnett, W.R.
Little Caesar
New York: Dial Press, 1929; Cape, 1929

by depicting the criminal underworld in all its power and ruthlessness. It follows the rise and fall of Cesare Bandello, known as Rico, an ambitious Italian gangster in Chicago whose diminutive stature belies his toughness and lack of compassion. It tells also of the urban society that fosters such men, and so explains something of the emergence of the racketeers who were later to dominate Chicago. Just as the moviegoer will never forget Edward G. Robinson's final words as the screen's Little Caesar – 'Mother of God, is this the end of Rico?' – so the book itself will remain a classic.

Twenty years later, in

Burnett, W. R.
The asphalt jungle
New York: Knopf, 1949; Macdonald, 1950

Burnett again led a field which has since become extensive, or perhaps opened a vein which is now overworked. It is the classic 'big heist' story, showing the planning and execution of a complex robbery which ultimately founders when a mistake is made.

Sadly, it has to be said that Burnett was followed by many bad writers, which made the work of William McGivern (1920–82) even more refreshing. A former newspaper man, McGivern could tell an excellent story while raising some uncomfortable questions. For him there were no moral absolutes, and his policemen were as human and open to temptation as were his criminals. Frequently the message of McGivern is that prejudice and corruption exists on both sides of the law, but still the law must survive as the final arbiter if the city is not to degenerate into a human jungle, where the strong and ruthless survive and the weak and innocent perish. Of many fine works, pride of place goes to

McGivern, William
Rogue cop
New York: Dodd, Mead, 1954; Collins, 1955
for its portrait of Sergeant Mike Carmody, who is in the pay of mobsters. In contrast there is his younger brother Eddie, an honest cop who intends to testify against the mob. When Eddie is murdered, Mike reaches the point where he has to make a choice, and from that point McGivern presents a masterly story of revenge and mounting suspense combined with a fine and compassionate eye for human relationships.

Before examining the modern private eye novel, which is the legacy of Hammett and Chandler, two more outstanding books in the gangster field must be mentioned. The first, by Eleazar Lipsky (b. 1911), became a classic film, and it is a pity that the book itself is not better known today. The central character of

Lipsky, Eleazar
The kiss of death
New York: Penguin, 1947; Penguin, 1949
is a hardened criminal called Vanni Bianco; his environment, and the fact that as a boy he saw his father gunned down by a cop, has ensured that crime is a normal way of life to him. He believes that an informer is the lowest of the low, but this short novel shows how Bianco, while retaining the highest code of honour, becomes an informer himself. The Assistant District Attorney, with his symbol of the open door to a happy family existence, leaves Bianco little choice. But for a man with such a record, finding himself between two camps, there can be no real freedom. This is an exciting story of hard men, and yet one of the most poignant crime novels one is likely to come across.

Like Lipsky's novel, that of William Wiegand (b. 1928) is not as well known as it deserves to be.

Wiegand, William
At last, Mr Tolliver
New York: Rinehart, 1950; Hodder & Stoughton, 1951
tells of an elderly and discredited ex-doctor who lives in a seedy boarding house, once a doctor to hoodlums but now having to eke out an existence in a shop selling stamps and coins. He has a dream, the only thing which means anything to him – to carry out medical work in Brazil, and to set up a laboratory there. When one of his fellow boarders is murdered and suspicion falls upon everyone in the house, it is likely that the boorish Lieutenant

110

Carmichael will unearth Tolliver's past, and the old man's dream looks less like becoming a reality. So Tolliver himself begins to investigate the murder, to use his knowledge of the underworld to expose the killer, but behind him constantly is Carmichael. The figures of the unscrupulous Carmichael and the sympathetically portrayed Tolliver combine to make this a memorable book. It has a harshness, and yet at the same time a tenderness, which few American crime novels display.

In the field of the modern private eye novel, one writer who is certain to survive the test of time is Kenneth Millar (1915–83). He wrote at first under his own name, but his series of Lew Archer mysteries was produced under the successive pseudonyms 'John Macdonald', 'John Ross Macdonald' and 'Ross Macdonald'. Most appeared under the latter pseudonym, and 'Ross Macdonald' has been hailed by critics over several decades as the foremost successor to Hammett and Chandler. Lew Archer, the Los Angeles private eye, is something special. It was clear from an early success,

Macdonald, John Ross
The ivory grin
New York: Knopf, 1952; Cassell, 1953

that Macdonald dug psychologically deeper than his predecessors in the hard-boiled tradition. In this case Archer is hired by a woman to find a coloured girl who used to work for her, and who left with some earrings and a necklace – but no case is ever that simple. Like Hammett and Chandler before him, Macdonald used the private eye to show the dirt beneath the surface glitter of some parts of American society.

As the series progressed, the subtlety of Macdonald's writing and his keen eye for character observation became increasingly recognized. He could be sympathetic and compassionate, but could also be bitterly critical of the ugliness in society and the attitudes which have passed from one generation to another. The crimes exposed by Archer frequently stem from a cover-up of earlier crimes or family scandals, and he has to delve into past history to find the roots before he can apportion guilt. In

Macdonald, Ross
The chill
New York: Knopf, 1964; Collins, 1964

Archer is hired to trace Dolly, a runaway bride. He discovers that she has been working as companion to old Mrs Bradshaw,

wealthy mother of Dr Roy Bradshaw, the dean of a college some
forty miles from Los Angeles. The problems of the newly-weds
prove to be connected with a trail of murder that spans a con-
tinent, and complex family relationships keep Archer guessing until an unlikely murderer is revealed in a dramatic
conclusion.

Missing persons frequently provide the starting point of
Archer's cases, before murder and other complications arise.
This is so in

Macdonald, Ross
The far side of the dollar
New York: Knopf, 1965; Collins, 1965

in which the principal of a private reform school asks Archer to
find a missing boy. At first it appears to be a straightforward case
of juvenile delinquency, but it soon becomes a horrific mixture
of murder and extortion.

Not to be confused with John Ross Macdonald, John Dann
MacDonald (b. 1916) entered the field at roughly the same time
but has been much more prolific, with many of his books being
published as paperback originals in the USA. He too is more than
a superb teller of private eye tales, dealing with pressing moral
issues and the unacceptable face of the commercial world, as well
as frequently setting his hero up against the corrupt individuals
who masquerade as benevolent businessmen or democratic politicians. This hero is Travis McGee, an attractive man who was
once a pro football player, who carries out his investigations
from his home base on board his boat *Busted flush* at Fort
Lauderdale in Florida. McGee ostensibly earns his keep by carrying out salvage operations which tread a thin line between legality
and illegality; but in matters of real crime and in his personal
relations he is inherently honest, the champion of the underdog
threatened by corruption and violence. Indeed, he salvages more
than material goods from this very imperfect world.

Sometimes McGee has little liking or tolerance for his clients,
but is instead motivated by sympathy for others caught up in the
case. A good example is

MacDonald, John D.
The quick red fox
New York: Fawcett, 1964; Hale, 1966

in which, after a wild party, actress Lysa Dean receives pho-
tographs and a blackmail demand. McGee would not normally

be enthusiastic about taking the case, and has little regard for Lysa and her problems, but he is drawn to others who are implicated. Before long, he has to become involved himself.

The world in which McGee frequently finds himself is tawdry and evil beneath the tinsel, and his mission is to oppose the encroachment of moral and environmental barbarians. Particularly powerful in this respect is

MacDonald, John D.
The green ripper
Philadelphia: Lippincott, 1979; Hale, 1980

where the mystery plot concerns the death of his lover Gretel Howard, murdered by the Church of the Apocrypha, a cult which fronts for revolutionary terrorists. The implications are of course far wider. The horror of the situation lies in the fact that Gretel is a mere pawn, and the people who hold life to be cheap will not hesitate to kill if their security is threatened.

Not so well known today is the work of Len Zinberg (1911–68), who wrote some thirty private eye novels as 'Ed Lacy'. He was one of the first writers to introduce a black private detective, and to do so was a considerable risk before private eyes and policemen from ethnic minorities became almost a commonplace. Lacy showed great understanding for the position of his hero Toussaint Moore in

Lacy, Ed
Room to swing
New York: Harper, 1957; Boardman, 1958

and his sympathetic treatment of Moore's problems earned him a Mystery Writers of America award for the year's best crime novel. Moore, often out of work or filling in as a postal worker, proves to be a good private detective but is often unhappy about what he has to do. When a murder case takes him from Harlem to a town rife with racial prejudice, he finds that his search for a murderer is the least of his worries. There are many enemies and few friends, and this arises more from the colour of his skin than the fact that his investigation endangers the security of some local people.

Another competent writer, Henry Slesar (b. 1927), provided with his first novel an excellent example of the mystery story set in the world of advertising. This always seems to give a most effective background to a tale of murder and detection, and in this case it may be said that Slesar's own experience in the field enabled him to invest the story with colour and authenticity. Dave Robbins in

Slesar, Henry
The gray flannel shroud
New York: Random House, 1959; Deutsch, 1960

is an ad-man who has to turn amateur sleuth when a colleague is murdered, although he is frequently and humorously sidetracked by his work on the Burke Baby Foods account. It is a fast-paced story of chicanery and murder, with that feel for the setting which Dorothy L. Sayers had shown for its earlier English counterpart in *Murder must advertise*. The principal differences are Slesar's raciness and lightheartedness, rather than merely his nationality.

An entirely different direction was taken by Donald E. Westlake (b. 1933), who turned from standard hard-boiled novels to crime and gangster stories laced with comedy. Simultaneously he has maintained a prolific output of stories of violence and private eyes under pseudonyms including 'Tucker Coe' and 'Richard Stark'. It is for the Westlake world of fall guys and bungling criminals, however, that he has been highly praised. While occasionally causing the reader to ponder or to be affected by the pathos of a situation, they are unique examples of warm humour in a subgenre which is usually all too serious. American slang provides the title for

Westlake, Donald E.
God save the mark
New York: Random House, 1967; Joseph, 1968

A mark is an easy victim, a ready subject for the confidence trickster, in short a sucker. The narrator of this story, Fred Fitch, is the archetypal mark, and no con artist visiting New York considers his trip complete until he has called on Fred. Maybe Fred's luck has changed, as his long-lost Uncle Matt has died and left him $300,000; but maybe not, as Uncle Matt was murdered and someone has the same thing in mind for Fred. The pursuer pursued, Fred recounts this brilliant mixture of suspense and laugh-aloud comedy.

A phenomenon of the 1960s and 1970s was the emergence of the novel in which the protagonist was an avenger, a vigilante, a man who met violence with violence and with whom the reader identified in spite of his particular brand of lawlessness. Again the theme attracted numerous bad writers whose intention was primarily to glorify violence, but there were two novels which specially demonstrated that a good author could have something more to say.

Joe Gores (b. 1931), before turning to high-quality private eye stories, produced something special in his first novel

Gores, Joe
A time of predators
New York: Random House, 1969; W. H. Allen, 1970

The central character is sociology professor Curt Halstead, whose wife commits suicide after being gang-raped by four young thugs. Halstead rediscovers in himself the animal instincts he had experienced when he was a commando, and seeks revenge on the rapists because he cannot rely upon the law taking its course. The pacing and development of tension is superb, but the questions it raises are very important – can there be moral justification for violence, especially when it is premeditated as in Halstead's case, and are we really aggressive animals beneath the accumulated layers of civilised training? Much the same questions were raised in readers' minds by Brian Garfield (b. 1939) when he wrote

Garfield, Brian
Death wish
New York: McKay, 1972; Hodder & Stoughton, 1973

In clipped prose which adds to the readability and suspense, Garfield shows why accountant Paul Benjamin comes to reject the civilized standards he previously accepted and assumes the role of a murdering vigilante. Benjamin's wife and daughter are savagely attacked, and his wife dies from her injuries. It is a crime which he realizes is becoming all too common in New York, and of a type which provides the police with few leads. It transforms Benjamin from ordinary citizen to grieving victim, and then to summary executioner. In this powerful study of the paranoia of big city life, New York becomes the lone man's private battleground.

To return to the private eye novel, it is quite likely that the demise of this sector of crime fiction could have been predicted many years ago. After Hammett and Chandler and their numerous followers, it might have been reasonable to suppose that this particular well was likely to run dry. This has been confounded in the past twenty years by the arrival on the scene of many new writers, some of them excellent, and a minority of whom are clearly more than imitations of the early masters. Moreover they are writers with messages to convey, as well as good stories to tell.

Dennis Lynds (b. 1924), in addition to producing pulp novels and private eye tales under various pseudonyms, introduced his best character under the 'Michael Collins' label. The one-armed investigator Dan Fortune burst on to the scene in

Collins, Michael
Act of fear
New York: Dodd, Mead, 1967; Joseph, 1968

and was highly praised by Ross Macdonald for originality as well as for the author's skill in characterization. As the intelligent and honest Fortune pursues the cases of a mugged policeman, a missing boy and the murder of a young woman, the background of Chelsea in New York is brought vividly to life. Once a young tearaway, Fortune brings to his work an inherent courage and the compassion of a thinking man, with a toughness not manifested in brutality but in his ability to face up to many problems and understand them without running away. The so-called tough private eye, who settles matters by frequent use of firearms or fists, could learn much from Dan Fortune's gentle but strong approach to getting results.

Perhaps the unique investigator of recent years is the middle-aged and sometimes weary Dave Brandstetter, created by Joseph Hansen (b. 1923) in

Hansen, Joseph
Fadeout
New York: Harper & Row, 1970; Harrap, 1972

Brandstetter works as an insurance investigator for Medallion Life in Los Angeles, and is also a director of the Homosexual Information Center. He is himself homosexual, and his relationships both within and outside his cases enable readers to gain a greater understanding. Indeed, Hansen realized that homosexuals had for too long been treated badly in crime fiction, portrayed either as vicious criminals or as pitiable figures. A love affair for Dave Brandstetter is presented by Hansen in a way which provokes neither pity nor revulsion, but at the least an acceptance that Brandstetter is a real person rather than the stereotyped homosexual of fiction.

In *Fadeout* Brandstetter investigates the case of Fox Olsen, whose automobile has plunged into a flooded creek. Olsen has the reputation of a family man, entertainer and local hero, but Brandstetter needs to probe deeply beneath the facade. His difficulties with the case are magnified by his own depression, following the death from cancer of his life partner, an interior decorator called Rod. In

Hansen, Joseph
Skinflick
New York: Holt, Rinehart & Winston, 1979; Faber & Faber, 1980

death comes to Gerald Dawson, a little man with an ambition to change those unsavoury aspects of the world which he dislikes and fears. His killer, the police believe, is the owner of a porno shop which Dawson wrecked. Dave Brandstetter is not convinced, and his investigation takes him into the worlds of evangelism, blue films, teenage drugs and prostitution. It is a tarnished society making people rich, and Brandstetter has to be very determined to uncover the truth.

Michael Z. Lewin (b. 1942) is an American writer who for some years has been resident in England. His private eye stories nevertheless have the authentic American tang, and his series character Albert Samson is a delightful addition to the list of memorable detectives. Operating in Indianapolis, Samson is seedy, impecunious and self-mocking. His clients are few, but they can rely upon his wholehearted personal attention to their problems. He carries no gun and is unlikely to get into a fight, but he gets results by dogged persistence and by displaying a thick skin to those who have something to hide and would be rid of his questions. As with many of Ross Macdonald's plots, those of Michael Z. Lewin normally begin with the detective accepting a case which appears trivial and domestic; by the final page, Samson frequently exposes crimes of great seriousness or scandals of some enormity. In his first case,

Lewin, Michael Z.
Ask the right question
New York: Putnam, 1971; Hamish Hamilton, 1972

Samson is hired by teenager Eloise Crystal to find her biological father, and some hesitant checking on the rich Crystals convinces him that all is not what it seems. From the mere matter of a youngster with a question which she might be better advised to ask of her mother, it soon develops into something more sinister and criminal.

Although Lewin has generally concentrated upon novels with Samson as the narrator, in

Lewin, Michael Z.
Night cover
New York: Knopf, 1976; Hamish Hamilton, 1976

his central character is an Indianapolis policeman, Lieutenant Leroy Powder, a prickly but shrewd man who prefers to work the night shift. Here, among other problems, he has to cope with a string of murders. This is in fact an excellent police procedural novel rather than a private eye story, although Albert Samson makes a brief contribution to Powder's investigation and a link is thus created with Lewin's other work.

On those occasions when a new writer of hard-boiled detective stories received the approbation of Ross Macdonald, it was a sure sign that something special had arrived on an otherwise rather stale scene. One such writer is Roger L. Simon (b. 1943), and the book which caught Macdonald's eye was

Simon, Roger L.
The big fix
San Francisco: Straight Arrow, 1973; Deutsch, 1974

In many respects modelled upon Macdonald's work, it is nevertheless a product of the modern school. The young Jewish private eye Moses Wine is a Berkeley radical, a hirsute and denim-clad rebel who smokes pot and proclaims his Marxist philosophies and his pacifism. The milieu of Southern California provides him with much to attract his disapproval, and like Macdonald's Lew Archer he finds many social evils when he digs beneath the surface of the crimes he investigates.

In *The big fix* Moses Wine is visited by a former girlfriend from college days, Lila Shea, who is a supporter of Senator Miles Hawthorne. The chances of Hawthorne winning the Democratic presidential nomination in the California primary are being damaged by the unwelcome support of Howard Eppis, leader of the Free Amerika Party. Wine agrees to investigate the motives of Eppis, who has himself gone to ground. Although at first reluctant to become embroiled in the dirty business of politics, Wine becomes personally committed when Lila Shea is murdered. It is the start of an intriguing and disturbing puzzle, which demonstrates on almost every page the differences between the old and the new manifestations of the hard-boiled mystery story.

Bill Pronzini (b. 1943) is difficult to categorize, having

produced many short stories and several novels which are not strictly in the hard-boiled tradition. Nevertheless, his best-known creation is the San Francisco private eye to whom Pronzini gives no name other than Bill, who has appeared in novels of a uniformly high standard. For one of the most interesting, Pronzini was in double harness with police procedural writer Collin Wilcox.

Pronzini, Bill and **Wilcox, Collin**
Twospot
New York: Putnam, 1978

thus provides an opportunity to see the two subgenres linked and to identify the contrasts between them. As Pronzini's Bill works on the case with Wilcox's Lieutenant Frank Hastings, it is interesting to compare the freedom of the private detective with the policeman's need to observe standard procedures; the loyalty and confidentiality permitted to the private detective, as opposed to the wider public interest which the policeman must serve; and above all the loneliness and vulnerability of Bill, compared with Frank's back-up machinery and relative security.

Another novel with a joint author,

Pronzini, Bill and **Malzberg, Barry N.**
The running of beasts
New York: Putnam, 1976

shows why Pronzini can not easily be categorized. Here he moves away from the private eye story, as he has frequently done, and presents a crime novel of superlative suspense and horror. It centres upon four men, one of whom is a homicidal maniac. The problems of providing such a small group of suspects and managing to keep the reader guessing must be considerable, yet here is a book which gives to even the most demanding reader a remarkable fusion of psychological suspense and the traditional twisting whodunit. Pronzini always achieves a wholly professional product, and his versatility is quite remarkable.

One of the most exciting arrivals on the recent scene is Gregory McDonald (b. 1937), whose books have featured a journalist called Fletch and a Boston policeman called Flynn. Intelligent and witty, McDonald's work has also embodied suspense and ingenious situations. His principal character Irwin Fletcher (Fletch) is an investigative reporter in his middle thirties, physically attractive and emotionally if not financially carefree after two failed marriages, with a charm and persuasive tongue which can get him out of many a tight corner. In his first adventure,

McDonald, Gregory
Fletch
Indianapolis: Bobbs-Merrill, 1974; Gollancz, 1976
Fletch is working undercover in pursuit of a drug ring, when he is offered a small fortune by a dying millionaire to kill him. Although the purpose of the deal is to ensure that the millionaire's wife will benefit from a hefty insurance policy, all is not so simple. McDonald's technique is to avoid descriptive passages, and the story moves at rapid pace by means of excellent and gripping dialogue. It is a technique which seems to work, for this and subsequent Fletch novels have made him one of the most popular writers in the field today.

Almost reckless originality was brought to the private eye novel in the 1970s by Andrew Bergman (b. 1945). It was clearly an original idea to set his stories back in the 1940s, and so associate himself quite positively with the early masters. It was doubly original to introduce real politicians and movie personalities of the period, rather than just fictional characters. The recklessness arose from the risk that it might not work, or that readers would find the technique contrived or otherwise unacceptable. In the event it was a complete success, with even the aficionados regarding Bergman's books as affectionate historical novels rather than offensive parodies. Indeed it is the highest praise to say that they read as if they were written in the 1940s, and there is no sign that the style has been specially formulated to ape Chandler.

Following the success of *The big kiss-off of 1944* (New York: Holt, Rinehart & Winston, 1974; Hutchinson, 1975), Bergman produced an even better book,

Bergman, Andrew
Hollywood and LeVine
New York: Holt, Rinehart & Winston, 1975; Hutchinson, 1976
With a wit, abrasiveness and plotting ability that would not have disgraced Chandler's own pen, Bergman launches private eye Jack LeVine on his second case amid the first rumblings of McCarthyism in Hollywood. It is a mystery, with LeVine investigating the alleged suicide of his former college friend Walter Adrian. But it is also a fact that Adrian has become a top movie screenwriter, and when he is found hanging on the jailhouse set it has already been established that sinister forces are at work in the

studio. It is thus a historical novel, which is made more effective because today's reader knows the truth of the matter, and can see the intimidation and paranoia of the witch-hunts as an appropriate backcloth for a fictional tale of corruption and murder.

Finally, there can be little argument about the identity of the most significant exponent of the private eye novel today. Robert B. Parker (b. 1932) entered the field in 1974, with books which display all the finest qualities of Hammett, Chandler and Ross Macdonald, together with a detective who is assured of a secure place in the history of the genre. Spenser of Boston is a man of contrasts, a casual wisecracker who can also be deeply compassionate, a tough operator who adopts the bull-like approach when necessary but can also bring to bear his moving concern for the vulnerable, and whose devotion to physical fitness and sport is balanced by his cultured tastes and his dedication as a gourmet. He is his own man with his own moral code, unsullied by those who seek to influence him, a chivalric figure aptly named by his creator after the flower of English Renaissance poetry, Edmund Spenser. He is, therefore, a well-rounded and carefully conceived character, bearing no comparison whatsoever with those many private detectives of fiction who are distinguished from one another mainly by their attitudes to rye or bourbon, blondes or redheads, automatics or revolvers.

On Spenser's first appearance in

Parker, Robert B.
The Godwulf manuscript
Boston: Houghton Mifflin, 1974; Deutsch, 1974

he is hired to find a fourteenth-century illuminated manuscript, stolen from a Boston university and being held for ransom. It is believed that an organization called the Student Committee Against Capitalist Exploitation is responsible, but Spenser finds that the case develops many complications and widens to involve drug-peddling and murder. A lone hero with sufficient character and style to endure most pressures, Spenser is nevertheless sorely tried by unfriendly policemen, a university interested primarily in preserving its own reputation, and the hoodlums who are at the root of the problem.

It must have been clear from this debut that Robert B. Parker would soon be a contender for an award from the Mystery Writers of America. In fact it was his fourth book,

Parker, Robert B.
Promised land
Boston: Houghton Mifflin, 1976; Deutsch, 1977
which was judged the best crime novel of its year. Here Spenser is hired by Harv Shepard to find his wife Pam, the apparently happy mother of three. When he locates Pam living with two radical feminists, it is only the beginning of a complex web of murder, bank robbery and embezzlement. From a seemingly innocuous domestic case, Spenser finds himself in conflict with a notorious loanshark mobster called King Powers. The irony of the book's title lies in the fact that Spenser discovers promises without value and dreams which can not be fulfilled, culminating in crimes which reflect this world's imperfections rather than a romantic conception. Acerbic wit pervades the book, as indeed is the case with Parker's stories generally.

SOLIHULL
SIXTH FORM
COLLEGE

9

FLIGHT FROM MAYHEM PARVA: MODERN CRIME FICTION

Dashiell Hammett's best work appeared in the early 1930s. It coincided with another refreshing deviation from conventional detective themes which was given life by Anthony Berkeley in England. He had already flouted the rules or sailed close to the wind in several of his novels, two of which were cited earlier. It was in his books as 'Francis Iles', however, that his ideas reached full development. The first was

Iles, Francis
Malice aforethought: the story of a commonplace crime
Gollancz, 1931; New York: Harper, 1931

and this was followed by

Iles, Francis
Before the fact: a murder story for ladies
Gollancz, 1932; New York: Doubleday, Doran, 1932

'It was not until several weeks after he had decided to murder his wife that Dr Bickleigh took any active steps in the matter.' 'Some women give birth to murderers, some go to bed with them, and some marry them. Lina Aysgarth had lived with her husband for nearly eight years before she realized that she was married to a murderer.'

These are the opening passages respectively of the first two Iles titles, and significantly indicate that they presented something entirely different in the world of detective fiction. The mind of the murderer was established as more important than his identity, and indeed, his identity was revealed on the first page rather than the last. Although Iles was not the first to use the technique, these two novels provided the inspiration for a whole new school of crime fiction exemplified by many later writers.

In both books we are made to feel that murder is not a sensational subject. In fact it is planned in the cosy drawing rooms of English suburbia just as painstakingly as in the dens of the criminal classes. The examination of the murderer's mind, and the gradual revelation of how he proceeds with his plans, makes the Iles technique just as enthralling as a detective novel in the classic mould. The element of surprise regarding the murderer's identity has been replaced by the questions: will the murderer carry out his plan, and will he get away with it? But this would be too simplistic a definition of the Iles methods, as he shows that there are more ways of springing surprises than even the most seasoned reader will appreciate.

C. S. Forester (1899–1966), better known for his sea stories, produced an early novel which is not only pre-Iles but also pre-Hornblower.

Forester, C. S.
Payment deferred
Bodley Head, 1926; Boston: Little, Brown, 1942
concerns Mr Marble, an impecunious bank clerk who finds it increasingly difficult to support his family in their modest South London home, and sees the ideal opportunity to pay off his debts when a wealthy nephew arrives from Australia. The visitor is young and alone in the world, and murder occurs quite naturally in this commonplace setting of suburban normality. Mr Marble, having murdered, finds himself being dragged further into the mire together with his family, and the denouement is shattering.

The crime novel which poses questions other than 'whodunit?' is very much a phenomenon of the past forty years, and is much in evidence today. Although many of the authors owe much to Francis Iles, he was himself anticipated by a much earlier book by R. Austin Freeman, who made the first significant attempt to break away from the conventional puzzle format.

Freeman was in any case something of an innovator, in that his Dr Thorndyke employed scientific methods in the detection of crime far more than any other investigator, including Holmes, had done previously. His principal innovation, however, was the creation of the 'inverted' detective story, the first examples of which were collected in

Freeman, R. Austin
The singing bone
Hodder & Stoughton, 1912; New York: Dodd, Mead, 1923
Freeman asked himself, to quote from the preface,

> Would it be possible to write a detective story in which,
> from the outset, the reader was taken entirely into the
> author's confidence, was made an actual witness of the
> crime and furnished with every fact that could possibly be
> used in its detection? Would there be any story left to tell
> when the reader had all these facts?

He was convinced that the idea would be successful, and was
proved correct. Indeed, it established a type of detective story
which later became fully accepted. The idea was to be improved
upon, and to be elaborated in various directions, by many other
writers.

The element of surprise, and of the reader being caught
unawares by a clever detective, is of course absent. The reader is
nevertheless compensated by being in a position of superiority,
of knowing all the facts before the detective is even called in, and
a different kind of satisfaction is derived from observing the
detective at work. The question is 'how will the detective prove
the criminal's guilt?' rather than 'whodunit?'

In her introduction to *Great short stories of detection, mystery
and horror* (Gollancz, 1928), published in New York as *The
omnibus of crime* (Payson & Clarke, 1929), Dorothy L. Sayers
remarked that 'Mr Freeman has had few followers, and appears
to have himself abandoned the formula, which is rather a pity.'
It was not until later that Freeman's idea was to bear fruit in
the work of other writers, who succeeded in establishing the
'inverted' detective story as something far more than an intriguing experiment.

The master of the form was Roy Vickers (1889–1965). A collection of his stories was published in New York as *The Department of Dead Ends* (Spivak, 1947), but the standard and larger
collection is

Vickers, Roy
The Department of Dead Ends
Faber & Faber, 1949; New York: Detective Book Club,
1949

In these stories we know the murderer from the start, we see his
motive and the workings of his mind, and we observe the crime

being committed. The surprise element is embodied in the question – how will the police crack the case? The Department of Dead Ends at Scotland Yard contains the files of unsolved cases, together with clues and objects which have not hitherto been fitted into their places in the respective puzzles. Inspector Rason, sometimes years after the event, has the job of connecting the unconnected and breaking the unbreakable alibi. Normally it is a small everyday object – be it a yellow jumper or a baby's toy trumpet – which brings the murderer to book, and this adds to the stories a fascination all their own. There is, too, a tinge of sadness without sentimentality, most of the murderers being ordinary citizens rather than vicious killers. Even the staunchest advocate of capital punishment should finish these stories with a feeling of sympathy and compassion. A further volume of excellent cases appeared as

Vickers, Roy
Murder will out: nine Dead Ends stories
Faber & Faber, 1950; New York: Detective Book Club, 1954

Richard Henry Sampson (1896–1973), using the name 'Richard Hull', wrote fifteen crime novels in the wake of Francis Iles, the first and best of them being

Hull, Richard
The murder of my aunt
Faber & Faber, 1934; New York: Minton, Balch, 1934

Hull made no secret of the fact that he was so impressed by the technique of Iles that he set out to follow the same course. He wrote in the first person, and this was no doubt to enhance the reader's appreciation of the motive and mind of the murderer. Some of his narrators have minds which are far from cosy. Their intentions are more frequently the sort of deliberate and coldblooded murder with which the reader cannot sympathize, rather than the elimination of someone whose demise would be a distinct gain to society. The aunt in his first book is not everyone's favourite type, but we nonetheless have difficulty in associating with the nephew who plans to murder her. As with Iles, the interest lies in observing the potential murderer's plans step by step, proceeding at a leisurely pace until we are stopped in our tracks by the neat twist at the end.

Another interesting contemporary of Iles, not the least for his touches of black comedy and an intelligent wit, was C. E. Vulliamy (1886–1971). In the 1930s his novels were published under the pseudonym 'Anthony Rolls', but he later reverted to his own name. Particularly effective was

Rolls, Anthony
The vicar's experiments
Bles, 1932

which was published in Boston as *Clerical error* (Little, Brown, 1932). Later editions used the American title, an inspired improvement upon the original, and acknowledged C. E. Vulliamy as the author. Some authorities consider it a *tour de force*, others a mere imitation of Iles. In fact there can be little doubt that it is a clever work, a most compelling study of a clergyman who turns to murder because he believes that he has 'been chosen by the Inscrutable Purpose to be the destroyer of Colonel Cargoy'. The reader is taken each step of the way with a killer who has many likeable qualities, and a victim who can claim little sympathy. As the plot twists and turns, the vicar's mind is seen to be affected by the act he has committed and the further acts which are necessary as a result. In all it is not to be taken too seriously, but it is a polished example of the inverted tale.

The renowned wine expert Raymond Postgate (1896–1971) also wrote several detective novels. Noticeably following the trend against the accepted classic form is

Postgate, Raymond
Verdict of twelve
Collins, 1940; New York: Doubleday, Doran, 1940

which has survived as an outstanding book. There have been others which use the courtroom as a setting, but none in quite this way. The case concerns the poisoning of a small boy, for which his aunt is put on trial, and the evidence is presented from the viewpoint of each member of the jury. The character of each juror is sketched by means of flashbacks, which show why each might interpret the evidence in his or her own peculiar way. As the trial proceeds, and the time draws nearer when the life of the accused will be in the hands of these twelve people, the drama of the situation is more skilfully conveyed than in most other courtroom novels.

A specially fine and realistic crime novel is

Hamilton, Patrick
Hangover Square, or the man with two minds. A story of darkest Earl's Court in the year 1939
Constable, 1941; New York: Random House, 1942

---

which explores the mind of a man driven to murder. Patrick Hamilton (1904–62) wrote such evergreen stage melodramas as *Rope* and *Gaslight*, but here he brilliantly evokes the atmosphere of 'darkest Earl's Court', and draws with sympathy and consummate skill the feckless members of the gang with which the unfortunate George Harvey Bone becomes involved. As a novel of London, and as a horrifying picture of a man's decline, this must surely be a prime example of the sort of book which has shaken the world of crime fiction out of its prewar cosiness.

At this point it is well worth examining the work of five women writers, four American and one British, who made signal contributions to the modern crime novel as we know it today. The first, Vera Caspary (b. 1904) is still best known as the author of

Caspary, Vera
Laura
Boston: Houghton Mifflin, 1943; Eyre & Spottiswoode, 1944

which was immortalized as a movie classic but is still a superlative novel in its own right. It is not an inverted tale, since the facts of the crime are not in the reader's possession at the outset, but it is a modern crime novel by virtue of the fact that it relies for its effect upon a detailed study of personality which makes the whodunit element subordinate. The central character is Laura Hunt, beautiful and romantic but remaining an enigma for most of the story. Lieutenant Mark McPherson begins to investigate Laura's murder, and is consumed with a fascination which turns to love. When Laura stuns him by reappearing, and it is learned that the corpse is that of her rival, McPherson has to conceal his emotions and to regard her as a suspect.

Together with Mark McPherson, several of the people in Laura's circle of close acquaintances act as narrators in turn. This technique is the book's principal strength, as the author contrives to get inside the skin of each narrator, and to delineate character with wonderful sharpness. Their individual modes of expression, the ways in which they recount their versions of events, and their views of Laura and other characters all serve to convince the reader that real people are speaking while the author recedes into the background. Particularly effective is the narrative of the aesthetic columnist Waldo Lydecker, exuberant in style and sometimes cruel in wit, leaving little doubt of his own self-esteem and his contempt for lesser mortals.

The long career of Helen McCloy (b. 1904) has seen a change of style from relatively conventional detective stories to novels of terror and suspense, often with horror being injected into a commonplace situation. In all cases she has brought to her work a high standard of writing, and an enviable ability to pace her narrative so that the tension mounts inexorably. Dr Basil Willing, a psychiatrist who serves as medical assistant to the New York District Attorney, has appeared in many of her novels, but has proved more at home where there is a mystery to be solved. Although her contribution to the modern crime novel is to be seen at its best in the psychological thrillers of recent years, it is tempting to mention here a superlative example of her earlier form,

McCloy, Helen
The goblin market
New York: Morrow, 1943; Hale, 1951

The setting is Puerto Vieja in the Caribbean, a refuge for people with something to hide. Philip Stark offers to replace Peter Halloran as correspondent on the island for Occidental News Service, but Halloran has been murdered and someone is determined that his successor will meet a similar fate. Stark is not only a man in danger but something of a mystery himself, and there is a final revelation which is totally unexpected.

Of Helen McCloy's later work, particularly commendable among many fine examples is

McCloy, Helen
The sleepwalker
New York: Dodd, Mead, 1974; Gollancz, 1974

in which strange and terrifying things happen to Marian Tansey. She suffers from loss of memory, and has no idea of her true identity. Her new car is being borrowed at night from her garage, by an unknown person for an equally unknown purpose. Finally she begins to sleepwalk, which comes to a head one night when she wakes to find herself in her car many miles from home. Does she really want to uncover the secret of her past, or is she running away from it? Gradually a story of murder unfolds, and it is impossible not to feel strongly for Marian as she tells of her chilling experiences.

Further instances of suspense, terror in civilized surroundings and brooding mystery came from the pen of Charlotte Armstrong (1905–69) over some thirty years, with

Armstrong, Charlotte
Mischief
New York: Coward-McCann, 1950; Peter Davies, 1951
finding a well deserved place on the roll of honour. It is a
superbly horrifying picture of a babysitter with psychopathic
tendencies, and the reader is kept on tenterhooks until the final
few pages. Taking a perfectly everyday situation, that of a young
child left alone with an outwardly normal and pleasant teenage
sitter, Charlotte Armstrong turns it on its head and gradually
exposes the girl's streak of insanity. The tension builds toward
the point when a destructive and murderous act will be inevitable. A threat to an innocent child is always calculated to attract
the reader's concern and involvement, but in this case the author
squeezes every ounce of fear from the situation and defers a
climax unbearably.

Abnormal psychology also figures in the key contribution of
Helen Eustis (b. 1916), although

Eustis, Helen
The horizontal man
New York: Harper, 1946; Hamish Hamilton, 1947
is additionally an excellent whodunit. The masterly combination
of various elements has made it a classic of the genre, described
by Anthony Boucher as 'a highpoint in modern murder'. The
scene is Hollymount, a women's college, and in the early pages
the reader witnesses the murder of Professor Kevin Boyle by his
lover. Left unaware of the killer's identity, the reader is then able
to go on to explore the effects of Boyle's death on several people.
Amid the flurry of academic gossip, the role of detective falls to
Kate Innes, editor of the college newspaper, together with a
young reporter. Literate, realistic and absorbing, *The horizontal
man* passes the test as a mystery novel that can be read more than
once.

There are many similarities between the work of these four
American women and that of their English counterpart Nancy
Bodington (b. 1912). Her novels as 'Shelley Smith' might appear
on the surface to be essentially English and occasionally almost
genteel, but beneath it all there lurks much evil which she gradually teases out with icy menace. Characterization and criminal
psychology replace the puzzle element, although the surprising
twists of her plots are more than sufficient compensation for the
loss of the whodunit flavour.

Smith, Shelley
Come and be killed
Collins, 1946; New York: Harper, 1947
is a good example of her early work. It tells of Florence Brown, a markedly neurotic spinster, who enters a nursing home following a suicide attempt. She discharges herself from the home, and it becomes a clear case of 'out of the frying pan . . . ' when she meets the plump and motherly Mrs Jolly. For Mrs Jolly is a murderess.

A later work,
Smith, Shelley
The Lord have mercy
Hamish Hamilton, 1956; New York: Harper, 1956
is one of the best novels of mystery and suspense set in an English village. Life goes on, sometimes passed in trivial pursuits, but underneath there are passions and evil thoughts, sexual and social frustrations, which eventually erupt. Satirical wit is here mixed with horror, as Shelley Smith paints a chilling picture of the probing eyes and clucking tongues. Nice Dr Mansbridge's wife dies from an overdose of barbiturates, and the village gossip and suspense escalate to a startling climax.

Returning now to the American scene, the unusual idea employed by Kenneth Fearing (1902–61) in
Fearing, Kenneth
The big clock
New York: Harcourt, Brace, 1946; Bodley Head, 1947
has gained it a permanent place among the great crime novels. Earl Janoth, a rich and unspeakable magazine proprietor, kills his mistress and then discovers that someone saw him go to her apartment just before the murder. He employs one of his staff, George Stroud, to find the witness – which happens to be Stroud himself. The predicament of appearing to carry out a search for oneself, yet striving deliberately to fail, is well thought out. Stroud realizes, however, that Janoth's vast resources will ensure that his identity as the witness will inevitably be revealed. Naturally he fears the consequences, and this makes an enthralling crime novel of considerable pace.

Sadly unrecognized as a major contribution to crime fiction, and amazingly not published in the author's native America until almost twenty years after its British appearance, was

Bardin, John Franklin
Devil take the blue-tail fly
Gollancz, 1948; New York: Macfadden, 1967
Fortunately the cause of John Franklin Bardin (1916–81) has been ably championed by Julian Symons, whose authoritative views on modern crime fiction have come to be internationally respected. It will still be a tragedy if the importance of this particular novel continues only to be recognized by a limited band of enthusiasts, for it is one of the pre-eminent studies of schizophrenia and unlikely to be bettered. This battle between two worlds will haunt the reader who experiences it for the first time, many long hours after the last page has been reached. From the moment Ellen Purcell wakes on the morning of her discharge from hospital and finds the friendly nurses strangely reluctant to turn their backs on her, to the final terrifying sequence, it is a work of great power which makes considerable demands upon its audience.

It would not be derogatory to state that the one major contribution of Ira Levin (b. 1929) was less demanding and more entertaining, for it is still a classic of the field with an appeal which remains fresh more than thirty years later. Although Levin has since produced bestsellers outside the crime field which have brought his name to the attention of readers worldwide, we are here concerned with
Levin, Ira
A kiss before dying
New York: Simon & Schuster, 1953; Joseph, 1954
It was his first novel and may still be regarded as his best, irrespective of the popularity of his better-known and cultish *Rosemary's baby*, *The Stepford wives* and *The boys from Brazil*.

The physical construction of *A kiss before dying* is truly inspired. In the first part, we see events through the eyes of a young man who kills his pregnant girlfriend so that he is free to marry into a rich family, but the reader is left in the dark as to his identity. In the second part, we follow the investigation by the sister of the murdered girl, who finally becomes the second victim. In the third part, we meet another sister and her boyfriend, and see their pursuit of the investigation to a bitter end. It is at once an ingeniously constructed mystery story, and a convincing picture of a charming yet coldly arrogant young killer.

Ursula Curtiss (1923–84) was a writer of some originality, with an enviable ability to create frightening situations. Often she would present an ordinary person with whom her readers could identify, and then catapult that person into a deadly dilemma. Sometimes the protagonist goes into the danger zone of his or her own accord, as in

Curtiss, Ursula
The noonday devil
New York: Dodd, Mead, 1951; Eyre & Spottiswoode, 1953
in the case of Andrew Sentry. In a conversation with an unknown man in a bar, Andrew learns that his brother Nick, killed while trying to escape from a Japanese prison camp, was betrayed by one of his own comrades. This was murder, described as the devil that works at noonday, and Andrew sets out to find the man responsible.

A more typical example of the Ursula Curtiss style is

Curtiss, Ursula
The deadly climate
New York: Dodd, Mead, 1954; Eyre & Spottiswoode, 1955
which concerns an innocent bystander, Caroline Emmett, who sees a woman murdered one night but cannot see the killer's face. The beam of a torch tells her that the killer has seen hers, from which point the story is breathless and unremitting in its suspense. The author has the capacity to force the reader to share Caroline's fearful isolation as a stranger in a small New England community, exposed to the danger of an unknown pursuer who needs her silence.

Dorothy Salisbury Davis (b. 1916), contemporaneous with Ursula Curtiss and another competent practitioner in the field of suspense rather than detection, has drawn many sympathetic portraits of criminals. For her there is often a question-mark, rather than an absolute right or wrong; environmental stresses and influences are realistically conveyed, rather than the simple choices of good and evil to be found in the work of so many other writers.

Davis, Dorothy Salisbury
A gentle murderer
New York: Scribner, 1951; Corgi, 1953
is a book which displays her great understanding and her ability to explore character. When a killer confesses to a priest, who must then pursue him to ensure that no further violence is done,

the basic situation presents an opportunity to analyse the two men which Mrs Davis uses to the full. In a later novel,

Davis, Dorothy Salisbury
A death in the life
New York: Scribner, 1976; Gollancz, 1977

she was still using one of her favourite themes, the pressures of city life. Indeed it is probably an even more relevant and justified theme in crime novels today. With typical compassion she here introduces a new series character Julie Hayes, a drifter who describes herself as having been fired by even her psychiatrist. Julie establishes a fortune-telling business in a vice-ridden district of New York, and it is against this background of urban decay that she meets a motley assembly of gangsters, pimps and hookers. The murder of her closest friend, a stage designer, finds Julie turning to amateur detection, but the book excels more for its sympathetic presentation of real people in the city jungle than for its mystery element.

Having identified some notable predecessors and successors of Francis Iles, it might be useful at this juncture to define some of the factors inherent in the modern crime novel as compared with the classical form. Basically it is important to realize that, whereas the pure detective story asks 'who?' and sometimes little else, the modern crime novel allows 'why?' and 'how?' to assume greater significance. There are other basic differences, and an excellent tabulation appears in Julian Symons's *Bloody murder*.

It must be appreciated that the modern crime novel is a hybrid. While some show crime at its most violent, others are as cosy as their predecessors of the 1920s. Again it must be emphasized that the identity of the criminal is not always revealed at the outset, and in some cases it even remains a mystery. The tracking down of the criminal is seen sometimes from the viewpoint of the pursuer, and sometimes from that of the pursued. There is clear interest in criminal psychology; in the little man or woman involuntarily drawn out of their depth into a criminal situation from which there is no escape; and in the humdrum, everyday scene where an ordinary person is driven to uncharacteristic violence.

A generalization, however, would draw attention to the modern crime novel's fascination with the cause of a crime, to its characterization as opposed to the often cardboard figures of detective fiction, and above all to its status as a novel worthy of

serious consideration. It is a marked contrast to the puzzle story
of yesteryear, the typically English whodunit of Agatha Christie
and her successors, whose settings and style led Colin Watson to
dub them 'the Mayhem Parva school' in his brilliant study *Snobbery with violence.*

One of the most interesting features of the modern crime novel
is that it is prepared to question police methods, showing policemen who are by no means the shining lights which some writers
of pure detection make them out to be. Again there is a refreshing
tendency to prick the bubble of infallibility which surrounds the
British legal system. One of the earliest to do so was Edgar
Lustgarten (1907–78), who established a reputation as a skilled
commentator on criminal trials and the machinery of justice, and
whose work was presented in almost every medium. Understand-
ably, therefore, he brought to his handful of novels a unique
knowledge.

Lustgarten, Edgar
A case to answer
Eyre & Spottiswoode, 1947
which was published in New York as *One more unfortunate*
(Scribner, 1947), is a thought-provoking example. A Soho prostitute is murdered and mutilated, and a man is placed on trial. He
is a respectable family man, holding a good position with a reputable city firm, yet he was connected with the dead woman and
the police have evidence against him. Edgar Lustgarten takes us
through the trial, and we see it from the standpoint of the police,
the witnesses, the judge and counsel. The verdict is finally
reached, but there is more to come.

Very far removed from the classic detective story, but aligned
with the contributions of Iles and Lustgarten, is

Grierson, Edward
Reputation for a song
Chatto & Windus, 1952; New York: Knopf, 1953
Grierson (1914–75) produced at once a competent study of a
domestic murder and a fine example of courtroom drama.
Robert Anderson is a stolid and reputable solicitor in a small
town, with a fairly typical family life. It is his son Rupert, however, whose contempt for his father develops into a rankling
hatred which culminates in murder. The narrative builds up skilfully towards the crime, after which we witness the attempts of
various members of the family to secure Rupert's acquittal.

Their ends can only be achieved by blackening the reputation of the deceased, to impress upon the jury that the case is one of self-defence rather than premeditated murder. Whether viewed as a domestic tragedy or as a trial drama with the verdict on the final page, it is a perfect example of the new direction in crime writing.

Although Grierson's contribution would have been recognized if he had written nothing else, he added to his stature as a crime novelist by turning to a completely different subject in

Grierson, Edward
The second man
Chatto & Windus, 1956; New York: Knopf, 1956

The legal scene is still here in abundance, but it is essentially a study of one central character rather than one case. That character is barrister Marion Kerrison, who is engaged in two battles – the need to assert her position as a woman in a predominantly male profession, and to clear a man accused of murder who appears to be his own worst enemy.

The first and decidedly best book by 'John Bingham', the family name of Lord Clanmorris (b. 1908), is

Bingham, John
My name is Michael Sibley
Gollancz, 1952; New York: Dodd, Mead, 1952

in which the author was controversial for the time in his portrayal of police officers. It is frightening, to say the least, although one might feel that Michael Sibley has only himself to blame in his gruelling encounter with the law. His friend Prosset has been murdered, and he is himself under suspicion; but his attempts to extricate himself are gradually revealed as lies and subterfuge. The police are convinced of his guilt, and subject him to a series of harrowing interviews. We follow his various changes of mind, and know his innermost feelings, in this first person narrative of a man who is innocent but feels the weight of the law bearing down upon him.

Bingham's menacing policemen are again in evidence in

Bingham, John
A fragment of fear
Gollancz, 1965; New York: Dutton, 1966

which first finds crime writer James Compton recuperating in Italy after a car accident, and becoming interested in the apparently motiveless murder of an elderly English woman. Back in

London, Compton is threatened by mysterious telephone calls and letters written with his own typewriter, and he suspects also that he is under surveillance. This is where the suspicious, insinuating, unhelpful policemen enter the picture and increase Compton's frustration and anxiety with their scorn. Is his persecution real or imaginary? Compton's dilemma provides a compelling story, which is the more suspenseful because of its lack of physical violence.

An intriguing writer of several good novels, Margot Bennett (1912–80) was in top form in

Bennett, Margot
The man who didn't fly
Eyre & Spottiswoode, 1955; New York: Harper, 1956

Four men propose to fly to Dublin, but only three of them are on the plane when it crashes. Who and where is the fourth, and why did he disappear? It is necessary to delve into the past lives of the four in order to fit the pieces of the puzzle together, and it is here that Miss Bennett scores with her perceptive drawing of people. There is even a mystery to be solved in the true deductive manner. Although less conventional than her earlier works, this novel displays the full range of her wit, ingenuity and command of dialogue.

Further evidence of Margot Bennett's best qualities, including her exquisitely apt turns of phrase and her delicious observation of character, is to be found in

Bennett, Margot
Someone from the past
Eyre & Spottiswoode, 1958; New York: Dutton, 1958

which is again a fine mixture of mystery and suspense. It introduces to the reader four men from the past of a murdered woman, any one of whom could be her murderer. Their characters and relationships are analysed against a background of suspicion, jealousy and fear, and the tension mounts toward the final revelation.

Again in Britain, Celia Fremlin (b. 1914) has produced some excellent work in the field. On some occasions she has not needed to rely upon murder being committed in order to satisfy the reader's need for excitement, but has found it sufficient merely to suggest that violence will eventually happen. There are few writers who can do this so effectively, and moreover she does it indirectly, with the merest nuances and indications and a brooding atmosphere that promises horrors to come. It says much for the quality of her writing that if that horror does not come the reader never feels cheated; the trip, even without a bloody climax, is sufficient in itself to keep the reader gripped. As with many other writers discussed earlier, she excels with the story set in an everyday domestic scene with which the reader can easily identify, and which is even more terrible for that. In her highly acclaimed first novel,

Fremlin, Celia
The hours before dawn
Gollancz, 1958; Philadelphia: Lippincott, 1959
Louise Henderson is a harassed London housewife. The hours before dawn always find her comforting her crying baby, while during the hours of daylight she is beset by her other demanding children, her unresponsive husband, irritating friends and complaining neighbours. The turning-point, for good or ill, occurs when the enigmatic Vera Brandon arrives as the tenant of the Hendersons' upstairs room. Louise's fatigue and inability to cope develop into suspicions and incidents which indicate to others that she is losing her mind. The secret of her new lodger, and the explanation of why she has deliberately sought out the Hendersons, provide a shattering conclusion.

Winston Graham (b. 1909), a writer of great versatility who began in the 1930s, has produced successful historical novels as well as books in the crime fiction field. This interest in history might perhaps explain why many of his mysteries have links with the past, concerning crimes which have their roots in earlier events. His versatility is evident even within his crime fiction, as they range from detective stories to thrillers and embrace espionage and psychological suspense. With excellent descriptive passages and plenty of atmosphere, Graham sets against his carefully observed backgrounds an implicated protagonist rather than a neutral investigator, and so has little use for conventional detectives. In

Graham, Winston
The little walls
Hodder & Stoughton, 1955; New York: Doubleday, 1955
Philip Turner investigates the apparent suicide of his archaeologist brother, with only a letter from an unknown woman and a diary to provide him with leads. He soon finds himself involved in a net of mystery and danger, in richly varied locations from

138

Holland to Italy, as well as in England. It is of course a thriller, but also ranks as a skilful study of human motivation and morality.

Perhaps his best-known novel is

Graham, Winston
Marnie
Hodder & Stoughton, 1961; New York: Doubleday, 1961
which is a rare instance of a novel in which the protagonist is virtually impossible to categorize. Amoral, kleptomaniac, victim of circumstances? Good or evil, detective or criminal? In spite of the beautiful Marnie's character deficiencies and antisocial tendencies, no reader can fail to be intrigued by her. The effects are there to see, but the causes of Marnie's troubled mind have to be found. When she delves into her past to find these causes, the quality of writing means that it is not fanciful to suggest she needs our support every step of the way.

The work of Julian Symons (b. 1912) as a historian and critic in the field of crime fiction is well known. In journal articles, and of course in his invaluable book *Bloody murder*, he traces the development from detective story to crime novel. His own books have followed this pattern. After some competent detective stories in the classic tradition, which were but examples of a very large field, he turned to the crime novel. The 'why?' and the 'how?' began to assume greater importance in his books than the 'who?', although the latter sometimes remained a factor. In some cases the identity of the murderer remains doubtful at the end of the book, and this apparent failure neatly to secure all the loose ends is a marked difference between the detective story and the crime novel.

The first book to show Symons's transition to the full was

Symons, Julian
The colour of murder
Collins, 1957; New York: Harper, 1957
which was judged by the Crime Writers' Association to be the best crime novel of its year. In the first part of the book, which is John Wilkins's statement to a consultant psychiatrist, we see a picture of an unexceptional suburban husband with a bitchy wife. Wilkins strikes up a relationship with an assistant in his local library, and begins to create around her a world of fantasy in which his wife has little part. He is a frustrated man, and also suffers from blackouts. It is almost inevitable that murder occurs

to create the break in the triangle, although events do not perhaps develop in the way the reader expects. The second part of the book, in which Wilkins faces trial for murder, displays the author's ability to communicate the courtroom atmosphere which his subsequent books were to confirm and improve upon. With regard to the outcome of the case, it is sufficient to say here that it emphasizes the new direction in crime writing.

Few contemporary writers can produce a genuinely absorbing *roman policier*. Symons can and consistently does, a noteworthy example being

Symons, Julian
The progress of a crime
Collins, 1960; New York: Harper, 1960

On Guy Fawkes night, around the bonfire on the village green, motorcycle thugs from the city are an unwelcome intrusion. When the motorcycles leave, a man lies stabbed to death. From this point develops a painstaking investigation and murder trial, throughout which the author provides thumbnail sketches of a host of journalists, police, and characters savoury and unsavoury. The central character, a reporter following the best story of his career, finds it impossible not to become emotionally involved. The reader too, as with most of Symons's work, will be unable to bestow his sympathies or condemnation lightly. In this imperfect world it is not always a question of simple right or wrong.

A further example demonstrating Symons's craftsmanship – and possibly his supremacy – in the field of the contemporary crime novel in Britain is

Symons, Julian
The end of Solomon Grundy
Collins, 1964; New York: Harper & Row, 1964

in which a 'model' (say no more) is murdered in a London mews flat, and the trail leads to a suburban middle-class housing estate called The Dell. Solomon Grundy is a misfit in The Dell, and it soon becomes obvious that the police regard him as their prime suspect. Many of his so-called friends and neighbours can well believe it, their antagonism fuelled by his irascibility and failure to conform. As a piece of social commentary it is first-class, and as a courtroom drama it is riveting. But as a question – what *was* the end of Solomon Grundy? – it will long remain in the reader's mind.

During the 1970s and 1980s Symons has displayed versatility and a willingness to experiment, sometimes delving back into historical crimes and presenting his own fictional reconstructions. Still the most impressive, however, have been his modern stories of the violence which simmers beneath the respectable surface of society, human relationships reaching crisis point, and the exposure of weaknesses in characters previously unblemished. In

Symons, Julian
The man who lost his wife
Collins, 1970; New York: Harper & Row, 1971

publisher Gilbert Welton has a settled existence with a charming wife and a fine house. This world begins to crack when his wife departs to Yugoslavia and fails to return. Perhaps she has come to grief, or perhaps she has deserted Gilbert for a lover. The search provides a story of unfolding jealousy and suspicion, intrigue and suspense, but there is also ample opportunity for Symons to exercise his sharply satirical wit on contemporary subjects.

A further example of character analysis and soul-searching,

Symons, Julian
The plot against Roger Rider
Collins, 1973; New York: Harper & Row, 1973

shows two characters who are starkly contrasting. Roger Rider's strength of personality and Geoffrey Paradine's weakness have been apparent from their school days, and Roger has become a successful businessman whereas Geoffrey has become his employee. Geoffrey's affair with Roger's wife may be seen as his revenge – but when Roger disappears while on holiday has Geoffrey gone too far? It is a baffling puzzle with a shock ending.

Another writer who must be mentioned in connection with the transformation from detective story to crime novel – Paul Winterton (b. 1908), writing as 'Andrew Garve' – has occasionally devised the purely intellectual type of puzzle. Some of his earlier books had more of a whodunit flavour than most of his work in the 1960s and 1970s, although he has kept his options open and returned to straight detection from time to time. Particularly commendable is

Garve, Andrew
Frame-up
Collins, 1964; New York: Harper & Row, 1964

which was praised by the discerning American critic Anthony Boucher. Chief Inspector Blair, pursuing the murderer of artist

John Lumsden, knows that one of his suspects must have faked an alibi. But how was it done? The answer is most ingenious.

Many of Garve's stories, however, concern ordinary people who become enmeshed in situations from which they must escape, be it an involvement in murder or some other complex criminal machinations. To do so, they must seek out the truth, and often with little assistance from the police. In others the central character is a rogue, as is the case with

Garve, Andrew
Murderer's fen
Collins, 1966

which appeared in New York as *Hide and go seek* (Harper & Row, 1966). Here the rogue in question, Alan Hunt, seduces a young woman while on holiday and expects never to see her again. He is mistaken, which poses a serious threat to his plans for marrying the daughter of a property tycoon. Ruthless and disreputable, Hunt concludes that murder is his only solution. In showing that all is not so simple, Andrew Garve combines cleverness and mounting suspense to keep the reader guessing.

Garve is a remarkably versatile writer, who ties himself to neither a series character nor a recurrent central idea. For example, in

Garve, Andrew
Boomerang
Collins, 1969; New York: Harper & Row, 1970

we see a young city wheeler-dealer, in prison for dangerous driving, making useful contacts for pulling off a clever but hazardous plan. He needs at least £100,000 to conceal his embezzlement, and they all set off for Australia to put the plan into effect. But, as the title implies, complications set in.

In complete contrast is

Garve, Andrew
The late Bill Smith
Collins, 1971; New York: Harper & Row, 1971

in which a successful salesman knows that someone wants him dead, and can only escape and uncover the truth by disappearing on a 'permanent' basis.

Among the foremost American contributors to crime fiction today is Patricia Highsmith (b. 1921). Rather artificially classified, her books come under the umbrella of the psychological thriller, were it not for the fact that they do not set out to thrill.

On the contrary, there is a 'there but for the grace of God . . . ' quality about them which makes them frankly disturbing. The central character of

Highsmith, Patricia
The blunderer
New York: Coward-McCann, 1954; Cresset Press, 1956
is a young lawyer, Walter Stackhouse, who would dearly like to be rid of his wife. Could he, he wonders, copy a murder recently committed by another man? From the moment his mind turns to thoughts of murder, he begins to sink deeper into a chasm from which there is no escape. Lieutenant Lawrence Corby is determined to obtain confessions from both men, and has no qualms about the methods he employs. He plays them one against the other, with tragic and appalling results.

Patricia Highsmith is adept at putting her characters under a magnifying glass, exposing their deepest and most sinful thoughts. Throughout her work there is an obsession with guilt, although sometimes it is the concept of complete amorality and absence of guilt which interests her. This is particularly to be seen in

Highsmith, Patricia
The talented Mr Ripley
New York: Coward-McCann, 1955; Cresset Press, 1957
which is a well-plotted study of a charming young American who is also a remorseless criminal psychopath. Tom Ripley murders his rich acquaintance Dickie Greenleaf in Italy, and then takes over his identity. It is scarcely conceivable that the reader can sympathize with Ripley, yet Highsmith manages to endow him with an attractiveness which gave him a strange fascination for the reader and resulted in his reappearance in other books. Perhaps in some perverted way we envy his freedom, his refusal to be shackled by laws, which results in the sort of anarchy where it is only a question of degree between the petty pilferer and the murderer.

Another triumph,

Highsmith, Patricia
The two faces of January
New York: Doubleday, 1964; Heinemann, 1964
explores the brittle relationship between two men against the background of Greece. Rydal Keener sees petty crook Chester MacFarland attempting to dispose of a body, but does not react

like a member of conventional and orderly society. Instead he attaches himself like a leech to Chester and his wife.

Patricia Highsmith ranks extremely highly in the field under discussion. Two other Americans who, like Highsmith, do not produce stories in which detection is the key element and certainly do not set out to provide solace and comfort for their readers, are Margaret Millar and Stanley Ellin. Margaret Millar (b. 1915), the widow of 'Ross Macdonald', moved from detection to suspense in mid-career and has been in the forefront for many years since. Her key work,

Millar, Margaret
Beast in view
New York: Random House, 1955; Gollancz, 1955

was judged to be the best crime novel of its year by the Mystery Writers of America, and even at this juncture it would be unfair to reveal details of the plot. The starting-point is when Helen Clarvoe, who lives reclusively in a hotel, enlists the aid of her lawyer Paul Blackshear following the receipt of annoying phone calls from her childhood acquaintance Evelyn Merrick. All is clearly not as it seems, but it is not until the reader reaches the most shocking denouement imaginable that pieces of the mystery fall into place. The simplicity of the writing gives to the narrative tremendous power and compulsion, and this particular book demonstrates why Margaret Millar has since become acknowledged as one of the leading women in American crime fiction, vying only with Patricia Highsmith for the premier position.

It is considered by some authorities that

Millar, Margaret
How like an angel
New York: Random House, 1962; Gollancz, 1962

is her finest book. The central character, Joe Quinn, is a former cop in a Reno casino who moves into the very different world of a Californian cult called the True Believers. His job is to investigate the disappearance of a man called Patrick O'Gorman, and the case is a good and engrossing example of the crime writer's art. What really sets it apart from run-of-the-mill mystery, however, is the thoughtful picture it paints of the cult and its members, and the way in which the relationships between the characters are so credibly and compassionately presented.

Stanley Ellin (1916–86) developed over the years into a novelist of some significance. While most of his books concern

144

crime in one form or another, it would be inaccurate or at best restrictive to describe him as a crime novelist. He nevertheless produced some books which are well within the genre, and on many occasions presented stories of suspense and horror in a style which is most distinctive. At first he was acclaimed as a writer of short stories, with a run of award-winning contributions to *Ellery Queen's mystery magazine* beginning with the wickedly bizarre tale *The specialty of the house*, which has become a classic. Ellin devoted more care and attention to the writing of one short story than many other writers would lavish upon a novel, and as a result the end product is almost always a perfect example in form and content, a small masterpiece of villainy or grotesqueness or human fallibility. For this reason,

> **Ellin, Stanley**
> Mystery stories
> New York: Simon & Schuster, 1956; Boardman, 1957

is not only a feast for the reader, but a collection of all that is best from this superlative craftsman. Julian Symons described Ellin's work as 'a landmark in the history of the crime short story', and this collection was selected as 'one of the two hundred best and most important titles published in the United States' for presentation to the White House library.

Ellin soon demonstrated that he was also a master of the novel, gaining early approbation for

> **Ellin, Stanley**
> The eighth circle
> New York: Random House, 1958; Boardman, 1959

which is a portrait of private eye Murray Kirk. Far more than a detective story, it asks pertinent questions about such a man's role in modern American society. When Kirk seeks evidence to get a crooked policeman off the hook, his own motives are not all pure.

Ellin went on to produce a remarkable range of novels, bringing to them an inventiveness and imagination as well as an enviable facility for subtle character observation. One of the best of his later works,

> **Ellin, Stanley**
> Star light, star bright
> New York: Random House, 1979; Cape, 1979

is in the classic private eye tradition, narrated by detective Johnny Milano and in many respects in the Chandler mould.

Milano's job is to protect Kalos Daskalos, astrologer and high priest to the movie people who gather at billionaire Andrew Quist's mansion in Florida. Daskalos has received a death threat, and barbarous incidents which have already occurred are evidence of the unknown enemy's serious intent. It is an intricate plot with a mystery requiring a solution, and Ellin does not disappoint in bringing matters to a marvellously riveting conclusion. As is expected of such a fine writer, however, he gives much more to the reader by subtle character analysis.

The modern crime novel has also been developed by Continental writers, but few have been translated into English. Of the exceptions, the Swiss writer Friedrich Dürrenmatt (b. 1921) makes use of police detectives, but his books cannot be described as police procedural novels. In Dürrenmatt's case the policeman is used as a symbol, a means of ensuring that everything is subordinated to the ends of justice. In one of his most widely quoted books,

Dürrenmatt, Friedrich
The judge and his hangman: translated from the German
by Cyrus Brooks
Herbert Jenkins, 1954; New York: Harper, 1955
Inspector Barlach, old and ill, works toward the final confrontation with the monstrous criminal to whose downfall the detective's whole career has been dedicated. Barlach's own life is running out, and the normal processes of law cannot be relied upon to give him the ultimate satisfaction of a lifetime's work. Dürrenmatt's skill at building suspense, his mastery of the bizarre situation, and his use of the classical surprise denouement are all overshadowed by the force of his moral argument that evil must be punished by any possible means. In this case Barlach, officially investigating the murder of a young police officer, feels that he can serve the ends of justice only by appointing himself judge and by planning an execution.

There is rather more of the puzzle element in the works of the French writers Pierre Boileau (b. 1906) and Thomas Narcejac (b. 1908). Although they normally present a mystery, and build up the atmosphere of suspense until they spring the final surprise, they are still far from the classical approach. There is no systematic investigation or sifting of evidence. Instead the Boileau-Narcejac novels demonstrate a mixture of human relationships, with a crime and a detective of some sort who becomes

personally more than professionally involved. Their best work
is
Boileau-Narcejac
The living and the dead: translated by Geoffrey Sainsbury
Hutchinson, 1956; New York: Washburn, 1957
which was adapted as the Hitchcock film *Vertigo*. It starts as an
apparently simple case of a man hiring a detective to watch his
wife, whom he believes to be suicidal. But the complications of
the plot, and the ingenuity of the story when all is revealed, place
Boileau and Narcejac among the few consistently good crime
writers to have been translated from the French.

Also from France, award-winning novelist Jean-Baptiste
Rossi (b. 1931) as 'Sebastien Japrisot' has produced several outstanding crime novels, with a startling flavour all their own. They
might be better known to British and American audiences
through the medium of the cinema, but their idiosyncratic struc-
tures and brooding atmosphere can only be experienced to the
full through the printed page. A master of misdirection who
would doubtless be more than competent even if he restricted
himself to classic whodunits, Japrisot takes the process a stage
further. It is not always clear what crime has actually been committed, or indeed if there has been a crime at all. The reader is
sometimes left for long periods uncertain of the principal character's function, with the tantalizing need to discover if that person
is to be the murderer or the victim being the force which holds the
interest. For example, in
Japrisot, Sebastien
The lady in the car with glasses and a gun: translated by
Helen Weaver
New York: Simon & Schuster, 1967; Souvenir Press, 1968
when Dany Longo borrows her employer's car and drives to the
South of France, various people recognize her as someone they
met there earlier. It is in fact her first visit, or so we are given to
believe by Dany herself. The mad pattern of events escalates, and
then she discovers the body of a man in the car boot. A logical
explanation seems impossible, as the story rushes from scene to
scene with no relaxation of the mounting tension and horror.

To return to Britain for a complete update, mention must be
made of two women novelists who entered on the scene in the
1970s and are now very highly regarded. Margaret Beda
Nicholson (b. 1924), writing as 'Margaret Yorke', began with

straightforward detective stories featuring literary don Patrick Grant, but found her true *métier* with

Yorke, Margaret
No medals for the major
Bles, 1974

Clearly she had decided that the exploration of character was more important than the puzzle element, the 'why?' more interesting and relevant than the 'who?' Here she presents a marvellously credible character in retired Major Johnson, a fish out of water who finds village life too great a change from military precision and comradeship. He is implicated in a crime of which he is innocent, and rife rumour forces him to face the village utterly alone. Not without suspense, humour and a mystery to be explained, the novel is essentially an exercise in the observation of human nature and has great poignancy.

Margaret Yorke has continued to produce books about real people, rather than the cardboard characters of so many mystery novelists. She explores their motives and their reactions to violent events, often against the background of an English country village or small town, but they are miles away from the stereotyped setting of 'Mayhem Parva'. In a recent example which maintains her high standard,

Yorke, Margaret
The smooth face of evil
Hutchinson, 1984; New York: St Martin's Press, 1984

the central character is not calculated to engage our sympathy at first, but we feel for him nonetheless when he becomes a victim of circumstances. Young Terry Brett is a thief, a blackmailer and a womanizer. Although a thorough rogue, he has always shunned violence and achieved his ill-gotten gains by the use of stealth, charm and deception. It is therefore ironic when the chance acquaintance with a woman in a minor motor accident leads to his involvement in domestic murder, and more than ironic when he becomes enmeshed in crimes of which he is entirely innocent.

For her part, Jacqueline Wilson (b. 1945) takes a conventional domestic situation and then introduces into it a criminal or abnormal element. Unlike Margaret Yorke her settings are normally suburban, but the common factor between these two writers is that they fill their books with credible characters and leave the reader with a feeling that this is reality rather than make-

believe. Sometimes Jacqueline Wilson will begin with a comparatively inconsequential event, then rapidly build it into something terrifying, as in

Wilson, Jacqueline

Truth or dare

Macmillan, 1973; New York: Doubleday, 1974

which begins when young housewife Claire Townsend accepts a
lift from a middle-aged man. His assault on her is minor and little
more than pathetic, but her husband insists upon informing the
police. From that point the story develops into a nightmare of
deceit and murder.

Some of Jacqueline Wilson's work is sexually explicit,
although this is invariably required by the circumstances of the
plot and is always honest, never merely for the sake of effect. In

Wilson, Jacqueline

Making hate

Macmillan, 1977; New York: St Martin's Press, 1978

the subject is rape, and the presentation is frank but compassionate, without sensationalism. It tells of Simon, who has
joined the police force as a civilian scenes-of-crime officer following the failure of his marriage. Briefly a suspect in a case of
rape, he is immediately cleared but is afraid that his relationship
with his daughter could be damaged as a result. The reader shares
the innermost thoughts of the rapist, as the attacks continue and
the hunt intensifies, while Simon has to become deeply involved
in pursuing the case to its conclusion.

10

THE POLICE PROCEDURAL

Police officers made their appearance in detective fiction at a very early stage. They were, for example, to be found in the pages of Dickens or engaged in friendly rivalry with Sherlock Holmes. Generally speaking, however, these policemen served one of two functions. They were either a somewhat bewildered foil to the gifted intellectual detective, as is Inspector Lestrade to Sherlock Holmes, or they were themselves individualistic central detectives who displayed the flair and logical analysis which made them indistinguishable from the erudite amateur. This remained the case until the mid-1940s, when a new type of detective story was born and took its place alongside the other forms of crime fiction already discussed. As with the hard-boiled detective novel, it has remained popular to this day.

It has become known as the police procedural story. Unlike the story which relegates the official detective to the role of a somewhat inept supporting actor, it presents him (or her) as a working member of a skilled force. Unlike the classic mysteries of such writers as Ngaio Marsh or even Georges Simenon, where one official detective is very much the hero and sometimes unconventional in his approach, the police procedural shows one or more officers within a complex machine which is often bedevilled by regulations. Teamwork is the order of the day. While there is room for flashes of brilliance as displayed by the classical detectives, or for hyperactivity and physical toughness as displayed by the private eye, they are contained within a framework of standard procedures.

Most police procedural stories show these standard working methods to the reader, together with the scientific resources which are in reality more likely to catch criminals than the ratiocinative gifts of a single detective. It can also be said of most police procedural stories that they present to the reader all relevant facts as they emerge, and that there is no great detective who keeps the salient points to himself in order to unmask a totally unexpected criminal with an unfair flourish.

Successful writers of the police procedural have overcome one potential difficulty of great importance. Much of police work is routine and uninteresting, and a case may be solved by the methodical questioning of large numbers of people, by the tests carried out in the laboratory, or by the use of informants. It may be felt, with some justification, that rather more reading pleasure can be derived from following the activities of a great detective who is superior to an ordinary and fallible mortal, or the racy exploits of a private eye who is comparatively unshackled in his behaviour.

This difficulty has been overcome in a variety of ways which make the best police procedural stories anything but dull. The very process of gradually constructing a case against a suspect has been made gripping and suspenseful by several writers. Again, they do not necessarily abandon the whodunit element, and the systematic process in many cases leads to a surprising conclusion. Finally, the best of the procedurals are fascinating in their exploration of the police officers themselves, real people in a real world. Often they are shown as existing in two worlds: within the sometimes hard and demanding world of professional law enforcement, and within their own domestic environment. In showing these two worlds, the writers concerned are able to explore more deeply the personalities and relationships of their central characters. Indeed, in some instances it is seen that the two worlds are incompatible.

This trend began with Lawrence Treat (b. 1903) in the USA, although it is unlikely that he set out with the positive intention of creating a new type of detective novel which would become an important subgenre. It is nevertheless accepted that

Treat, Lawrence
V as in victim
New York: Duell, Sloan & Pearce, 1945; Rich & Cowan, 1950

was the first police procedural novel. Against the background of the New York Police Department, it shows the very different methods employed by detectives Mitch Taylor and Jub Freeman. Taylor is not particularly intelligent, but gets his results by the systematic breaking down of suspects. Freeman is a scientist, whose methods in the laboratory can lead to conclusions which are at variance with those achieved by Taylor's approach. Lawrence Treat shows the rivalries and disputes thus caused, and brings added realism to his characters by showing them also grappling with their own domestic problems and the thorny aspects of public relations.

On the scene shortly afterwards, this time in England, was Maurice Procter (1906–73). Again, the mainspring of his stories was not the crime itself, but the documentary treatment of police work. Procter examined the relationships within the force, the conflicts between policemen as individuals and their duties to the community. His own career of almost twenty years as a policeman gave him the necessary background, and enabled him to present the policeman's life down to the last authoritative detail. In his first book,

Procter, Maurice
No proud chivalry
Longmans, Green, 1946

he charts the progress of Pierce Rogan from the day he joins the Otherburn Borough Police as a constable, and one can almost smell the boot-leather.

Procter's portrayals of city life in the North of England, particularly the criminal elements, was first-class. Against this background he described in detail a dedicated police force committed to maintain law and order, and within that force he presented officers as human beings who were sometimes fallible. His experience gave him an understanding of the villains, and the conventional and unconventional police procedures required in order to apprehend them. Many of Procter's books are set in the fictional city of Granchester, which has some of the features of Manchester and Liverpool, and his principal series character is Chief Inspector Harry Martineau. Introduced in

Procter, Maurice
Hell is a city
Hutchinson, 1954

which was published in New York as *Somewhere in this city* (Harper, 1954), Martineau arrived on the police procedural scene slightly ahead of J. J. Marric's George Gideon and the 87th squad of Ed McBain. Here he must cope with a violent robbery and murder, and with a vicious criminal who poses a personal challenge. Martineau is shown to be no law enforcement machine, but a sympathetic man who does not always like what he has to do. Similarly, the story itself is full of human interest, but this in no way reduces the suspense of the plot. The meticulous investigation and questioning of suspects and informers is never dull, but provides an enthralling read and is well balanced with action.

Another good series of solid modern novels of police procedure came from perhaps a surprising source, that underrated writer John Creasey (1908–73). As is well known, Creasey used many pseudonyms, and produced a long list of thrillers which made him probably the most successful writer in the field since Edgar Wallace. Indeed, his work resembles that of Wallace in many ways, including economy of style, fast action, plenty of dialogue, and almost total lack of characterization. Most of his books, like those of Wallace, come within the field of the action thriller rather than detective fiction. He made a major breakthrough, however, under the name 'J. J. Marric' when he created George Gideon. In the first of what was to become a phenomenally popular series,

Marric, J. J.
Gideon's day
Hodder & Stoughton, 1955; New York: Harper, 1955
Gideon holds the rank of detective superintendent at New Scotland Yard. He is a dependable character of greater credibility than Creasey's other heroes, and was to develop in stature and in rank as later novels appeared. Gideon's working day involves him in dope-peddling, robbery, murder and gang violence. The style was at the time something new, as the story switches from one case to another until finally all the loose ends are tied up, and it presents a complex picture of the life of a busy detective.

This book was no flash in the pan, and was quickly followed by

Marric, J. J.
Gideon's week
Hodder & Stoughton, 1956; New York: Harper, 1956
in which the central case is a mass prison escape. One of the fugitives is bent on revenge, but there are many more crimes to occupy Gideon's attention.

As the series progressed, finally amounting to over twenty titles, Marric drew an authentic portrait of Gideon's developing career and that of his colleagues. It was all the more realistic for the many glimpses into Gideon's personal life, and the opportunities given to the reader to share in the pleasures, trials and tribulations of what became the best-known family of a fictional detective.

A further example of the solid and dependable policeman has appeared for many years in the books of Alan Hunter (b. 1922). The thoughtful Chief Superintendent Gently, who in his own way is something of a philosopher as well as a razor-sharp detective, was introduced in

Hunter, Alan
Gently does it
Cassell, 1955; New York: Rinehart, 1955
In his dogged pursuit of the killer of an elderly timber merchant, and in his refusal to accept the obvious solution, Gently impressed readers with his patience and tolerance.

Characterization is sound in the Gently novels, of which there are now more than thirty titles, and few patently cardboard creations appear in these well-written works. Hunter has also moved with the times, realistically linking his crimes with contemporary social problems.

Geoffrey Horne (b. 1916), writing as 'Gil North', made a worthwhile contribution to the list of great detectives when he created Sergeant Caleb Cluff. He appeared in a long series of novels beginning with

North, Gil
Sergeant Cluff stands firm
Chapman & Hall, 1960
in which the peaceful market town of Gunnarshaw is disturbed by a woman's suicide, and Cluff is suspicious. Cluff is obstinate but wholly likeable, with a love of the Yorkshire countryside matched by his love for his fellow man. He knows everyone in Gunnarshaw, and they know him. Cluff is motivated to right wrongs rather than to demand retribution, and he breaks his cases by exercising a persistence and endurance reminiscent of Maigret. His methods work, although sometimes Inspector Mole might disapprove.

'Jeffrey Ashford', one of the pseudonyms adopted by Roderic Jeffries (b. 1926), presented a picture of the life and duties of a country divisional detective inspector in

Ashford, Jeffrey
Investigations are proceeding
John Long, 1961
which appeared in New York as *The DI* (Harper & Row, 1962). There are several crimes under investigation at any one time within his jurisdiction, and he has to keep a finger on each of these threads. As with the Gideon series, this book conveys an impression of authenticity without pretentiousness.

In Britain, as in the USA, there have been a number of televised police procedural series which set out to present the realism of police work as a contrast to the more glamourized approach of other series, and to show the teamwork and complex machinery of law enforcement as an alternative to the attractive lone cop who seems unaccountably able to work with the unrestrained freedom of the private eye. Allan Prior (b. 1922) was in the forefront of this revolution in television drama, contributing over 150 hours of superlative scripts to the series *Z cars, Softly softly* and *The sweeney*. It can therefore only be assumed that lack of time has prevented him from writing more novels, but he nevertheless produced one of the best police procedural novels ever in

Prior, Allan
The interrogators
Cassell, 1965; New York: Simon & Schuster, 1965
It shows the police of an industrial town called Arkley in Northern England, hunting the man responsible for the rape and murder of a child. The principal characters are Jack Eaves, a young detective, and his case-hardened superior Savage, whose personalities and beliefs are analysed with great precision. As the investigation proceeds, and the police machinery comes into play, we see that absolute honesty and moral incorruptibility do not necessarily make a successful policeman. Jack Eaves learns this as he observes the methods of the veteran Savage, often to his horror. The clash of personalities is marked, in spite of the fact that the men share the same objective. It is Savage's last case, with his obsession to make this a triumphant end to his career blinding him to all else, and he concentrates fanatically upon wrenching a confession from his suspect.

The detective stories of Michael Gilbert have already been featured in Chapter 7, but this formidable and consistent contributor to the field of crime fiction has also carved a special place for himself in the police procedural area. Almost thirty years ago, in

Gilbert, Michael
Blood and judgement
Hodder & Stoughton, 1959; New York: Harper, 1959

he introduced Detective Sergeant Patrick Petrella of Q Division in the Metropolitan Police. He is young and industrious but sensitive and poetic, with an abiding fear that misjudgements and miscarriages of the law can take place. When a woman is murdered and a roughneck called Boot Howton is charged, Petrella feels there is more to the case than meets the eye. To the displeasure of his superiors, he probes further. Petrella later appeared in a collection of interlinked short stories,

Gilbert, Michael
Petrella at Q
Hodder & Stoughton, 1977; New York: Harper & Row, 1977

which further enhanced Gilbert's reputation as a master of police procedure, and showed how the flair of an individual detective need not necessarily be stunted by the routine formalities of an investigation.

Another Gilbert detective, Chief Inspector William Mercer, did not become a series character but is an interesting creation in his own right. In

Gilbert, Michael
The body of a girl
Hodder & Stoughton, 1972; New York: Harper & Row, 1972

the remains of a girl are found buried on an island in the upper reaches of the Thames. It could be one of two girls who disappeared many months earlier, and it is Mercer's task to identify the body and find the killer. Superimposed on this plot is the battle between the police and criminal gangs, and there is suspicion among Mercer's colleagues that he has something to hide. All is cleverly interrelated in a startling climax, but not until Gilbert has shown scenes of violence which are a stark contrast to his earlier work in the pure detection genre.

The 1980s have shown Michael Gilbert's remarkable staying power, with several novels in various subgenres which show no deterioration whatsoever in his skill, originality and ingenuity. In particular

Gilbert, Michael
Death of a favourite girl
Hodder & Stoughton, 1980
which was published in New York as *The killing of Katie Steel-stock* (Harper & Row, 1980), is a police novel of the highest order. The murder victim is a glamorous and popular television personality, who still lives with her family in the village of West Hannington. When she is killed after leaving the tennis club dance, the police might not need to look any further than one of the local young men with whom she has had romantic entanglements. To the ambitious Chief Superintendent Knott of Scotland Yard the case offers the prospect of promotion, and he is a thorough and uncompromising investigator who quickly unearths the fact that Katie was quite a different person at the London end of her life. Knott is a human steamroller, whose tactics make him unpopular with West Hannington people and with the local policemen who have to assist him. It could be that Knott, and indeed the reader, is in for a surprise.

One of the foremost writers of the British police novel, and one whose own career in the force serves him well, is John Wainwright (b. 1921). His first,

Wainwright, John
Death in a sleeping city
Collins, 1965
exposed the brutality of organized crime in a North of England city. That city, or the region around it, has been the setting of many Wainwright novels since then, and he has proved to be a prolific writer without a consequential lowering of his standards. Some of the men of his city police force are tough, some are scared, but all are human. In a major work

Wainwright, John
The last buccaneer
Macmillan, 1971
the central character is Jules Morgan, a madman who claims to be a descendant of the pirate Sir Henry Morgan. As his ancestor plundered, so Jules intends to plunder. In an unusually long novel, we follow the actions of the criminals and the police until the final holocaust.

While Wainwright comes through as the blunt Yorkshireman, he also displays great compassion for the underdog, the homosexual, the ordinary person pushed to commit an act of violence, and the sexual pervert without an understanding friend in the world. Although regarded as a police procedural writer, he normally concentrates upon one major case in each book rather than following the classic practice of presenting a team of detectives working simultaneously on interlinked cases, but a notable exception is

Wainwright, John
All on a summer's day
Macmillan, 1981; New York: St Martin's Press, 1981

This follows a day in the life of his Northern policemen, who have to cope with crime both petty and serious. It is a picture of teamwork, but within the team there are men who are hard and soft, industrious and lazy, cruel and compassionate. In their work and in their domestic lives there is humour, sadness, excitement and tedium.

Wainwright is an expert at presenting the extremes of criminal violence, and he concentrates his analyses as much on the actions of the criminals as on those of the police. Often he has something significant to say about law and morality, and he raises many an uncomfortable question. He is prepared to explore the limits beyond which policemen might go, and he has no compunction about revealing the human weaknesses of his series characters. Indeed, he is even willing to kill them off, but sometimes his deceased policemen reappear in novels covering a long timespan, such as

Wainwright, John
Blayde R.I.P.
Macmillan, 1982; New York: St Martin's Press, 1982

At the outset Chief Superintendent Robert Blayde, a regular Wainwright character, is dead. From the funeral, the story flashes back to cover his entire life. It is a fascinating career from constable to high ranking detective, a life of triumphs and disappointments, solid police routines and violent encounters. Then at last Wainwright pulls the final stroke, and reveals the circumstances of Blayde's death.

A number of other British police procedural writers, like Procter and Wainwright, have been able to bring their own professional experience to bear in enhancing their novels. Three such are the late Hamilton Jobson, Roger Busby and John Rossiter.

Hamilton Jobson (1914–81) was a police officer for thirty

years, and brought great credibility to his stories of the Fore-
bridge CID. Arguably the best is

Jobson, Hamilton
The evidence you will hear
Collins, 1975; New York: Scribner, 1975

which begins with a report that a child is missing from home,
setting in train a hunt intensified by the fact that three other local
children have been abducted and murdered. The daily lives of
many ordinary people are affected by the investigation, which
has an ironic and shattering conclusion.

Roger Busby (b. 1941) has written procedurals with the added
authenticity stemming from his experience as a crime reporter
and subsequently public relations officer for a county police
force. They mostly feature Detective Inspector Leric, an individ-
ualist with views about his own colleagues as well as an ability to
get under the skin of the villains. In

Busby, Roger
Deadlock
Collins, 1971

Leric and his opposite number from Scotland Yard have reached
an impasse in their investigation into the murder of a young girl.
Then Leric transfers his attention to a seemingly routine case of
safe-cracking, and he notices certain anomalies. One of the best
Leric novels is

Busby, Roger
Pattern of violence
Collins, 1973

which looks incisively at the problem of armed violence, perhaps
even more topical today than when the book was written. It
concerns not only the question of armed criminals, but the fact
that a largely unarmed police force has to contend with them.

John Rossiter (b. 1916), who was a high-ranking detective for
many years, went on to produce some fine police procedurals
under the pseudonym 'Jonathan Ross'. Under his own name he
has written mainly of a British agent called Roger Tallis, together
with the occasional police novel. He pulls no punches, writing in
a direct style and showing city life as it is. A fine example,

Rossiter, John
The manipulators
Cassell, 1973; New York: Simon & Schuster, 1974

concerns a scheme to blackmail a dedicated policeman into

collaborating with criminals. It is entirely credible, leaving the disturbing impression that the undermining of the law by highly organized means is a real possibility in this age of the sophisticated criminal.

The 'Jonathan Ross' novels feature a detective called George Rogers, who rises in rank as the series progresses and is a well-developed character. Crime is uncomfortably near to home for Rogers in

Ross, Jonathan
Dark blue and dangerous
Constable, 1981; New York: Scribner, 1981
when the promising Sergeant Proctor is found drowned in an icy industrial canal. Rogers is convinced that he has been murdered but is less sure of the motive, or whether the killing has arisen from Proctor's private life or police activities. It requires a characteristically thorough investigation, detailed and absorbing, before he knows the answers.

Generally agreed to be an excellent detective novelist, and working in the grey area between the police procedural and classic detective fiction, Reginald Hill (b. 1936) deals on occasions with subjects that would be of little interest to the reader who yearns for the comfortable golden age of the whodunit. As an English graduate with long experience in the academic world, it is not surprising that his writing is characterized by literary ability and careful construction, but this does not mean that they are set in an unreal world or that they are intellectual puzzles. They are in fact about very real people, set mainly in Yorkshire, and concern cases which are very much of today. Pertinent questions are asked, comments about modern society are made, and all are wrapped up into complex and intriguing plots. Most of them feature the large and coarse Superintendent Dalziel and the sensitive graduate Sergeant (later Detective Inspector) Pascoe, and much of the pleasure of Hill's books lies in observing the contrasts between these two men. In

Hill, Reginald
Ruling passion
Collins, 1973; New York: Harper&Row, 1977
Sergeant Pascoe feels that a reunion in the country with four old friends might be a soothing prospect, especially as he has eleven unsolved burglaries occupying his mind. In the isolated cottage in Oxfordshire there are only three friends waiting for him, and

they are all dead. It is a good mystery, but for a more appropriate instance of how Hill tackles some of the more sordid aspects of society one must mention

Hill, Reginald
A pinch of snuff
Collins, 1978; New York: Harper & Row, 1978

Here Pascoe and Dalziel are drawn by murder into the world of 'snuff' movies, a nauseous combination of sex and violence. The plot centres on a private cinema club, where the murder victim is a former headmaster who is found with the marks of a thrashing on his body. At times amusing and at times alarming, it is proof that Hill does not shy away from difficult subjects.

High standards have also been seen in the work of Laurence Henderson (b. 1928), whose gritty style makes his policemen and criminals come alive in the tradition of the realistic television series mentioned earlier. In Henderson's work, today's crime is not a game, played between the cops and the robbers, but a very serious struggle where the soft lose out. In fact, one of his best books,

Henderson, Laurence
Major enquiry
Harrap, 1976; New York: St Martin's Press, 1976

does not concern organized crime at all. Five girls have been found murdered in North East London, and the police machinery is poised for the sixth. When another girl is found dead, it proves to be someone known to Detective Inspector Arthur Milton since her childhood. He is well acquainted with her family and has a feeling for all the personalities involved, whereas his superiors are concerned only with precise facts and evidence. Milton's search for the truth creates major conflicts for him, and he is torn between his personal and professional responsibilities.

One of the most exciting arrivals on the British police procedural scene in the past decade is William McIlvanney (b. 1936), with his tough Glasgow stories featuring Detective Inspector Jack Laidlaw. In

McIlvanney, William
Laidlaw
Hodder & Stoughton, 1977; New York: Pantheon, 1977

Laidlaw made a great impact as a compassionate cop, an unconventional and brilliant addition to the ranks of fictional policemen. So many police novels had been set in London or

Northern cities or in the English counties, and McIlvanney's obvious affection for the streets of Glasgow lent something new. Indeed it may be said that the city itself is the central character. Laidlaw is a thinker, believing that the criminal needs to be understood rather than hunted like an animal. This cuts no ice with his rival Inspector Milligan, who has no patience with Laidlaw's approach, and in his search for the murderer of a teenage girl Laidlaw finds himself in competition with the orthodoxy of Milligan. It also becomes apparent that time is short, as others are similarly looking for the murderer. As Laidlaw pursues his investigation and questions those who can help him, we are shown the whole spectrum of Glasgow's daily life. It is a masterly novel, highly praised by the great Ross Macdonald for its style and for the character of Laidlaw himself, and it is sad that six years elapsed before the appearance of

McIlvanney, William
The papers of Tony Veitch
Hodder & Stoughton, 1983; New York: Pantheon, 1983
Here Laidlaw is called to the hospital bed of dying vagrant and alcoholic Eck Adamson, who mumbles the cryptic message that 'The wine he gave me wisny wine'. Old Eck also provides the names of two people and a pub, together with a phone number. Laidlaw is Eck's only friend in the Glasgow police, and takes a personal interest in following up the clues relating to this old reprobate's death. As with the earlier novel, the atmosphere of the city – with its ordinary hard-working people and its criminal elements – is conveyed to perfection. It provides the reader with much more than a mystery story, and with ample food for thought.

Before turning to the genre's principal American writers, mention must be made of a British police procedural writer with a difference. Some excellent detective novels and Gothic mysteries have been produced by Gwendoline Butler (b. 1922), and these are mentioned elsewhere in this book. Whereas the police procedural novel in Britain is a predominantly male preserve, Mrs Butler has contributed some excellent examples under the guise of 'Jennie Melville'. They feature Inspector Charmian Daniels of Deerham Hills, a new town in the Thames valley, who is a credible investigator without gimmicks. She is also a very feminine woman in a man's world, without being obsessively feminist. In one of her more recent cases,

Melville, Jennie
Murder has a pretty face
Macmillan, 1981

she tackles a new and frightening threat. At first the crimes appear conventional enough, with a corpse in the river and the robbery of a furrier. Then the situation takes an unusual turn, as Inspector Daniels finds she is up against a group of pretty women who are willing and able to match men in their criminality, and prepared even to bring social disorder to Deerham Hills.

Thoroughly American cops appear in the novels of Hillary Waugh (b. 1920), of which the first,

Waugh, Hillary
Last seen wearing . . .
New York: Doubleday, 1952; Gollancz, 1953

has become a classic. It concerns the sudden disappearance of eighteen-year-old Marilyn Lowell Mitchell from her college in Massachusetts, and provides a sharply authentic narrative of step-by-step police investigation in the American style.

The police novels which have come out of the USA have too often been excessively brutal or contrived, whereas Hillary Waugh has succeeded in producing police tales which rouse the reader's excitement by their very meticulousness, by the very routine which is ninety per cent of any investigation. No series characters were developed from *Last seen wearing . . .* , but Waugh went on to create two teams of detectives working in very different environments.

The police chief in the Connecticut town of Stockford is Fred Fellows, a folksy and patient man with a great understanding of human nature. His sharp mind belies his rural manner, and he is able to take a personal role in many of the cases arising in his small community of 8,500 inhabitants served by a force of eighteen policemen. Among the many excellent Stockford procedurals may be mentioned

Waugh, Hillary
Pure poison
New York: Doubleday, 1966; Gollancz, 1967

in which the assistant superintendent of schools, Roger Chapman, sits down to dinner with his wife and later dies of strychnine poisoning. It is discovered that the poison has been administered by a method so indiscriminate that it must stem from an insane hatred. There are no direct leads to the killer, but painstaking

163

investigation by Fred Fellows reveals that the respectable Chapman has been leading a double life. Taunted by the unknown killer, Fellows uses forensic science and a process of elimination to narrow numerous suspects down to just one.

In absolute contrast are the New York police procedurals featuring Frank Sessions of Homicide North, introduced in

Waugh, Hillary
''30'' Manhattan East
New York: Doubleday, 1968; Gollancz, 1969

There can be little similarity between the brutal crime of the big city and the genteel mayhem of sleepy Stockford, and the divorced womanizer Frank Sessions bears no resemblance to the comfortable Fred Fellows. Nevertheless, the two men share a strong sense of right and wrong, an inherent morality, and the persistence and analytical skill to wear down a case until the perpetrator is revealed. In his first case, Frank Sessions investigates the death of bitchy columnist Monica Glazzard. At first it is thought to be suicide, but medical evidence proves that she was strangled. Sessions works his way through superbly described police routines, leading to a surprise ending which has about it that indefinably unique Hillary Waugh touch.

Probably the best-known team of American cops, however, is that created by Evan Hunter (b. 1926) under the pseudonym 'Ed McBain'. The 87th Precinct novels have extended over three decades into a series of major importance and high standard. The first three are featured here as excellent introductions to the characters and style. In

McBain, Ed
Cop hater
New York: Permabooks, 1956; Boardman, 1958

someone is killing the cops of the 87th Precinct, and McBain shows for the first time the teamwork of Steve Carella and his fellow officers, together with the descriptions of authentic police methods which were to make the series a winner. The central case of

McBain, Ed
The mugger
New York: Permabooks, 1956; Boardman, 1959

involves the hunting of a man who mugs women, treating them with a strange mixture of brutality and courtesy. The race is on to trap the criminal before it becomes a murder case, but they are too late.

The third case of the 87th Precinct men,

McBain, Ed
The pusher
New York: Permabooks, 1956; Boardman, 1959
begins with the death of the boy Aníbal Hernandez, which looks
like suicide by hanging. When it is proved to be an overdose of
heroin and the fingerprints on the syringe are not those of the
victim, the case develops into one in which at least two members
of the 87th squad become very personally involved.

The attraction of the 87th Precinct novels on both sides of the
Atlantic lies in the author's versatility, and in his successful com-
promise between the dull routine of detective work and the sensationalism displayed by so many other writers. His versatility is
evident in the fact that the books display brutality and pathos
on some occasions, turning almost to knockabout comedy on
others. We see the detectives as human beings with private lives,
as fallible beings with loves and hates and the almost impossible
onus to remain impartial. A thinly disguised New York, with its
violent crime, provides ample employment for the men of the
87th squad, and each of McBain's novels shows them coping
with an interrelated set of cases. Indeed, in *Hail, hail, the gang's
all here!* (New York: Doubleday, 1971; Hamish Hamilton, 1971)
there are no fewer than fourteen separate story lines.

Thomas Walsh (b. 1908), another American writer, is
unaccountably seldom mentioned as a master of the police procedural. This may arise from the fact that his output has been
comparatively small, and his books display a versatility which
makes them resistant to categorization in one subgenre or
another. He is nevertheless a superb writer of the police story,
with an ability to show the districts and peoples of New York in
a vividly authentic manner which is matched by few writers. His
economical style probably stems from his experience as a newspaper reporter, and his books have a welcome readability as a
result. The first was recognized with an award from the Mystery
Writers of America, and
Walsh, Thomas
Nightmare in Manhattan
Boston: Little, Brown, 1950; Hamish Hamilton, 1951
is a classic of tension, with the story taking place within a period
of just forty-eight hours and the clock moving inexorably toward
a potential tragedy. It concerns the kidnapping of a six-year-old
boy, and much of the action is confined within the Manhattan

Depot (a fictionalized Grand Central Station). Not that the locale is too restricted, for Walsh makes tremendous use of the complexities of the building. He also uses the setting to provide a police procedural novel with a difference, placing the investigation in the hands of the terminus police.

On the border lines of several types of crime fiction, but with the elements of the police procedural well to the fore, is

Walsh, Thomas
The eye of the needle
New York: Simon & Schuster, 1961; Cassell, 1962

It is a compelling study of a priest's dilemma, faced with the suspicion that his own brother might be a murderer. He wants neither to lie to the police, nor to be guilty of betrayal. Running through the novel is a powerful duel of wits and endurance between Father Ed McDonald and Inspector Neil Bresnahan, with much to be pondered about the complexities of right and wrong.

Robert L. Fish (1912–81), who also wrote as 'Robert L. Pike', produced under both names some most commendable police procedurals. His first, which was highly acclaimed and presented police working in an unusual setting, was

Fish, Robert L.
The fugitive
New York: Simon & Schuster, 1962; Boardman, 1963

Captain José da Silva of Rio de Janeiro is on this occasion involved in the question of Nazis who have escaped to South America. He went on to appear in several novels which maintained a good standard, and was often accompanied by the contrasting figure of Mr Wilson of the American Embassy. The books have the added interest of well-described Brazilian locales, and peoples both ancient and modern.

Rather more conventional was the 'Pike' series, relating the cases of Lieutenants Clancy of New York and Reardon of San Francisco.

Pike, Robert L.
Police blotter
New York: Doubleday, 1965; Deutsch, 1966

is in the classic police procedural format. Although Lieutenant Clancy and detectives Kaproski and Stanton have to deal with the major threat of professional killers planning to assassinate a United Nations delegate, they are simultaneously wrestling with numerous other cases which fall to the lot of New York's 52nd

Precinct in the space of a few days.

The policeman created by John Ball (b. 1911) is original because he is black. Virgil Tibbs first appeared in

Ball, John
In the heat of the night
New York: Harper & Row, 1965; Joseph, 1966

in the distinctly unfriendly surroundings of a bigoted small town in the deep south, where the locals do not like murder but where some of them dislike negroes even more. John Ball's picture of racial prejudice gives the book added punch. Nevertheless there has been a killing, and Virgil is a detective who has specialized in homicide. His temporary secondment is unpopular, at least initially, with the local police chief – but things improve as Virgil shows what he is made of, and solves the case in classic style.

Chester Himes (1909–84) introduced two black detectives, Coffin Ed Johnson and Grave Digger Jones, who appeared in a series of novels of which the best known is

Himes, Chester B.
Cotton comes to Harlem
New York: Putnam, 1965; Muller, 1966

Johnson and Jones make maximum impact on the reader with their crude methods, their fighting of fire with fire, and Himes presents a mixture of humour and violence which is most unusual. He is starkly realistic, at times appalling and at times sad, and his situations would be even more harrowing if comedy did not occasionally intrude.

Another original setting, together with an unusual detective and an intriguing theme, have resulted in thought-provoking stories by Tony Hillerman (b. 1925). His long association with the Navajo and Pueblo Indians has led not only to a detailed knowledge of their lives and customs, but also to a deep understanding of their codes of justice and personal beliefs. His central character is Joe Leaphorn, a lieutenant of the Navajo police whose cases occur in 25,000 square miles of reservation in Arizona. Joe is working within a social order vastly different to that of his colleagues in other police procedural series, and must do this work without the benefit of their sophisticated technology and ordered methods.

Hillerman, Tony
Dance hall of the dead
New York: Harper & Row, 1973; Pluto Press, 1985

167

was awarded the Edgar of the Mystery Writers of America as the best crime novel of its year. A principal theme is the contrast in tribal beliefs between the Navajo and Zuni religions, as typified by two young friends Ernesto Cata and George Bowlegs. When Ernesto is murdered during his stringent training for the Shalako ceremony role of the Little Fire God, George disappears and is suspected of the murder. It is a compulsive mystery with tremendous atmosphere and suspense, since Joe Leaphorn has to race against time to prevent a further tragedy from occurring. In the process the reader learns much about the local landscape, the ancient Indian cultures, and the natural history of this vast territory. It is also significant, again in contrast with other police novels, that two sets of laws or two types of justice are in play. Joe has to uphold the formal law, but he is also thoroughly conversant with tribal law. In Hillerman's books, wrongdoers are contending with both.

More conventional in setting, but most incisive in the questions they pose, are the novels of Lawrence Sanders (b. 1920). He came to prominence with his highly successful first novel,

Sanders, Lawrence
The Anderson tapes
New York: Putnam, 1970; W.H. Allen, 1970
which is a 'big caper' story narrated by means of reports and other documentary evidence. It shocks as a picture of the underworld, but for some it will shock even more by its exposure of the means used to fight back on behalf of society. The reader has to come to terms with electronic eavesdropping and its implications for civil liberties and privacy, and to decide if a society which uses such methods can fairly be described as civilized.

Sanders made further impact with his second book,

Sanders, Lawrence
The first deadly sin
New York: Putnam, 1973; W.H. Allen, 1974
which might on the surface appear to be a straightforward police procedural story. Certainly it is a classic contest between Captain Edward X. Delaney of the New York Police Department and Daniel Black, who has degenerated into brutal acts of unmotivated murder. The reader follows each man, seeing Black's crimes and Delaney's methods of tracking him down. Its central theme, however, is reflected in the book's title. In Black the sin is the obsessive vanity which tells him he is not vulnerable to the

process of law, although such a sin is probably inconsequential compared with the magnitude of his crimes. But Delaney has to look into his own heart also, to decide if similarly pride is his motivating force.

New York is again the setting of most of the novels by Thomas Chastain, featuring Inspector Max Kauffman of the 16th Precinct. In Chastain's case, however, he introduces variety by producing the hybrid police procedural and private eye story, the latter being represented by investigator J. T. Spanner. This combination has been specially effective in the 'big caper' tale, most particularly

Chastain, Thomas
Pandora's box
New York: Mason & Lipscomb, 1974; Cassell, 1975
which concerns a plot to plunder the Metropolitan Museum of Art in Manhattan.

Rex Burns (b. 1935) has rung the changes by setting his stories in Colorado. Detective Gabriel Wager of the Denver Police Department provides the reader with much insight into the problems of the ethnic minority cop, suffering the intolerance of his white colleagues and the suspicion of the Chicano community. His Spanish-American origins combine with his job to make Gabriel Wager a man in the middle ground, a thoroughly professional and intelligent cop who has to adopt a hard veneer to survive and to get results. Highly praised by Hillary Waugh, who should know what makes a good police procedural novel, the first Rex Burns title was

Burns, Rex
The Alvarez journal
New York: Harper & Row, 1975; Hale, 1976
Here Wager is investigating the Rare Things Import Shop, having received a tip that it is a front for marijuana smugglers. It is not little old Mr Montoya, the owner of the shop, in whom Wager is specially interested. He really has his sights on Rafael Alvarez, a bigger fish who has previously been arrested on suspicion but has so far eluded the clutches of the law. A later Wager novel,

Burns, Rex
Angle of attack
New York: Harper & Row, 1979; Hale, 1980
finds him in the thick of mobster killings when he reopens the

investigation into the shooting of Marco Scorvelli. Wager's lead comes from an old informant known as Tony-O, who links the killing with a young man named Frank Corvino. Then Frank's body is found, and Wager goes to war with men who will not hesitate to kill again.

The good, the bad and the ugly are to be found among the policemen of Joseph Wambaugh (b. 1937). Formerly a detective in the Los Angeles Police Department, he shows police officers with all the warts. The Wambaugh men cover a wide range – the ingenuous rookie, the embittered veteran, the highly motivated, the lazy, the pure and the sado-masochistic alcoholic. Their work provides situations to which they react as human beings rather than machines, and their specific reactions give us cause for laughter or for raised eyebrows. Wambaugh's books are perhaps novels about policemen rather than police procedural mysteries, but he is an important writer who serves to balance some of the glamour presented by other writers. Above all, he shows how the men themselves are affected by the work they do, by what society expects of them, and by the people with whom they come into daily contact. In spite of their individual characters and styles, there is a bond which ties them together, and which sadly relates them more to each other than to their friends and families outside the force, a fact which is poignantly conveyed in

Wambaugh, Joseph
The choirboys
New York: Delacorte Press, 1975; Weidenfeld & Nicolson, 1976

Here there is the comic yet pathetic situation in which the cops meet after duty hours in MacArthur Park to drink and commune, rather than go about their private lives. There are many cases in the book that are exciting, funny or intriguing, but pervading all is the dehumanized and regimented cameraderie of the 'choirboys' which is moving and disturbing.

Collin Wilcox (b. 1924) was mentioned earlier in respect of his collaborative novel *Twospot* with Bill Pronzini. He is best known, however, for his series featuring the stubborn and industrious Lieutenant Frank Hastings of San Francisco Homicide, together with his sidekick Lieutenant Pete Friedman. They have firmly established Wilcox as a top police procedural writer, a key factor in his success being the care with which he conveys the personal history and attitudes of Frank Hastings to the reader. Hastings thus becomes as much the subject of the books as the cases he investigates, whereas many fictional detectives are merely vehicles for transporting the reader through an investigation. We see these cases so much through Hastings's eyes that we begin to know him and understand his own problems. Son of a broken marriage, husband of a broken marriage, immersed in his work as an escape from the loneliness and alcoholic solace of his past, he is a real character with whom we can sympathize. Wilcox is also good at exposing the sociological and psychological problems of people in a big city, and his crimes are never reflections of the simplistic absolutes of good and evil. In some of the books Hastings is working on various cases simultaneously in true police procedural tradition, but those which concentrate on a single case are equally effective. A fine example of the latter is

Wilcox, Collin
Doctor, lawyer . . .
New York: Random House, 1977; Hale, 1978
in which he faces a major crisis, no less than a death threat to the Chief of Police which holds the city itself to ransom.

In the USA, as in Britain, the police procedural scene has been a predominantly male preserve. This makes it doubly important to mention three women who have made outstanding contributions to the field. The first of these, Elizabeth Linington (b. 1921), bore the distinction of being a woman writer of police procedurals for so many years that she received the title (attributed to Allen J. Hubin) of 'Queen of the procedurals'.

Elizabeth Linington uses the pseudonyms 'Dell Shannon' and 'Lesley Egan' in addition to her own name. They are all labels for competent police procedurals, but the 'Dell Shannon' series, featuring Lieutenant Luis Mendoza and the Los Angeles Homicide Squad, just have the edge. The first,

Shannon, Dell
Case pending
New York: Harper, 1960; Gollancz, 1960
was praised by the critics, and can still be cited today as a first-class example of the form. Not only did this novel and its successors depict police work with accuracy, but they also provided Dell Shannon's brand of social comment. Violence in the Mendoza stories is shown to be stupid, and throughout the books there is a strong sense of morality which invests the cops with a

responsibility for bringing order out of urban chaos. There is a relatively uncomplicated war between good and evil, and a clear distinction between the two which is seldom found in other police procedural writers.

Case pending sees Mendoza searching for the link between two female corpses, each with one eye mutilated. Interwoven plots cover crimes such as illegal adoption, blackmail and narcotics. These are balanced with details of Mendoza's private life and loves, while later books show him settling down as a happily married family man. Sometimes the many subplots become confusing, but Mendoza is always a comforting link. In

Shannon, Dell
Murder with love
New York: Morrow, 1972; Gollancz, 1972

the squad has a mixture of murders with which to contend, and an earthquake does nothing to help. As usual the domestic life of some of the detectives creates a welcome contrast to the often grisly aspects of their daily work.

Following on the heels of Elizabeth Linington came two other women writers of police procedurals, who are also significant for the introduction of investigators who are themselves women. Lillian O'Donnell (b. 1926) is the creator of Norah Mulcahaney of New York, and the novels show the development of her career and details of her home life as well as including some good and original mysteries for her to investigate. Married to Lieutenant Joe Capretto, Norah is an attractive and ambitious young woman who pursues her job with dedication and initiative, sometimes thwarted by male attitudes but never being presented as an ardent feminist. In short, she is a detective who gets on with the job and is prepared to be judged by results. One novel which deals particularly with sex discrimination is

O'Donnell, Lillian
No business being a cop
New York: Putnam, 1979; Hale, 1980

where the subplot concerns the need for the police department to reduce numbers as a result of a budget cut. The women cops bring an action for discrimination, which leads to more strained relations between the sexes than is normally found in O'Donnell's novels. Indeed, sex discrimination in the extreme is the theme of the main plot, as an obsessive murderer seems dedicated to killing every woman on the New York police force.

In an eerily atmospheric conclusion, Norah goes alone to an empty Madison Square Garden to face the killer, and to learn the identity of the person who thinks women have no business being cops.

Women police officers in fiction, as presumably in real life, are often relegated to the role of dealing with juvenile cases. In some respects Norah Mulcahaney does just this in

O'Donnell, Lillian
The children's zoo
New York: Putnam, 1981; Hale, 1982

but it is a case with all the violence associated with the worst manifestations of modern society. Norah is faced at the outset with a series of wanton acts of vandalism and intimidation, and there are pointers to a classy private high school in Manhattan. This escalates to the horrific destruction of the animals in the children's zoo in Central Park, but appears also to be linked with a number of murders. It is a story of depravity among children who have both too much and too little.

Dorothy Uhnak (b. 1933) was a policewoman for some fourteen years. This experience in the field gave her, like her counterpart Joseph Wambaugh, a detailed knowledge of police procedures and the ability to show the unglamorous aspects of the work. She shows the worst features of society, the deprivation which leads to crime, the cruelty and greed which spawn acts of violence against ordinary people from the youngest to the oldest. It is a society in which police officers cannot be disinterested observers, in which justice might be blind but those who have to enforce the law are likely to become case-hardened or even brutalized. Against this background Dorothy Uhnak places Christie Opara, a young policewoman attached to the staff of the district attorney in Manhattan. Compassionate and fair-minded, Christie has to make a positive effort to retain such qualities following the killing of her policeman husband, and in her daily observation of the depths to which some people will sink. She first appeared in

Uhnak, Dorothy
The bait
New York: Simon & Schuster, 1968; Hodder & Stoughton, 1968

and was acclaimed as a welcome addition to the roll of fictional investigators. Here she suspects that a pattern exists between three apparently unrelated murders, and embarks on the only sure way of trapping the killer by offering herself as bait.

Dorothy Uhnak's masterpiece, however, is a book which deserves to become a classic of crime fiction,

Uhnak, Dorothy
Law and order
New York: Simon & Schuster, 1973; Hodder & Stoughton, 1973

This major work covers three generations of a New York police family called O'Malley. It contains much crime, but can in no way be described as a mystery story. Instead it shows what one family has given to the police force, and what the police force has done to one family. The O'Malleys, like any family, are a group of individuals. Although Irish Catholics, they do not consist of the folksy Irish cops beloved of the cinema in the 1930s. They can be dedicated, disillusioned, prejudiced or compassionate. All are covered in detail and with feeling, as is the important contribution made by the O'Malley women.

Many fictional policemen have been shown at work in Britain and the USA, but it is worth drawing attention to the fact that some excellent police procedural novels have been set in such diverse locations as Holland, Sweden, Denmark, South Africa and the West Indies.

The novels which F. R. E. Nicolas (b. 1927) wrote as 'Nicolas Freeling', and which feature Piet Van der Valk, are realistic in their acceptance of the fact that crime is a part of life. It is sometimes in the open, sometimes behind the masks of the respectable businessmen. Freeling does not dwell upon police procedure, and his Inspector (later Commissioner) Van der Valk of Amsterdam is so much more than a cipher. We can assess his relations with other officers, with his French wife Arlette, and with the characters with whom he rubs shoulders daily. If he must be denied a class of his own, he must rank with Maigret – we see Amsterdam through the eyes of Van der Valk as vividly as we see Maigret's Paris.

Nicolas Freeling is outspoken. His penetrating analysis leads us towards a more understanding view of social problems, and particularly those relating to crime. Beginning with *Love in Amsterdam* (Gollancz, 1962; New York: Harper & Row, 1962) and ending when Van der Valk is killed in *A long silence* (Hamish Hamilton, 1972), Freeling presented a series of uniformly high standard which was as memorable for raising difficult questions and pricking hypocrisy as for its mystery content. The last Van der Valk title was published in New York as *Auprès de ma blonde* (Harper & Row, 1972). In some of his later books, Freeling has either retained Van der Valk's widow Arlette or featured a French detective called Henri Castang.

Of the Van der Valk books,

Freeling, Nicolas
Gun before butter
Gollancz, 1963

appeared in New York as *Question of loyalty* (Harper & Row, 1963). When a stabbed corpse is found in a house in Amsterdam, the cleaner identifies him as her employer Stam. The problem for Van der Valk is that nothing more is known of the man, his personal life or his business activities. Enquiries take Van der Valk into Germany and Belgium, and into contact with a rich assortment of characters. All are used to the full to display Freeling's shrewd wit, and his perceptive exposure of the bogus and the bureaucratic.

Freeling, Nicolas
Criminal conversation
Gollancz, 1965; New York: Harper & Row, 1966

concerns the murder of a painter, and analyses the art world of Amsterdam with biting comment and caustic humour. It also sees Van der Valk posing as a patient in order to secure the confidence of Dr Van der Post, a principal suspect in the case. As ever, Van der Valk risks unconventional methods to achieve results.

Another widely acclaimed title,

Freeling, Nicolas
The king of the rainy country
Gollancz, 1966; New York: Harper & Row, 1966

begins after Van der Valk has been wounded by a sniper's bullet, and then recounts the events leading up to the attack. There is little promise of violence or even of crime when Van der Valk, on the instructions of his superiors, undertakes a private commission to trace a disappearing millionaire. This takes him from Amsterdam to Germany, Austria and France, leading to three corpses and his own brush with death.

Some years later on the scene, Janwillem van de Wetering (b. 1931) has also taken Amsterdam as the setting for his police novels. Although a resident of the USA and writing in English, he was born in Holland and was an officer of the Amsterdam Police. He has also written books on his experiences as a Zen Buddhist, which does much to explain the depth and imagery of his novels. Some readers might indeed find them to be an acquired taste, although they may still be read and enjoyed for their careful portrayal of police procedure and subtle characterization. The central detectives are Adjutant Henk Grijpstra and Sergeant Rinus De Gier, who first investigated and philosophized in

van de Wetering, Janwillem
Outsider in Amsterdam
Boston: Houghton Mifflin, 1975; Heinemann, 1976

This concerns the murder of the leader of the Hindist Society, a suspect commune for lost young idealists. A bizarre group of characters figure in a case where eccentricity, intrigue and violent crime are well mixed. Much of the action seems incongruous against the beautiful and peaceful background of Amsterdam, while van de Wetering provides food for thought with his observations on life and human nature.

The Swedish writers Maj Sjöwall (b. 1935) and Per Wahlöö (1926–75) were again interested in the roots of crime and the contradictions and hypocrisies of modern society, rather than in merely presenting a police documentary or whodunit. In every respect they succeeded with their ten novels of the Stockholm Police, and they created a memorable character in Senior Detective Martin Beck. He is shown to be a thinker about Swedish politics and attitudes, as well as a family man and a dedicated police officer, and the men of the National Homicide Squad are frequently depicted as antiheroes, capable of terrible fallibility. In the first of the series,

Sjöwall, Maj and **Wahlöö, Per**
Roseanna: translated by Lois Roth
New York: Pantheon, 1967; Gollancz, 1968

Beck investigates the rape and murder of an American girl whose body is found in a canal. Persistent and systematic enquiries reveal the murderer, but there still remains the problem of extracting a confession. In this respect, if in few others, there is a similarity with the work of Georges Simenon.

A specially impressive police procedural is

Sjöwall, Maj and **Wahlöö, Per**
The man on the balcony: translated by Alan Blair
New York: Pantheon, 1968; Gollancz, 1969

which involves a massive hunt throughout Stockholm for a psychopath. The crime is the sexual assault and strangulation of little girls, and the novel has all the grim realism that such a crime entails. Perhaps their best-known work, however, is

Sjöwall, Maj and **Wahlöö, Per**
The laughing policeman: translated by Alan Blair
New York: Pantheon, 1970; Gollancz, 1971

involving the machine-gunning of the occupants of a Stockholm bus. In addition to presenting the story of a scrupulous and unrelenting investigation, the authors cause the reader to think about the psychology of the mass murderer.

It would be wrong to give the impression that Sjöwall and Wahlöö show only the horror and tragedy with which the police contend, since they are equally adept at light relief. While their locked room mystery in

Sjöwall, Maj and **Wahlöö, Per**
The locked room: translated by Paul Britten Austin
New York: Pantheon, 1973; Gollancz, 1974

is a serious affair, with Martin Beck facing one of his most difficult cases, his colleagues are hunting a gang of bank-robbers in fine style. The special squad, under the leadership of 'Bulldozer' Olssen, give a spirited imitation of the Keystone Kops. At what point, the reader wonders, will the two investigations collide? In the meantime we are treated to an extremely lively adventure, with Sjöwall and Wahlöö in entertaining mood.

Denmark is the setting for police procedurals featuring Detective Inspector Jonas Morck and his assistant Knud Einarsen, the creations of Poul Ørum (b. 1919). One of the most striking features is the marked contrast between the two men, Morck being an amiable and secure man with a loving wife, while Einarsen is a self-centred and often cruel man who suspects his wife of infidelity and is jealous of her success in business. Even more relevant in respect of their professional life is that Einarsen is a bully who takes advantage of his position, so that witnesses and particularly suspects suffer at his hands. Their first case,

Ørum, Poul
The whipping boy
Gollancz, 1975

was published in New York as *Scapegoat* (Pantheon, 1975) and concerns the murder of a nurse in a resort called Vesterso. The questioning of witnesses can, in the hands of some authors, be somewhat tedious. Ørum's principal skill, however, is that he can use such passages to develop suspense to a considerable degree. It can also be powerfully shocking, as in this case. The main suspect is an uneducated man with the mentality of a child, the whipping boy or scapegoat of the title. Guilty or innocent, it is clear that the world will never be the same for him again.

James McClure (b. 1939) sets his detective novels in South Africa. The principal detective, Lieutenant Tromp Kramer, is an Afrikaaner; his assistant, Sergeant Mickey Zondi, is a Zulu. Their cases are modern versions of classic detection, but naturally the question of apartheid is one which it is impossible as well as undesirable to ignore. In their first case,

McClure, James
The steam pig
Gollancz, 1971; New York: Harper & Row, 1972
there is confusion at the undertakers in Trekkersburg because a post mortem is carried out on the wrong body. Moreover, a wound is found, possibly made by a bicycle spoke.

McClure has maintained a high quality as a detective novelist, and has also asked questions about South Africa rather than treating it merely as a picturesque background. In

McClure, James
The Sunday hangman
Macmillan, 1977; New York: Harper & Row, 1977
someone is doing the South African state executioner's job for him. Kramer and Zondi pursue the hangman, and in doing so must themselves examine the idea of capital punishment in order to enter the mind of this extraordinary killer. Intensified pressures at both national and professional levels threaten to divide Kramer and Zondi. This is a substantial book, giving a vivid picture of rural Natal as well as the familiar city of Trekkersburg.

There is often a touch of the bizarre in McClure's work. In

McClure, James
The blood of an Englishman
Macmillan, 1980; New York: Harper & Row, 1981
Kramer dismisses the fairy tale that a homicidal giant is on the rampage, attacking victims at random, until the gruesome discovery of a murdered Englishman whose injuries suggest a killer of superhuman strength. This gripping mystery is laced with humour, and enhanced with interesting and carefully observed characters.

As a final example to demonstrate the cosmopolitan nature of the police procedural, there is the British author Christopher Nicole (b. 1930) in his guise of 'Andrew York'. Perhaps this pseudonym is still best known for the secret agent novels featuring Jonas Wilde, the Bond lookalike known as the Eliminator. More impressive and more relevant here, however, are the cases of Munroe Tallant, commissioner of police on the island of Grand Flamingo in the West Indies. The author spent his early life in the islands, and brings a fine and exotic authenticity to his settings as well as much local warmth and humour, intriguing characters and colourful dialect. In

York, Andrew
Tallant for trouble
Hutchinson, 1977; New York: Doubleday, 1977

the commissioner has to track down a murderer in the midst of simmering revolution and terrorism. He shows himself to be a powerful new detective creation, a man with a questioning attitude to those who are in authority over him, strong and independent but capable of compassion towards those who need his protection.

11
History With Mystery

A form of crime fiction which has become very popular, although it is not sufficiently extensive to be described as a subgenre, is that in which crime is shown against the background of a past age. A variation of this is the novel which takes a nonfictional criminal case of the past and transfers it to modern times, sometimes giving the characters fictitious names and providing the author's own solution or interpretation. These books may be presented as detective novels in the classic mould, or as crime novels in which motive and character are more important than the mystery element, or even as police procedural stories. In short they traverse several of the forms already discussed.

There is nothing new in this approach. Some writers of the golden age, including Agatha Christie and John Dickson Carr, produced a number of creditable historical mysteries with settings ranging from ancient Egypt to Victorian England. Again there are major crime novelists of today, such as Julian Symons and H. R. F. Keating, who have shown great versatility by devising historical mysteries to add to that body of work for which they are best known.

Here, however, we are concerned with those authors who have made a speciality of fictional mysteries with a historical background, or conversely real cases given modern fictional dress. The chapter will also cover some major individual titles which have been widely recognized as key contributions to the field.

To take the examples in chronological order of subject, and to begin with a series which transported the reader to very early times, it is important to recognize the unique works of Robert van Gulik (1910–67). He was a Dutch diplomat and expert on Chinese history, and his ancient tales of Judge Dee attracted a large following. Van Gulik's interest was fired when, in the 1940s, he translated into English a traditional Chinese story from the seventh century which concerned the judge Ti Jen-chieh, and this inspired him to invent his own stories. A magistrate in various provincial cities, Judge Dee also fulfils the function of bringing the wrongdoers to book, and is therefore the principal detective as well as the judiciary.

The volumes produced by van Gulik are all fascinating, but excellent examples are

van Gulik, Robert
The Chinese nail murders
Joseph, 1961; New York: Harper & Row, 1962
and
van Gulik, Robert
The haunted monastery
Heinemann, 1963; New York: Scribner, 1969
In keeping with other books in the series, they include three novelettes which are interlinked. This was a genuine Eastern story device, to which van Gulik gave added verisimilitude by using drawings in the text, and by basing Dee's procedures on the ancient customs and laws of China which he had scrupulously researched. His clues can sometimes be found in the drawings, as well as in the narrative. The plotting and characterization are good, as is the enormous amount of information he imparts about the China of Dee's time; but detection as we know it is sometimes a trifle thin. Even that is excusable, for the real Dee would have used his own methods to extract the evidence he required. These included intimidation and acceptance of the fact that agencies of the supernatural were on the side of the magistrate, which made it relatively easy to prise confessions from the impressionable lower orders of society. All such techniques are to be seen in van Gulik's books, which must rank as the most unusual and instructive of historical mystery stories.

The crimes devised by Ellis Peters, who is mentioned again in Chapter 12, often have their roots in the past. Of special interest here, however, is the fact that in recent years she has turned her attention to England in the twelfth century and produced a remarkable series of mysteries featuring the monk Brother Cadfael. The atmosphere is superb, and the historical detail impeccable. A good example,

Peters, Ellis
Monk's-hood
Macmillan, 1980; New York: Morrow, 1981

is set in Shrewsbury in 1138, where Gervase Bonel plans to give his valuable manor to the Abbey, in return for life tenure in one of the houses owned by the Benedictines. Before the deeds are signed and sealed, he is poisoned with monk's-hood. Brother Cadfael is an expert on plant life, no mean exponent of the art of understanding humankind, and rapidly becoming highly proficient in the science of detection.

Turning to fourteenth-century Italy, there is room to debate the justification for including in this book

Eco, Umberto
The name of the rose: translated by William Weaver
New York: Harcourt, Brace, 1983; Secker & Warburg, 1983

It is, after all, not primarily a detective story but a major historical novel which became a bestseller throughout Europe and the USA. The fascination of Eco for his native Italy and its past is very evident, and the novel bears all the hallmarks of the scholarship of this professor at the University of Bologna who is distinguished in the fields of history, philosophy and literature. He has used his expertise in all these fields to the full in this novel, providing an absorbing glimpse into the politics and religion of his country, showing the contrasts between rich and poor and telling it with compassion and humour. The critics drew comparisons with Voltaire, Rabelais, Cervantes, Sterne, Melville, Dostoevsky, and other literary giants, yet it can still be maintained that *The name of the rose* also ranks as a fascinating detective story. It is a long work with many subplots, but its basic plot concerns a series of bizarre murders at a prosperous Italian abbey, investigated by an English friar called William of Baskerville and a German monk called Adso of Melk. Secret manuscripts and a mysterious library add to the haunting atmosphere. It is a superb book, a reading experience of a kind which seldom occurs.

Turning to a significant British contributor to the field, the comparatively small output of Elizabeth Mackintosh

(1896–1952) as 'Josephine Tey' ranged from classic detection to the modern reconstruction of historical *causes célèbres*. It is extremely difficult to specify her major achievement, but some authorities would cite

Tey, Josephine
The Franchise affair
Peter Davies, 1948; New York: Macmillan, 1948

for its credible characterization and the skilfully drawn setting in a small English town. It is a mystery without a murder, based on the eighteenth-century case of Elizabeth Canning but given modern dress. The peace of young lawyer Robert Blair's comfortable existence is shattered when he agrees to defend the Sharpes, a mother and daughter who allegedly held prisoner a teenage girl called Betty Kane. The mystery element is ever-present in the uncertainty of the outcome of the case, but it is essentially a fine study of character and a convincing portrait of the young lawyer as he becomes emotionally involved with his clients. It is also a rare example of a detective novel which does not rely upon murder to generate and maintain suspense.

Other devotees would undoubtedly regard

Tey, Josephine
The daughter of time
Peter Davies, 1951; New York: Macmillan, 1952

as her best book. It is not only a unique contribution to the field of detective fiction, but is quoted in circles far wider than the genre itself. Inspector Alan Grant is forced into the role of armchair detective in a literal sense, when he is hospitalized after a fall. The case he chooses to occupy his mind is one which has intrigued many others before him. He reaches a solution which is not necessarily very original, but only after following up some fruitful lines of scholarly research. The case is one of England's longest-standing unsolved mysteries, that of the princes in the Tower and the guilt or innocence of Richard III.

American Lillian de la Torre (b. 1902), who has described herself as a 'histo-detector', has produced novels and short stories in which she reconstructs criminal cases of the past and provides her own solutions, a task to which she has brought painstaking research and a keen academic mind. She is probably best known, however, for her contributions to *Ellery Queen's mystery magazine* which feature a giant of English history and give him the role of detective. These stories were collected as

de la Torre, Lillian
Dr Sam: Johnson, detector
New York: Knopf, 1946; Joseph, 1948
a volume which was described by Ellery Queen in *Queen's quorum* as 'the finest series of historical detective stories ever written – in scholarship, humor, flavor, and compelling detail'. This is praise indeed, but it is that rare example of a literary project in which everything gells to perfection. Firstly there is the basic concept, a stroke of genius – Samuel Johnson and his biographer James Boswell, a ready-made combination as a sort of eighteenth-century Holmes and Watson. Then there are the real mysteries of the period, which were many and varied, together with other living personages and genuine London settings. All Lillian de la Torre had to do was to supply the ingenuity which devised the fictional solutions, and of course to be able to emulate the flavour and style of Boswell. The mode and manners of the good Dr Johnson are well known, but they are still difficult to bring to life without the appearance of pastiche or exaggeration. In fact, all this was achieved most cleverly and affectionately, resulting in a collection of stories which are pure pleasure.

The Victorian period has perhaps been the most fruitful source of material for mystery writers. Indeed, the Ripper murders of the late 1880s proved an inspiration for a novel when comparatively few years had elapsed since the gruesome events themselves,

Lowndes, Marie Belloc
The lodger
Methuen, 1913; New York: Scribner, 1913
Mrs Belloc Lowndes (1868–1947) makes a competent job of conveying the terror which existed in London while the unknown killer stalked the streets. Mr and Mrs Bunting have a new lodger, Mr Sleuth, and from the outset there is something odd about him. Clearly he is a gentleman fallen upon hard times to rent such modest lodgings, although he has money for rent in advance. But he turns all the pictures with their faces to the wall, and behaves in other ways which gradually begin to prey upon Mrs Bunting's mind. Could he be the Avenger, the maniacal killer whose sobriquet is on the lips of every Londoner?

An author of today, Gwendoline Butler, has shown a particular fascination for the melodrama of Victorian times. Her detective novels and police procedurals are mentioned elsewhere in this book, but here it is appropriate to commend

Butler, Gwendoline
A coffin for Pandora
Macmillan, 1973

which was published in New York as *Sarsen Place* (Coward-McCann, 1974). It is a novel of suspense set in nineteenth-century Oxford, in which she conveys the 'upstairs-downstairs' contrast of the rich and the poor, and presents a governess heroine whose life is at risk once she becomes involved in a mysterious death and a kidnapping.

Evelyn Berckman has similarly been mentioned for her detective novels and tales of suspense, but one of her best books has an eerie historical basis.

Berckman, Evelyn
The Victorian album
Hamish Hamilton, 1973; New York: Doubleday, 1973

tells how a 'latent' medium, Miss Teasdale, is impelled by an old album she finds in her attic to delve back into the past. She is rather curious about a death which, it seems, had been swept well under the carpet.

In recent years Anne Perry has written a series of mysteries set in Victorian London, beginning with

Perry, Anne
The Cater Street hangman
Hale, 1979; New York: St Martin's Press, 1979

which centres on the Ellison family. Sisters Charlotte and Emily are repressed by their typically Victorian father, protected from the outside world, forbidden to read newspapers, expected only to participate in the proper social and charitable activities of the day and to prepare themselves for good marriages. Charlotte suddenly faces the unacceptable aspects of life when one of their servant girls becomes the latest victim of a strangler, and shame is brought on the house by the visit of the police. Even more reprehensible is the fact that Charlotte is attracted to the investigating officer, Inspector Pitt. It is a good mystery, and a witty and observant portrait of Victorian society. Fortunately, Anne Perry went on to write others, with Charlotte becoming Mrs Pitt and less restrained by her father's influence. Thus we are able to hear more of her political convictions, and her compassionate views about the way the Victorians treat society's 'have nots', as well as her concern about the role of women.

The Inspector Lintott novels by Jean Stubbs (b. 1926) are set in late Victorian and early Edwardian times. Lintott is a Scotland Yard detective at the end of his career, a sound family man, and very much the proper Victorian who finds it difficult to understand the feminism of his daughter. Set slightly later than the books of Anne Perry, the Lintott novels show women beginning to cast off their shackles, but the first,

Stubbs, Jean
Dear Laura
Macmillan, 1973; New York: Stein & Day, 1973
is still essentially about the impotence of Victorian women as well as being a satisfying and haunting mystery story. In presenting a prosperous household, Jean Stubbs concentrates largely upon the character of Laura Crozier, mistress of the house and wife of Theodore. Family relationships are examined in depth, and we are also witness to the gossip below stairs, all set against a meticulously described background of London and its social scene in the 1890s. It is all convincing enough to be the recounting of an actual case, but is entirely fictional.

In later cases Lintott goes to Paris and San Francisco, but he is basically a Londoner. He knows the customs of the country, and the correct approaches to be made by him in careful recognition of the class structure. While he is a man of strong moral convictions, his work has made him familiar with the underworld, and with the aspects of Victorian society which people of quality prefer to ignore. Thus Jean Stubbs sets out to show the contradictions of the time, the attitudes and the behaviour which make present-day talk of 'Victorian values' somewhat hypocritical. Many women in London were cherished and protected in their fine houses, while 80,000 lived as prostitutes.

That seamy underbelly of Victorian London is also well known to Sergeant William Verity of Scotland Yard, the creation of Francis Selwyn (b. 1935) in

Selwyn, Francis
Cracksman on velvet
Deutsch, 1974; New York: Stein & Day, 1974
Verity is well acquainted with the underworld and with the sexuality of the times, but his puritan nature keeps him on the right path. The novels in which he appears cannot truly be described as mysteries, but are more in the nature of historical adventure stories. Nevertheless, they again show an authentic and

186

disturbing picture of the life and times of a Victorian policeman, and they frequently leave the reader with the impression that, even in matters of crime, it was the rich that got the pleasure and the poor that got the blame. For himself, like it or not, Verity is part of the system which upholds such injustice.

Without a doubt the biggest impact in the field of detective fiction set in the Victorian age has been made by Peter Lovesey (b. 1936). From his debut with *Wobble to death* (Macmillan, 1970; New York: Dodd, Mead, 1970), his popularity and influence have been unrivalled. His central characters, Sergeant Cribb and Constable Thackeray of Scotland Yard, are inspired creations. So too are the stories themselves, in which Lovesey has successively unearthed novel features of the Victorian way of life and then built mysteries around them, be it the music hall, ritual trips to the seaside, prizefighting, or indeed the endurance race which gave him his original idea.

Cribb is a shrewd investigator, sometimes achieving his results against all the odds. Stacked against him is the rigid class system, which can be seen in the bristly attitude of his superior Chief Inspector Jowett, and in the members of the middle and upper classes that Cribb must question in pursuance of his duties. Nevertheless Cribb invariably presses on, sometimes rather naively shocked by the evil he uncovers, until he reaches the solutions of mysteries that Peter Lovesey has planned with great skill and ingenuity. The atmosphere of Victorian England is there in the writing itself, and in the whole period feel of the books, perhaps most effectively in

Lovesey, Peter
Waxwork
Macmillan, 1978; New York: Pantheon, 1978

Here the aura and fascination of the Victorian *cause célèbre* is brilliantly evoked, from the lovely young woman in the condemned cell to the businesslike approach of the public hangman negotiating with Tussaud's waxworks for the disposal of her clothing. But is Miriam Cromer guilty? The Home Office receives evidence to suggest that there has been a grave miscarriage of justice, and Chief Inspector Jowett is only too pleased to leave Cribb the task of taking the matter further.

An excellent idea like the Sergeant Cribb novels can easily grow stale if taken too far and continued indefinitely; but Peter Lovesey has more recently turned to crimes of a slightly later era

and repeated his outstanding success. For example,
Lovesey, Peter
The false Inspector Dew
Macmillan, 1982; New York: Pantheon, 1982
was awarded the Gold Dagger of the Crime Writers' Association
as the best crime novel of its year, and is indeed a marvellously
stylish piece of work. Set in the London of 1921 and aboard the
liner *Mauretania* en route from Southampton to New York, it is
a murder mystery with echoes of the Crippen case. The fascination lies in the assorted passengers and their lifestyles, the
romance and the elegance, and the sudden intrusion of murder
and the false Inspector Dew. To give more than this cryptic
summary would be unfair.

In terms of detective fiction the essence of Victorian England
was, of course, Sherlock Holmes. Interest in Sherlockiana has
never waned, and one manifestation is that various writers
throughout the twentieth century have paid homage by producing pastiches, either introducing detectives with a close resemblance to Holmes or actually producing new Holmes adventures.
In quantity they have been impressive, in quality they have been
variable; but at this point it would be wrong to discuss the best
historical mysteries without mentioning several of the more
interesting examples.

One of the most voracious readers of the Holmes stories was a
young American named August Derleth (1909–71), who once
wrote to Conan Doyle enquiring if there would be any more
stories published. Conan Doyle, it may be recalled, had only
continued with Holmes after the turn of the century because of
massive public pressure, and it is not surprising that young
Derleth in the late 1920s received no commitment from the great
man. What followed is quite remarkable, for at the age of nine-
teen Derleth himself began to write the first of what was eventually to amount to some seventy stories. Strictly speaking they
did not feature Sherlock Holmes, but there was no attempt to
disguise the family likeness which was immediately apparent in
Mr Solar Pons of 7B Praed Street and his companion Dr Lyndon
Parker – quite the opposite in fact, for Derleth was unashamedly
paying his respects and perpetuating the tradition.

They are excellent stories, in which Derleth caught the flavour
of the original with something amounting to genius. Solar Pons,
physically resembling Holmes and displaying the master's brilliant

powers of deduction, investigates cases which have just the right period atmosphere. They have one additional quality which is not seen in many other Holmes pastiches – they are ingenious and well-plotted detective stories in their own right. Perhaps on consideration they should not be described as pastiches, since the word has come to be defined as embodying an element of irreverence or ridicule. It was not so with Derleth, who was besotted with Holmes and was determined that he should live on.

Following magazine publication, Derleth's stories were collected in book form by his own aptly named publishing firm, the first being

Derleth, August
In re: Sherlock Holmes
Sauk City, Wisconsin: Mycroft & Moran, 1945

Thirty years elapsed before this was published in London, as *The adventures of Solar Pons* (Robson, 1975), together with several of the other Pons volumes.

Special mention must also be made here of

Doyle, Adrian Conan and **Carr, John Dickson**
The exploits of Sherlock Holmes
John Murray, 1954; New York: Random House, 1954

The inside knowledge of Sir Arthur's son is here combined with the skill of a top storyteller with an uncanny knack of conveying the Victorian atmosphere, resulting in a quality one would expect. They are written in simulation of the original style, with each new plot based upon a case to which Dr Watson makes passing reference in the original stories. Although the complete Holmes fanatic might disagree, the task is accomplished rather well.

More recently an American in his twenties produced a new Sherlock Holmes novel which became a bestseller. Nicholas Meyer (b. 1945) was responsible for encouraging renewed enthusiasm for Holmes and Watson with the highly entertaining

Meyer, Nicholas
The seven per cent solution
New York: Dutton, 1974; Hodder & Stoughton, 1975

Not only do we stylishly renew the acquaintance of the men from Baker Street, arch-enemy Professor Moriarty and brother Mycroft, but the passage of time has permitted Meyer to introduce a character of some relevance who gives the story an added dimension – none other than Sigmund Freud. It can hardly be described as sycophantic, but it is an adventurous addition to the literature which will surely survive. Its success encouraged Meyer to follow up with *The west end horror* (New York: Dutton, 1976; Hodder & Stoughton, 1976).

John Gardner (b. 1926), a versatile British writer whose books include a series about antihero Boysie Oakes and several James Bond novels as the official successor to Ian Fleming, has also added a further slant to the Holmes stories. Taking as his fictional brief the journals of Professor Moriarty and the papers of Inspector Crow of Scotland Yard, he has produced two excellent novels with the original twist that they feature arch-enemy Moriarty as the central character.

Gardner, John
The return of Moriarty
Weidenfeld & Nicolson, 1974; New York: Putnam, 1974
presents the evil genius as a sort of nineteenth-century Godfather heading a criminal fraternity, the top man in the London underworld of the 1890s. He forms an unholy alliance with his opposite numbers in Berlin, Paris, Rome and Madrid, but the failure of an ambitious plot against the British royal family leaves him isolated from his allies. Hungry to prove himself, in

Gardner, John
The revenge of Moriarty
Weidenfeld & Nicolson, 1975; New York: Putnam, 1976
he concocts one complex scheme after another to bring the foreigners within his power, and to destroy the reputations of his enemies Inspector Crow and Sherlock Holmes. Whereas the original Holmes stories concentrated upon the brilliance of the great detective, Gardner indulges in an almost affectionate examination of Moriarty as a cunning tactician, master of disguise and superb commander of a vast criminal force. The aura of the underworld is evoked with care and much attention to detail, complete with criminal slang and sleazy locations.

Shortly after the Victorian period, in 1902, a housemaid named Rose Harsent was murdered in Suffolk, and the crime has since inspired several books speculating upon the truth, both fiction and nonfiction. American mystery writer Jean Potts (b. 1910) based her first novel on the case, and it received the Mystery Writers of America award as the best debut of its year. In

Potts, Jean
Go, lovely Rose
New York: Scribner, 1954; Gollancz, 1955
she updated the original and set it in a small American town in
the Midwest called Coreyville, where her Rose Henshaw is
pushed down some cellar stairs. The quality of the work lies both
in plot and characterization. It is a whodunit, with the murderer
pursued by the two detectives Sheriff Jeffreys and Mr Pigeon.
As in her later novels, however, Jean Potts concentrates on the
observation of her characters and their relationships. They are
ordinary people with whom any reader can easily identify, and
to whom murder comes as an intrusion and a totally incongruous event in the community. With much wit and careful planning, Jean Potts shows the heart-searching and the suspicions
which culminate in a well-rounded conclusion.

The turn of the century has also attracted the attention of one
of the best British detective novelists, the late John Buxton
Hilton (1921–86). He clearly had a deep interest in the past, as
many of his mysteries with modern settings turn out to be rooted
in history, and his Superintendent Simon Kenworthy often has
to look back several generations to find the clues to the solution
of today's murder. More direct, however, are his novels of
Inspector Thomas Brunt, set in Peak District villages in the early
1900s. They are murder mysteries which provide satisfaction for
the lovers of whodunits, but which also tell us much about the
social history and way of life of the people concerned. In the
small closed communities depicted by Hilton, there is an insu-
larity and a suspicion of outsiders, an ignorance and an intolerance, amounting almost to tribalism. In one of the best,

Hilton, John Buxton
Dead-nettle
Macmillan, 1977; New York: St Martin's Press, 1977
Brunt is in the village of Margreave in Derbyshire, near the
abandoned Dead-nettle lead-mine. Two outsiders at first appear
to be the salient figures in the case – crippled Frank Lomas,
wanting to turn to mining after his discharge from the army, and
the murdered woman from the south, Hetty Wilson. It would be
convenient for the locals if someone like Lomas were guilty of
the crime, but Brunt feels the answer lies in Margreave, and is
prepared to stretch his customary patience to the limit. Hilton
tells a story which is excellent on several counts, quite apart from

the mystery itself. He introduces romance with credibility and relevance; he gives details of country life and traditional lead-mining with the authority which clearly stems from careful research; and he shows how such a community breeds loyalties which are not always well placed.

The reputation of F. Tennyson Jesse (1889–1958) in the crime fiction field rests mainly upon

Jesse, F. Tennyson
A pin to see the peepshow
Heinemann, 1934; New York: Doubleday, Doran, 1934

This substantial novel bears the stamp of documentary fiction, being soundly based upon the Thompson and Bywaters murder case of 1922. Julia Almond, who is Miss Jesse's reincarnation of Edith Thompson, is portrayed as a girl of sheltered upbringing and romantic inclinations. Her marriage to an older man is unsuccessful, and her affair with the young Leonard Carr leads to flights of fantasy which seem inevitably to result in murder. The Thompson and Bywaters case was a *cause célèbre* which shook England, and here the reconstruction follows the same pattern as the real-life trial, the verdict and the shocking conclusion.

The infallibility of the British legal system was scarcely ever questioned by the writers of pure detective novels in the 1930s; the guilty rarely went free, and the innocent were never hanged. When the modern crime novel began to emerge, however, the reader was frequently left to draw his own conclusions, as in this case.

The exploration of criminal psychology is even more fascinating when inspired by real-life crime, and one example which will remain a cornerstone of the genre is

Levin, Meyer
Compulsion
New York: Simon & Schuster, 1956; Muller, 1957

Meyer Levin (b. 1905) here presents a superlative examination of the mind of the motiveless murderer, based upon the Loeb and Leopold case of 1924. Two Chicago students, both of wealthy families and above average intelligence, decide to commit the perfect crime. They kidnap and murder a millionaire's son, and we follow the story step by step; the murder, the trial, the verdict. It is a long novel, appalling but positively stimulating. The attitude of many readers to the case, as with its real-life counterpart, will be that such bestial killers ought to be put down like mad dogs. Levin psychoanalyses, however, rather than merely contenting himself with a crime documentary. 'I do not follow the aphorism that to understand all is to forgive all,' he says his foreword. 'But surely we all believe in healing, more than in punishment.'

It is a far cry from Levin to the cosy village murder in the English countryside, and it might also be questionable to include here two detective novels set in the 1930s and to describe them as historical mysteries. With a little licence, however, it is surely reasonable to admit works written in the 1970s which the authors have chosen to set some forty years earlier, irrespective of the fact that they are primarily intended as affectionate tributes to the golden age of mystery fiction. The first comes from a major writer, Kingsley Amis (b. 1922), who in

Amis, Kingsley
The Riverside Villas murder
Cape, 1973; New York: Harcourt, Brace, 1973
produced a book which can be highly·commended. The murder victim, dripping wet and with a terrible head wound, staggers through the french windows and expires. The mystery deepens, and further attacks indicate the presence in the small country town of a clever and ruthless killer. With wit and urbanity, but with fondness rather than sneers, Kingsley Amis takes the reader back into the atmosphere of the 1930s. For good measure he presents as unofficial detective a boy of fourteen, Peter Furneaux, who is hovering on the brink between sexual inexperience and initiation. Thus Amis also paints a sympathetic, and at times amusing, picture of a boy coming of age. It would certainly have been out of order in the golden stories of which this is a delightful reminder, but any disapproving reader will be consoled by the fact that this is also a really puzzling whodunit.

The other good example of 1930s nostalgia is

Anderson, James
The affair of the bloodstained egg cosy
Constable, 1975; New York: McKay, 1977
with its dirty deeds in an English stately home, fully equipped with secret passage and impeccable butler. In true Mayhem Parva tradition, the assorted characters gather for a weekend house party. Instead they get the obligatory thunderstorm, the

scream in the night, and the body in the lake. It is all reminiscent of Agatha Christie at her best, but nothing – not even the unconventional Inspector Wilkins – is meant to be taken too seriously.

12
MYSTERY FICTION TODAY

The best of today's writers in the fields of the hard-boiled novel, the modern crime story and the police procedural having been covered in the respective chapters of this book, it remains to consider today's exponents of the mystery story. The difficulties of doing so are twofold. Firstly, while many of the authors concerned produce classic whodunits, there are some whose books defy categorization other than the general description of 'mystery story', and there are others who display a versatility which crosses the various boundaries with almost every book they write.

Secondly, there is the problem inherent in period divisions. Many of the authors discussed earlier are still writing, and it might therefore appear dismissive to exclude them from a grouping entitled 'mystery fiction today'. Nevertheless, the general rule of thumb has been to restrict this chapter to the best writers of mystery fiction, mainly of the whodunit variety, who entered the field within the past twenty years and are still producing new work.

That said, an interesting point emerges. The vast majority of authors falling into that category are women, and there is no simple explanation for this. It could be suggested that some good male writers have been unaccountably excluded, but still there is little doubt that they are easily outnumbered by the women. It is contended that any exhaustive examination of the best of today's output will confirm the fact. The four 'queens of crime' are no longer with us, but their successors abound. They will therefore

195

be covered first, and sex discrimination in this final chapter appears to require no apology.

The many talents of historical novelist Edith Pargeter (b. 1913) may be seen in the fact that for many years she has also produced excellent detective novels under the pseudonym 'Ellis Peters'. Her early titles featured policeman George Felse, sometimes assisted or even overshadowed by his teenage son Dominic.

Peters, Ellis
Death and the joyful woman
Collins, 1961; New York: Doubleday, 1962
gained a much deserved award from the Mystery Writers of America, for it presented a sympathetic picture of Dominic experiencing the pangs of growing up, as well as being a creditable mystery. Music lessons give Dominic the opportunity to see more of heiress Kitty Norris, to whom he is attracted, and indeed music and young love are important features in this case of a murdered brewery baron.

Never afraid to experiment in her settings, and always showing a mastery of description and atmosphere, Ellis Peters has occasionally turned to India and produced some specially vivid and realistic writing.

Peters, Ellis
Death to the landlords!
Macmillan, 1972; New York: Morrow, 1972
is a powerful whodunit, derived from the fact that landlords are not beloved in India. Sooner or later brooding hatred gives way to murder, and on this occasion Dominic Felse and a party of young tourists become involved. It is a well-plotted mystery, but its background and implicit social commentary make it much more than this.

In recent years Ellis Peters has largely concentrated upon mysteries set in twelfth-century England, as mentioned in Chapter 11.

Another top British crime writer, Gwendoline Butler (b. 1922) has produced a series of detective novels concerning Inspector Coffin which have been deservedly popular. In

Butler, Gwendoline
A coffin from the past
Bles, 1970
Coffin investigates the death of Thomas Barr MP, concerning whom salacious rumours are rampant. Some of her later works

196

fall within the fields of the historical mystery and the Gothic novel, while as 'Jennie Melville' she has written some very sound police procedural stories. Other titles are therefore featured in the chapters on the police procedural and 'history with mystery'.

Although the sobriquet 'queen of crime' tended to be reserved for writers of longevity such as Agatha Christie, several women entered the field in the 1960s and 1970s who proved that the classic detective story was still a living force. One such is Patricia Moyes (b. 1923), having devised some ingenious plots featuring the pleasantly ordinary Chief Inspector (later Chief Super-intendent) Henry Tibbett and his wife Emmy. Among her best is

Moyes, Patricia
Who saw her die?
Collins, 1970

which is a piece of classic detection of the good old school, published in New York as *Many deadly returns* (Holt, Rinehart & Winston, 1970). The house party murder with suspects galore might seem old hat, but the author scores with her highly original murder method, and critics went so far as to compare her with Christie and Sayers.

Patricia Moyes is also adept at ringing the changes as far as her backgrounds are concerned, and

Moyes, Patricia
Season of snows and sins
Collins, 1971; New York: Holt, Rinehart & Winston, 1971

finds Tibbett on holiday in a Swiss ski resort. Each year the departure of the international set leaves a host of problems for the locals at the end of the season. This year it would appear to be a *crime passionel*, but Tibbett thinks otherwise.

Another literate and satisfying mystery novelist, Kinn Hamilton McIntosh (b. 1930) has produced a comparatively small number of highly acclaimed novels as 'Catherine Aird'. She is one of the writers who from the 1960s has breathed new life into the genre, concentrating mainly upon the cosy village puzzle of the golden age tradition but showing welcome unwillingness to maintain the rather colourless, unconvincing and formulaic approach of so many of her predecessors. Never allowing witty and creditable characterization to be subordinated to a genuinely puzzling mystery, she has made a commendable contribution to the survival of the detective story proper. Those who say that the modern crime novel heralded the demise of the traditional mystery story will continue to be confounded by writers of Catherine Aird's standard. Much the same can be said of Elizabeth Lemarchand (b. 1906), Felicity Shaw (b. 1918) as 'Anne Morice', and Honoria Tirbutt as 'Emma Page'.

A few examples will demonstrate that such excellent talent in a time-honoured field will today still find an audience and ensure the genre's survival. In

Aird, Catherine
The religious body
Macdonald, 1966; New York: Doubleday, 1966
we are introduced to the series character Detective Inspector C. D. Sloan of the Calleshire CID. Here he investigates the murder of a nun, whereas in

Aird, Catherine
His burial too
Collins, 1973; New York: Doubleday, 1973
he turns to matters of the modern world when the head of a secret scientific establishment is found dead in most original circumstances. The Fitton Bequest, a marble weighing several tons, is lying in pieces on top of the unfortunate Richard Mallory Tindall's body.

Elizabeth Lemarchand's Detective Superintendent Tom Pollard is a likeable character, and she provides details of his family life in successive novels which show her readers the many sides to this shrewd investigator. As a result he is seen as a credible and rather ordinary human being rather than a super sleuth, and so does not detract from the other interesting and well-drawn characters with whom his profession brings him into contact. One such is Olivia Strode, a local historian who figures almost as an amateur detective, and who first appeared in

Lemarchand, Elizabeth
The Affacombe affair
Hart-Davis, 1968
Here there are some thoughtful pictures of village and school life, with blackmail and other nefarious deeds beneath the surface gentility. The discovery of a body below the famous Monk's Leap leads to an investigation in which the local stalwarts, as well as the mysterious newcomers, find themselves and their relationships probed meticulously.

One of the delights of 'Anne Morice' is her amateur detective Tessa Crichton Price, a young actress married to a policeman.

The settings are many and varied, but always Anne Morice brings to them scrupulous observation and much witty social comment. When a character is shallow and colourless it is a reflection of true personality, rather than an acceptance that in detective fiction characterization is unimportant. In the first novel,

Morice, Anne
Death in the grand manor
Macmillan, 1970

the crimes occur in Roakes Common, a piece of London suburbia which is presented with all its false values and snobbery. Tessa's investigation centres on the *nouveaux riches* at the manor house, held in low esteem by the locals and finding that nasty things are beginning to happen. This novel has been followed by others which show this author's versatility, crafty plotting and sleight of hand.

Playwright Honoria Tirbutt turned to writing detective novels in 1970, and quality rather than quantity has been the keynote since then. In the Agatha Christie tradition, she sets her stories in small English towns and devises entertaining puzzles, but her characters and their environments are more clearly drawn than those of her illustrious predecessor. This gives to her work a credibility and a rapport with the reader, so that there can be no suggestion that she produces only a sort of guessing game with an artificial air. In her first novel,

Page, Emma
In loving memory
Collins, 1970

she set the standard by presenting a very real family in which suspicious death occurs. When the elderly, wealthy victim dies after taking a mixture of alcohol and tablets, there is a nice confusion of motives which the reader will greatly enjoy trying to sort out.

Jessica Mann (b. 1937) and Marian Babson are crime writers rather than detective novelists. Mann began with straight mystery novels, but soon began producing stories in which menacing events and character analysis displaced the puzzle element. Babson has displayed the remarkable versatility and prolificity which has resulted in some two dozen novels, ranging from classic detection through comedy thrillers to nail-biting suspense. In no case have they relied upon series detectives, preferring instead

the protagonist who is closely and intimately involved in what-
ever dark doings are afoot.

The purist will probably prefer Jessica Mann's first novel,

Mann, Jessica
A charitable end
Collins, 1971; New York: McKay, 1971

which tells of a comfortable group of Edinburgh citizens who run
a ladies' charitable organization, and are thrown into disarray by
an outbreak of poison pen letters. The apparently accidental
death of their chairman, Lady Gosset, is in bizarre circumstances
which lead their secretary to investigate further.

The range of the novels of Marian Babson, an American living
for many years in London, can only be demonstrated by citing
several of her books. Her work is typified by a lively imagination
and the ability to produce neat pen portraits of every character,
but she is also good at crisp action when required. She shows an
unusual skill at handling humorous situations together with the
most delicate of human problems. Her third novel,

Babson, Marian
Pretty lady
Collins, 1973

is a moving story of a mentally retarded man who becomes
involved in murder. While suspense is there in plenty, the memorable feature is the compassionate treatment of a difficult subject. Denny is strong and handsome but with the mind of a child,
and his happy and undemanding existence is threatened when he
meets a beautiful woman who wants to be rid of her husband.

Marian Babson's talent has become increasingly obvious over
the years. Even when she stays near to the well-trodden paths of
detective fiction, she always produces something a little different. It may be a novel twist, an intriguing central idea or a
criminous use of a modern social phenomenon. For example, in

Babson, Marian
Queue here for murder
Collins, 1980

which was published in New York as *Line up for murder*
(Walker, 1981), she brings death to the January bargain-hunters
at a London department store. One person in the queue at
Bonnard's plans to kill, but the author keeps us waiting for the
identity of the murderer and the victim. Firstly she examines the
diverse personalities at the head of the queue, and the relation-

ships that develop among them during the days and nights they spend encamped on the pavement.

When she turns to a somewhat tired theme, such as maniacal multiple murders, again Marian Babson makes it fresh and exciting. In

Babson, Marian
The cruise of a deathtime
Collins, 1983; New York: Walker, 1984

there is mayhem aboard the *Empress Josephine*, sailing from Miami with more than 500 passengers on board. As the deaths mount daily, it appears that one of them is insane. But is it so simple, or is the killer cunning and calculating?

Two welcome and original arrivals on the list of great detectives in the 1970s were the creations of Gwen Moffat (b. 1924) and Antonia Fraser (b. 1932). Experience as a mountain guide and expert on climbing has enabled Gwen Moffat to bring to her stories of Miss Melinda Pink an authority and detail which never descends to dullness, while Antonia Fraser has introduced in Jemima Shore one of the very best contemporary heroines.

A good example from the casebook of Miss Pink is

Moffat, Gwen
Persons unknown
Gollancz, 1978

in which the formidable yet gentle lady returns to one of her favourite spots on the wild Welsh coast in the hope of some peace and relaxation. Instead she finds a local family disrupted by the intrusion of a high-class prostitute, who is writing her memoirs. Two gruesome murders occur before Miss Pink's probing reveals all and peace is restored. As with the other adventures of this likeable lady mountaineer, there is much description of scenic beauty, flora and fauna; this gives the story a background which makes murder seem even more criminal, and the murderer even more dastardly.

Antonia Fraser, acclaimed as a popular historian, has now become even better known in wider circles for her entertaining stories of television journalist Jemima Shore. Attractively feminine, yet intelligent and incisive without being strident, Jemima is a well-conceived character. Her first case,

Fraser, Antonia
Quiet as a nun
Weidenfeld & Nicolson, 1977; New York: Viking Press, 1977

is a tale with elements of the Gothic. Jemima is summoned to her

Alma Mater, the Blessed Eleanor's Convent, to investigate strange happenings which include the starving to death of Sister Miriam in a ruined tower. Disrupter of the peace is the mysterious Black Nun, who roams the corridors at night.

It has already been suggested that women dominate the mystery fiction scene in Britain today. Three writers in particular ensure that this will prevail for the foreseeable future, so superlative are the works they produce in the classic tradition. They are June Thomson (b. 1930), P. D. James (b. 1920) and Ruth Rendell (b. 1930). In addition, their standards are now being equalled by two newer writers of considerable quality who are following in their footsteps, B. M. Gill (b. 1921) and S. T. Haymon.

June Thomson has since the early 1970s produced excellent mystery stories in which ingenious puzzles have been satisfyingly combined with thoughtful character analysis. Her people are shown in detail, their personalities and motivations examined with intelligence and sympathetic understanding. The environments in which they live, often but not always country villages, are not only described with feeling but are sometimes shown to influence their attitudes and behaviour. The novels of June Thomson, good from the beginning, have actually improved in quality as her career has progressed. Her series detective Chief Inspector Finch has been renamed Rudd in the American editions, presumably to avoid confusion with the Inspector Finch of Margaret Erskine. Whether Finch or Rudd, he now finds it even more necessary to dig beneath the skin of his suspects than in his earlier cases, so effectively has June Thomson introduced the elements of modern crime fiction while retaining the whodunit plot.

Thomson, June
Shadow of a doubt
Constable, 1981; New York: Doubleday, 1982
concerns the disappearance of Claire Jordan, the nervous and neglected wife of a successful doctor, from an expensive psychiatric clinic. Finch fears that it will develop into a murder case, and so it does – but it is the doctor's secretary who is found dead. In

Thomson, June
To make a killing
Constable, 1982
which appeared in New York as *Portrait of Lilith* (Doubleday, 1983), the body of an art dealer is discovered in an outhouse on the

202

property of old and bedridden artist Max Gifford. The family and friends of Gifford must have their relationships closely scrutinized by Finch before the murderer is exposed.

Never restricting herself to the cosy English murder or to domestic crimes, June Thomson introduced a feckless young criminal called Ray Chivers in

Thomson, June
Sound evidence
Constable, 1984; New York: Doubleday, 1985

Chivers is a homosexual, the lover of a senior civil servant, and from the outset he is destined to meet a nasty fate. He does so in a derelict house in Essex (truly June Thomson country), and soon afterwards there is another murder which appears to be linked. Finch needs to determine if the crimes are examples of gang violence, or if personal passions and jealousies are the motivating factors.

P. D. James is considered by many to be the finest exponent of the detective novel today. Some regard her as the new 'queen of crime', but this is inaccurate: the only feature she shares with Agatha Christie is that she writes whodunits. Others describe her as the intelligent person's mystery novelist, but this is patronizing both to the author and to the reader; her novels are well written but easily read, and the implication that they are specially suitable for intellectuals is quite false. If one finds it necessary to delve back into the history of the genre and to make comparisons, one can perhaps detect the influence of Dorothy L. Sayers and Margery Allingham. Certainly it is possible to see in the work of P. D. James the same scrupulous attention to detail and authenticity, not to mention atmosphere, displayed by Miss Sayers. Equally it is possible to find the capacity for social comment and depth of characterization which raised Miss Allingham above her peers, although without her lightness of touch and sheer irreverence.

In general P. D. James stands alone and can be judged by her own standards. These standards are exceptionally high, from her complex plots to her ability to bring every character to life, from her powers of description to the manner in which she has used so much of her own experience to provide the settings in which her murders occur. Finally, and not the least of her virtues, is the fact that she has created one of the most human and stimulating detectives in the history of the genre – a widower, poet, thinker, and dedicated policeman called Adam Dalgliesh.

Dalgliesh's personal life, with its occasional romances which seem destined never to see him return to the happily married state he once enjoyed, is as realistic as the cases he investigates, which frequently lack a happy ending or find him obliged to charge a murderer who is less reprehensible than the victim.

James, P. D.
Shroud for a nightingale
Faber & Faber, 1971; New York: Scribner, 1971
is set in a nurses' training school, Nightingale House, where we see the customary development of characters and relationships leading up to the deaths of two students. Dalgliesh meets a bewildering array of personalities, and an equally wide range of possible motives for murder. All are most sympathetically presented, from the insecure to the sexually frustrated; or they are honestly and fearlessly presented, from the bombastic to the cruel. It is not that all characters created by P. D. James are psychologically inadequate or unpleasant, but merely that she does not content herself with the artificially shallow people or stereotypes of bonhomie favoured by so many other writers.

In another of her best works,

James, P. D.
The black tower
Faber & Faber, 1975; New York: Scribner, 1975
Miss James again uses her knowledge of hospital administration and medical questions to set a scene for dark doings at Toynton Grange, a private nursing home for young disabled people. Dalgliesh is invited there by Father Baddeley, an old family friend, but arrives after the priest's death. Among the strange group of patients and staff, some of whom seem to be taking refuge from the outside world, Dalgliesh senses a brooding atmosphere from which springs blackmail, poison pen letters, sexual perversion, drugs and murder. After the reader has been given the mystery's solution, it is not easy to forget the chilly feel of the waves on the Dorset coast or, particularly, of the folly known as the black tower.

When one thinks of P. D. James, the name Adam Dalgliesh immediately springs to mind. She did, in fact, create another detective who was equally credible, equally inviting of self-identification on the part of the reader. Cordelia Gray, an attractive young woman who inherited a detective agency in *An unsuitable job for a woman* (Faber & Faber, 1972; New York: Scribner, 1973), did not reappear for ten years. But when she did so, in

James, P. D.
The skull beneath the skin
Faber & Faber, 1982; New York: Scribner, 1982

she did so in style. It is a lengthy and gripping work, certainly one of the finest detective novels of the decade. Perfection would not be too strong a word, for it contains all the best ingredients of the classic mystery in a beautifully balanced blend. The setting is an offshore island, where Cordelia's job is to protect a neurotic actress who has been receiving threatening notes. For almost half the book, the characters are developed in a strangely compelling atmosphere of impending horror, surrounded by their host's weird collection of Victoriana and mementoes of past murders. When murder comes it is as theatrical and horrific as the play for which the cast are preparing, or as the quotations about death which have been sent to the leading actress. The circle of suspects is smaller than P. D. James usually employs, and the island location contains them as tightly as in Agatha Christie's *Ten little niggers*. In the case of P. D. James, however, this setting provides the opportunity to examine the characters in detail, to look beneath the surface and expose all aspects of their personalities for good or ill. Without doubt it is a most accomplished book, and arguably her masterpiece to date.

Ruth Rendell has from the mid-1960s written a succession of superb crime novels which fall into two categories. Firstly there are the whodunits featuring Detective Chief Inspector Reginald Wexford of Kingsmarkham in Sussex, which nevertheless contain a standard of characterization and a psychological insight which in earlier years was not expected of the detective novel. Secondly there are the non-series novels of suspense, in which she looks at the causes and the effects of crime, and often examines with compassion the inadequacy and deprivation which leads a person to commit the sort of crime which would attract only disgust from those of little understanding and tolerance. It must not, incidentally, be assumed that only her whodunits are capable of providing the reader with a surprising denouement or an electrifying shock.

Reginald Wexford is a very ordinary, unglamorous detective. Middle-aged and intelligent, with a genuine interest in his fellow man, he is the sort of dependable person in whom one could place absolute trust. His comforting amiability must not be misunderstood, for he is a thorough investigator with a job which he takes very seriously. Occasionally Ruth Rendell will look more closely at subordinate series characters, such as Wexford's wife and daughters, and in

Rendell, Ruth
No more dying then
Hutchinson, 1971; New York: Doubleday, 1972

she turns her attention to Michael Burden, Wexford's assistant, who has been widowed and left with the responsibility for two children. In a book which is itself a good detective story, the running subplot is memorable for its exploration of Burden's reaction to his sudden loss, his need to overcome his loneliness, and his search for compensation by becoming emotionally involved in the case they are investigating. That case concerns the discovery of a child's body in the empty shell of a stately home, and the urgency which impels Wexford and Burden to reach a solution before another child is murdered.

In a more recent novel of skill and originality,

Rendell, Ruth
The speaker of Mandarin
Hutchinson, 1983; New York: Pantheon, 1983

Wexford takes a trip to China, a combination of consultancy and holiday, then returns to his home surroundings and the less exotic world of local murder. There proves to be a strong connecting thread, for Wexford has already met the murdered woman and her husband during his Chinese tour. As the investigation proceeds, his mind must return continually to clues which originated in that mysterious land.

A really powerful example of Ruth Rendell's non-series novels, and one for which she was awarded the Crime Writers' Association's premier prize of the Gold Dagger, is

Rendell, Ruth
A demon in my view
Hutchinson, 1976; New York: Doubleday, 1977

Its London setting, and particularly the rather seedy house divided into flats, is most effective. Among the tenants are two men with almost identical names, Anthony Johnson and Arthur Johnson, and both have sorely troubled minds. Anthony is having an affair with a married woman, and it has reached the point when she has to decide whether or not to leave her husband. Anthony is studying criminal psychology, and gradually begins to recognize familiar signs in Arthur. Arthur is a tenant of long standing who resents newcomer Anthony, spies on him and intercepts his correspondence. More serious, however, is the fact that Arthur is a psychotic killer of women who can only sublimate his desire by keeping a shop-window dummy in the basement and strangling it whenever the urge takes him. When the dummy is removed by others and burnt on a Guy Fawkes bonfire, Arthur is faced again by his particular demon and is unable to fight against it. The two men are examined in detail, their innermost thoughts exposed to the reader. In Arthur's case we see the events of his childhood, which gave him the hatred of women that later surfaced as murderous tendencies. The pressures besetting these two men gradually coincide, and the final scenes are shocking and brilliantly conceived.

The talents of Ruth Rendell have also been seen to good effect in the short story format, which has resulted in several superlative collections. Specially recommended is

Rendell, Ruth
The fallen curtain and other stories
Hutchinson, 1976; New York: Doubleday, 1976

Just a few years ago, one would easily have identified P. D. James as the answer to a crossword clue reading 'initially a fine crime authoress'. Now she has been joined by B. M. Gill and S. T. Haymon, both of whom have been placed by the critics in the James tradition. They share her concern for characterization and the examination of the roots of a crime, all of which enhances the mystery and whodunit element immeasurably. B. M. Gill's first novel,

Gill, B. M.
Death drop
Hodder & Stoughton, 1979; New York: Scribner, 1980

concerns the death of schoolboy David Fleming during a visit to a maritime museum. His blindfolded body is found at the bottom of a ship's hold. The school, anxious to avert a scandal, announces the tragedy as the accidental result of boyish pranks, but David's father is determined to learn the truth. He has to contend with closed ranks, and to overcome his own emotions. This is a story of suspense and mystery, with a beautifully drawn cast of characters providing an atmosphere of absolute credibility.

Even greater acclaim was given to
Gill, B. M.
The twelfth juror
Hodder & Stoughton, 1984; New York: Scribner, 1984
in which Edward Carne, television personality, is on trial for the murder of his wife. The facts of the case, and the guilt or innocence of Carne, are in themselves absorbing elements of mystery. Far more important, however, are the insights provided into the personalities and close-contact relationships of the twelve jurors, one of whom has a secret interest in the case they are trying.

S. T. Haymon sets her exquisite mysteries in and around the cathedral city of Angleby in Norfolk, readily identifiable as Norwich. While the action takes place in the present day,
Haymon, S. T.
Ritual murder
Constable, 1982; New York: St Martin's Press, 1982
concerns the death of a cathedral choirboy, murdered and mutilated in a manner reminiscent of the death of Little St Ulf in 1144. The murder in the Middle Ages had been followed by the slaughter of local Jews, and Detective Inspector Ben Jurnet is afraid that he might have to face a renewed outbreak of anti-semitism. A second choirboy disappears, and Jurnet's investigation is complicated by his own wish to convert to Judaism. This is a first-rate mystery, enhanced by the picture painted of the very human Jurnet and his agonizing.

Still in classic detective fiction country but with so much more to offer, Jurnet in
Haymon, S. T.
Stately homicide
Constable, 1984; New York: St Martin's Press, 1984
attends a party at the stately Bullen Hall to celebrate the curator's retirement, but his visit becomes official when a mutilated corpse is dragged from the moat. Against a beautiful and historic background, Jurnet dissects the characters of those who live and work at the Hall, uncovering their relationships of love and hate as well as their links with the past.

Much space has been devoted to those women novelists in Britain today who excel in the field of the classic detective story. While some of the men might be somewhat less classic in their approach, there are a number who have come to the forefront in the past twenty years and who consistently produce mystery novels of a high standard. Indeed, both the classical form and modern variations have been enhanced for over twenty-five years by a writer who now has a substantial list of reputable works to his credit, H. R. F. Keating (b. 1926). He exploded onto the scene with several detective novels of an intellectual flavour, each with distinctive settings or other features which stamped them as extraordinary. For example, in the first,

Keating, H. R. F.
Death and the visiting firemen
Gollancz, 1959; New York: Doubleday, 1973
a delegation from the American Institution for the Investigation of Incendiarism Inc. is met at Southampton by a stage-coach carrying a reception committee in nineteenth-century costume. The farce takes a different turn, however, when a highwayman is shot dead.

One of his most enjoyable detective novels is

Keating, H. R. F.
A rush on the ultimate
Gollancz, 1961
which is set in a boys' preparatory school during the summer vacation, when the annual croquet week is to be held. This very civilized game was clearly well researched by the author, and we are treated to a description of the match. The players, however, are destined not to complete their tournament. Not only has a convict escaped from Broadmoor, but someone has found an original use for a croquet mallet.

Following several entertaining and skilful novels, Keating created his own series detective – Inspector Ganesh Ghote of the Bombay police. Possibly the Ghote stories suffer a little by sometimes making the plots subordinate to the central character, although it must be admitted that Ghote is a truly inspired creation. He is a product of the middle class, a recipient of a British education who must nevertheless relate to the heritage and ancient traditions of his own country in his daily work. At home he is dominated by his superiors, his wife and the establishment figures of India's structured society – or so they all believe. When his cases take him abroad, he again gives an impression of being out of his depth and the reader is confident that this is self-created for the sake of effect. Outwardly diffident and somewhat comic, Ghote is really a shrewd, crafty and perceptive investigator. Keating received the highest award of the Crime Writers' Association for

Keating, H. R. F.
The Perfect murder
Collins, 1964; New York: Dutton, 1965
which was Ghote's debut. As its name might imply, it concerns
the murder of a Mr Perfect, who is the secretary of ruthless and
overbearing business tycoon Lala Arun Varde. It is not a welcome assignment, since Varde and his kind are the type of rogue
and bully that strike at all the honest Ghote stands for. He is
beset by many other day-to-day difficulties in this tale of
Bombay and its contrasts, its humour and its injustices.

The standard of the Ghote novels varies considerably, but a
specially good one is
Keating, H. R. F.
Inspector Ghote goes by train
Collins, 1971; New York: Doubleday, 1972
in which the Inspector travels to Calcutta to collect a prisoner,
and finds himself indulging in a guessing game with a fellow
traveller.

More recently Keating set a novel in India which does not
feature the Inspector, and which was something of an experiment. It paid off, as witness its recognition by the Crime Writers'
Association as the best crime novel of its year. A murder mystery
of the 1930s,
Keating, H. R. F.
The murder of the Maharajah
Collins, 1980; New York: Doubleday, 1980
is affectionately presented in the great Agatha Christie tradition.
As usual Keating communicates the atmosphere, the words and
the customs of India superbly. This time, however, he uses them
as background for a really clever whodunit. There is the time-
honoured technique of concentrating upon a small circle of suspects, visitors to the Summer Palace at Bhopore at the time of the
Maharajah's murder. It is delightfully tongue-in-cheek, and
indeed Keating finds it difficult to stop – after the killer is
revealed, he serves up a further bombshell in the very last line.

The novels of another award-winning British writer, Lionel
Davidson (b. 1922), show not only a major literary talent but an
almost bewildering versatility. He has produced polished novels
of suspense, international adventure and espionage, most of
which are outside the scope of this book. Yet it would be quite
wrong to ignore

Davidson, Lionel
The Chelsea murders
Cape, 1978
which was published in New York as *Murder games* (Coward-McCann, 1978). It can be judged as a brilliant detective puzzle or as a delicious pastiche of the classical whodunit, but by any standard it is excellent. Set in the arty student world of London, with a modern Chelsea terrorised by a maniacal killer, it has that ring of the murky London tale of yesteryear. The killer stalks, and sends taunting notes to the police which reveal a poetic bent. Bizarre and suspenseful, but with some satirical and comic touches, it is a wicked game between the author and the reader.

Then there is crime novelist Dick Francis (b. 1920), whose books have been categorized as everything from adventure yarns to detective fiction. There is actually a strong detective element in many of them, as they usually involve crimes which the hero needs to investigate – to right a wrong, to clear himself, to protect others or sometimes just to expose the villain. Champion jockey Dick Francis, who retired from steeplechasing in the 1950s, now has a long list of novels to his credit. His first,

Francis, Dick
Dead cert
Joseph, 1962; New York: Holt, Rinehart & Winston, 1962
was well received, and was followed by more with the world of racing as a backcloth. The dead cert of the title is an unbeatable horse, except that in this instance he falls and his rider is killed. Jockey Alan York, who knows that a tripwire has been used but is unable to convince the authorities, is determined to find the men responsible. This is a hazardous pursuit, as the gang will not hesitate to kill again, and it seems likely that their leader is one of York's friends or acquaintances.

His career as a crime novelist to date has seen Dick Francis enjoying enormous popularity throughout the world, and he has received the unusual distinction of also being the subject of considerable critical acclaim. He is properly regarded as a serious novelist, rather than cursorily dismissed as a genre writer. The quality of his writing warrants such recognition, but so too do his many and varied themes. Contrary to popular belief, his books are not simply about crime in the world of racing. His heroes, stoic and resilient, are reacting against the forces of evil. Yet they often need to find their true selves, or to use the adventure as a

means of clawing themselves back from the pit of despair following personal or financial misfortune. For example, his journalist
James Tyrone in

Francis, Dick
Forfeit
Joseph, 1968; New York: Harper & Row, 1969

is grappling with as nasty a bunch of criminals as any Francis
hero is likely to encounter, but he is also facing the agony of
choosing between his wife and his mistress. The principal villain,
who appears to have been thrown out of South Africa for being
too evil, is cruelly using Tyrone's invalid wife as a pawn in his
game.

Another feature of Francis is that he rarely uses a professional
detective. One notable exception is Sid Halley, private investigator and ex-jockey, who first appeared in *Odds against* (Joseph,
1965; New York: Harper & Row, 1966). When Francis reintro-
duced Sid Halley in

Francis, Dick
Whip hand
Joseph, 1979; New York: Harper & Row, 1980

the result was a triumph. Here Sid is tackling several interlinked
cases simultaneously, but one frightening theme runs through
the book. Sid, like any ordinary man rather than a super hero,
feels genuine fear and the inclination to back down. Having
earlier lost one hand, he is being threatened by one of his vicious
adversaries with the loss of the other.

Every Dick Francis book shows his skilful pacing, his good
and almost Chandleresque dialogue, and his meticulous plotting.
Occasionally he produces one which stands out for its simple
humanity and compassion, and often this makes the racing background almost superfluous. Just such a book is

Francis, Dick
Banker
Joseph, 1982; New York: Putnam, 1983

which is an absorbing novel, far more than just a story of crime.
Covering a span of three years, it is set in the worlds of merchant
banking and the breeding of top-flight racehorses. Banker Tim
Ekaterin and his client both face ruin when the progeny of a
multi-million-pound stallion are born deformed, and Tim must
determine who is interfering with nature and by what means. It is
also an extremely poignant love story.

Having mentioned the significant talents of Keating, Davidson and Francis, it is possible to single out some other men whose work is of a standard demonstrating that the ladies do not have it all their own way. The books of Michael Kenyon (b. 1931), for example, deserve greater recognition for their sympathetic characterization and competent plots. Several are set in Ireland and feature Superintendent O'Malley, with a skilful blend of humour and pathos. More recently he has introduced Inspector Henry Peckover, a poetic Cockney from Scotland Yard. His best work is nevertheless a non-series novel,

Kenyon, Michael
The rapist
Collins, 1977

which appeared in New York under the pseudonym 'Daniel Forbes' (Coward-McCann, 1977). This is a rich and chilling mixture of suspense, detection and comedy, telling of the hunt for a rapist in a small Irish town. Kenyon conveys the mounting fears of the inhabitants while lightening the tone with their eccentricities, but he never belittles the seriousness of the crime or underestimates the impact upon those with whom the rapist comes into contact.

Martin Russell (b. 1934) writes mystery stories, but their mystery often stems from complex and bizarre circumstances rather than from a simple whodunit element. Some of them form a series featuring a provincial journalist named Jim Larkin, a good example being

Russell, Martin
Deadline
Collins, 1971

in which Larkin becomes professionally involved in a series of murders in a small seaside town. Through Larkin we are able to witness the effects of front-page happenings upon a local community when sensational murder intrudes upon the small-time and normally unexciting atmosphere of the place, and Russell conveys this particularly well.

For original and really intriguing crime stories, however, it is necessary to turn to Martin Russell's non-series novels. Specially commendable is

Russell, Martin
Mr T
Collins, 1977

which was published in New York as *The man without a name*

(Coward-McCann, 1977). John Tiverton, a physicist, arrives home from work to find that his wife and children do not recognize him. Not only do they claim that he died in a car crash six months earlier, but this is confirmed by a neighbour and his professional colleagues. This puzzling situation is one which Russell uses to the full, gripping the reader's attention to the final page.

The novels of W. J. Burley (b. 1914) have, with few exceptions, featured the English West Country detective Superintendent Charles Wycliffe. They display many of the traits of Simenon, and indeed Wycliffe may himself be described as a sort of English Maigret. He is an individual rather than a regimented, procedural investigator. As with Maigret, he is deeply interested in the roots of a crime, which can often be uncovered only by exploring the history and personality of the victim. In a particularly good example,

Burley, W. J.
To kill a cat
Gollancz, 1970; New York: Walker, 1970

Wycliffe is drawn into a murder case while on holiday. In a seedy hotel, a girl is strangled and viciously disfigured. Wycliffe's probing reveals that she is far from an innocent victim, and like many of his cases it is the antithesis of the clean-cut whodunit of yesteryear.

Robert Barnard (b. 1936), for his part, might at first sight appear to be today's leading exponent of the donnish detective novel. His academic background, his career as a lecturer and professor at various universities, and his open admiration for Agatha Christie might seem to justify such a feeling, but in reality he has little in common with his conventional predecessors. While some of his mysteries are set in universities or colleges, such settings are far more than a venue for a murder puzzle. He exposes, often with acidity, the affectations and pretensions of academics, and he lays bare his characters to a far greater extent than did the classic detective novelists of the past. His first novel,

Barnard, Robert
Death of an old goat
Collins, 1974; New York: Walker, 1977

is set in the University of Drummondale in Australia, where a visiting professor from England is murdered. Inspector Royle is out of place and out of his depth among the moneyed classes and the smart academics, which provides Barnard with ample opportunity for wry observation of university life and the social scene before the mystery is solved.

It is often the case that Barnard's university types display greater loyalty to their institutions and to their students than to the law; and in several novels he has shown what happens when murder brings about the intrusion of an investigator from the outside world into a closed and almost incestuous community. On other occasions he has gone for a complete change of scene, as in

Barnard, Robert
Death in a cold climate
Collins, 1980; New York: Scribner, 1981

When a dog finds the body of an Englishman in the snow in the Norwegian town of Tromsø, Inspector Fagermo has to pick up a scent which is as cold as the climate itself. He must also pierce the wall of silence on the part of the local gentry.

Barnard is invariably witty and irreverent, as he deflates the pompous and aims his shafts at the more laughable features of middle-class England, or Australia, or Norway. He has needed to express himself more freely, and to vary his locations more widely, than he would have been permitted if he had used a series detective. It is to be hoped that his recent introduction of a regular character, Perry Trethowan of Scotland Yard, will not prove a restricting influence on this most refreshing writer.

In the case of Peter Dickinson (b. 1927), the use of series detective Superintendent James Pibble provided no restriction whatsoever. Although conventional whodunits, his novels are highly unconventional in their settings and characters. His books have been variously described as eccentric and odd, his people as grotesque and larger than life. All such terms were doubtless intended as complimentary, as indeed was H. R. F. Keating's view that 'in his power to create new worlds, Dickinson is the Tolkien of the crime novel'. He brought a welcome originality to the detective story, together with a vivid imagination and a sometimes esoteric use of words which almost perversely enhance the readability of his prose and the tension of his plots. This unusual combination of skills brought to Dickinson the unique distinction of receiving a Gold Dagger from the Crime Writers' Association for both his first and his second book. The first,

Dickinson, Peter
Skin deep
Hodder & Stoughton, 1968
was published in New York as *The glass-sided ants' nest* (Harper & Row, 1968). It tells of a New Guinea tribe, all named Ku, living in a house in London. Superintendent Pibble investigates when one is murdered with the heavy wooden figure of an owl, and this provides at once a classic whodunit and an anthropological and sociological study of an alien culture in the heart of a big city.

Dickinson selected one of the stock whodunit locations for his second novel,

Dickinson, Peter
A pride of heroes
Hodder & Stoughton, 1969
which appeared in New York as *The old English peep show* (Harper & Row, 1969). At a stately house, Pibble is faced with the mystery of a hanged manservant. Here ends any resemblance to the run-of-the-mill detective story, for the Dickinson world includes two highly eccentric knights of the realm, a man-eating lion, duels at midnight, and an ancient but efficient gallows. While Pibble pursues his knotty murder mystery, Dickinson provides a tongue-in-cheek look at some aspects of old England and some wicked swipes at the tourist trade.

Since the mid-1970s, Pibble has virtually disappeared from Dickinson's books. But still Dickinson has continued to maintain his reputation for fantastic settings, weird and wonderful characters, and detective puzzles with a flavour all of their own.

Roy Lewis (b. 1933) has proved since 1969 to be a prolific and very competent purveyor of mystery fiction, sometimes featuring the cadaverous Inspector John Crow. Lewis has been a lawyer, a teacher and an inspector of schools, and he has used all of this experience to good effect in his novels, both for authentic backgrounds and for the neat points upon which his plots hinge. Generally speaking, his non-series novels have been preferable, freeing him to explore his characters and locations in a way which is more difficult when the reader has to accompany a series detective through his investigation. For example,

Lewis, Roy
A fool for a client
Collins, 1972
is a tightly plotted story of a man in a terrifying situation. While

his actress wife is in America, young barrister Alan Armitage has a harmless relationship with a young woman who tells him she is a law student. When she is found dead, Alan is accused of the murder. Everything conspires against him, and his surprising decision to conduct his own defence stems from the fact that nobody else believes in his innocence. This is in spite of the old saying that the lawyer who defends himself has a fool for a client.

A Welshman by birth, Roy Lewis has shown special skill when painting the scenic beauty, together with many of the problems, of that fascinating land. His understanding of the Welsh people is very obvious from such novels as

Lewis, Roy
Witness my death
Collins, 1976

with its strong central character Taliesin Rees, a doctor in a mining valley. Rees refuses to believe that the murder of a pregnant local girl is the simple case accepted by the police, and in his investigation he exposes corruption and a rising tide of terror in a brooding environment.

Another bright light of the contemporary British detective novel is Simon Brett (b. 1945), whose tales of murder in the theatre and show business feature the unusual investigator Charles Paris, a seedy and impecunious actor well past his prime. Paris's vices are drink and women, not necessarily in that order, but while he displays few of the showbiz affectations he is only too willing to expose them in the stage characters with whom he frequently comes into contact. Simon Brett has an enviable knack of combining humour with some nasty crimes, and he presents real characters and credible situations in the worlds of drama, radio and television. His books are the best theatrical mysteries since Ngaio Marsh, but her Roderick Alleyn is a gentlemanly intruder whereas Charles Paris is a somewhat debauched and fully involved protagonist. From the beginning Brett has poked gentle fun at the acting fraternity, and his second book,

Brett, Simon
So much blood
Gollancz, 1976; New York: Scribner, 1977

is still one of his best. Here Charles Paris is on the fringe of the Edinburgh Festival, presenting his one-man show on the poet Thomas Hood. While he has a puzzling murder to solve, the book is memorable for its realistic picture of the city in high season.

More recently, in
Brett, Simon
Not dead, only resting
Gollancz, 1984; New York: Scribner, 1984
Brett proved that his rich vein was by no means exhausted. The smart restaurant called Tryst, run by Tristram and Yves, is not Charles Paris's usual scene at all, being expensive and fashionable and attracting the most successful and the gayest members of the theatrical profession. Paris samples the pleasures of Tryst as the guest of two wealthy collectors of theatrical memorabilia, and he is witness to a lovers' quarrel between Tristram and Yves. Later, while in his 'resting' occupation as an interior decorator, Paris discovers the mutilated corpse of Yves. It is a good plot, both witty and bizarre, liberally sprinkled with eccentric and colourful characters.

Colin Dexter (b. 1930) is similarly a leader in the field, and has been recognized by awards from the Crime Writers' Association. His complex and clever mysteries are set in and around Oxford, and they feature the very human Chief Inspector Morse of the Thames Valley Police. Perhaps Dexter's skill as a compiler of crossword puzzles provides the explanation for his great success in devising genuinely puzzling detective stories, which provide many a crafty surprise for the unsuspecting reader. In
Dexter, Colin
Service of all the dead
Macmillan, 1979; New York: St Martin's Press, 1980
deaths occur at the church of St Frideswide in the heart of Oxford, and Morse seeks the murderer among the officers and congregation of the church. They are convincing and rounded characters, and somewhere within this group lies the key to a series of murders. In
Dexter, Colin
The dead of Jericho
Macmillan, 1981; New York: St Martin's Press, 1981
a woman is found dead in an area of Oxford called Jericho. It has the appearance of suicide, but soon afterwards there is a murder in the same grim street. Again Morse's investigation brings him into contact with real people, convincingly drawn, and presents him with bewildering evidence and alibis to unravel.

Another of the new crop of fine crime writers, John Grant (b. 1933), has under the pseudonym 'Jonathan Gash' given us the lively Lovejoy, an antique dealer who frequently finds himself on the receiving end of all kinds of villainy. With equal fervour he pursues his twin passions, beautiful objects and willing women, and his wit and wisdom on both subjects is an educational experience for the reader. His adventures are romps, but intelligent romps for all that. In the first,

Gash, Jonathan
The Judas pair
Collins, 1977; New York: Harper & Row, 1977

Lovejoy is approached by a rich collector who wishes to acquire a pair of flintlock pistols known as the Judas pair. Assured by the client that these fabled weapons do in fact exist, and that they are currently in the possession of a murderer, Lovejoy sets out in pursuit of an unsolved mystery. In this debut by Gash, he provides not only a well crafted mystery but also a fascinating mixture of lore and cynicism in the world of antiques, a combination he has repeated with distinction in subsequent novels. In

Gash, Jonathan
Spend game
Collins, 1980; New Haven, Connecticut: Ticknor & Fields, 1981

Lovejoy, while in a compromising position with a married woman, witnesses the murder of a fellow dealer. It appears that someone is seeking items which the dealer bought from a local doctor, but there is nothing that seems important enough to warrant murder. With his own life threatened, Lovejoy has to delve into history to find the solution.

Roger Longrigg (b. 1929) has produced some excellent novels over many years, using several pseudonyms as well as his own name. Quite recently, however, he has made his most significant contribution to detective fiction as 'Frank Parrish', a pseudonym which was at first a closely guarded secret. The series character Dan Mallett is a truly inspired creation, a poacher and dropout from the rat race, an educated and intelligent young man who has abandoned a career in banking. He lives in a West Country village with his mother, to whom he is a great disappointment. On his first appearance in

Parrish, Frank
Fire in the barley
Constable, 1977; New York: Dodd, Mead, 1979

Dan assumes the somewhat incongruous role of detective, a

distinct change of scene for a man who habitually breaks a few laws. He is at first disgusted when protection racketeers burn crops and kill livestock, then he is galvanized into action when he finds himself under suspicion. A notable feature of the book, and one which has been evident also in its sequels, is the loving care with which Parrish evokes the atmosphere of rural life and describes many detailed facets of natural history. In

Parrish, Frank
Snare in the dark
Constable, 1982; New York: Dodd, Mead, 1982

Dan is caught redhanded on a poaching expedition by game-keeper Edgar Bland. It is unfortunate that the darkness and the torchlight in his eyes prevent Dan from recognizing Bland's companion, because the third person murders Bland on the spot and leaves Dan to take the blame. Dan's forte, however, is keeping one step ahead of the law, and concealing himself successfully while investigating a mystery.

It is a far cry from the rural scene of Dan Mallett to the sophisticated world of Mark and Molly Treasure, the wealthy banker and his actress wife who find themselves involved with serious crime wherever they go. The Treasure novels by David Williams (b. 1926) have gone from strength to strength, and some aspects have been compared by critics with the early Michael Innes and with Emma Lathen's Wall Street mysteries. Mark Treasure himself has been labelled as the successor to Ngaio Marsh's Roderick Alleyn. Two quite recent titles in the series give the essential flavour and show the author at his best, for in

Williams, David
Advertise for Treasure
Collins, 1984; New York: St Martin's Press, 1984

David Williams puts his own business background to effective use, beguiling and stunning the reader with the labyrinthine machinations of rival advertising agencies involved in a takeover struggle. Graft and other dirty doings abound, together with a seemingly accidental death which leaves Mark Treasure highly suspicious. Then, in

Williams, David
Wedding Treasure
Macmillan, 1985; New York: St Martin's Press, 1985

Williams concocts a country house whodunit of the old school, but still manages to produce a novel of today rather than a tired imitation of the works of a bygone age. Mark and Molly Treasure are invited to a wedding in the Herefordshire village of Much Marton, where they find a rich assortment of characters, much speculation about the hasty arrangements, a feud about the family fortune, and one unwelcome guest reopening old wounds. Murder is inevitable, but the murder method is highly original and the murderer well concealed.

Before turning to the American scene, mention must be made of an author who made a noteworthy impact with his first book about Superintendent Luis Bernal of the Spanish police. In

Serafín, David
Saturday of glory
Collins, 1979; New York: St Martin's Press, 1982

Bernal's suspicions are aroused when a young journalist falls to his death from a top-floor flat in Madrid. The whole affair, in the delicately balanced atmosphere of post-Franco Spain, is beset with the evasion of closed ranks. Even Bernal, dedicated to a task of which his superiors disapprove, finds his progress hindered by bureaucracy. It is more than a mystery of quality, as it presents a thought-provoking picture of contemporary Spain.

Finally, there are several of today's American practitioners in the field of classic detection whose books are very highly regarded on both sides of the Atlantic. In particular, an exceptional standard has been maintained for twenty-five years by 'Emma Lathen', who is in fact Mary Latsis and Martha Hennissart. These are conventional detective novels with a financial background, and the detective is the urbane and perceptive John Putnam Thatcher of the Sloan Guaranty Trust in New York. Some of the novels have a Wall Street setting, while others show Thatcher against different backgrounds which nevertheless have connections with his firm. The first,

Lathen, Emma
Banking on death
New York: Macmillan, 1961; Gollancz, 1962

finds Thatcher involved in the family affairs of the wealthy Schneiders. A relative's trust fund is to be distributed among them, but one of the beneficiaries has been missing for forty years. Unfortunately, a murderer is one step ahead of Thatcher in locating him.

Similarly excellent is

Lathen, Emma
Accounting for murder
New York: Macmillan, 1964; Gollancz, 1965
in which a little man called Clarence Fortinbras is agitating for an enquiry into the affairs of a large firm called National Calculating, and is murdered for his pains.

Perhaps Lathen's wittiest book, satirical and with unusual touches of compassion, is

Lathen, Emma
Murder against the grain
New York: Macmillan, 1967; Gollancz, 1967
It revolves around the threatened loss to the Sloan Guaranty Trust of one million dollars, when a shipment of grain for the Soviet Union has been loaded on the strength of forged documents. Naturally Thatcher investigates, which provides amusing and interesting contrasts between our hero and the men from the FBI, CIA and KGB. Replete with tart social comment and political barbs, it is a solid and memorable mystery.

The novels of Emma Lathen have been very highly praised, while it is a pity that greater recognition has not been accorded to those written by Columbia University's Caroline Heilbrun (b. 1926) under the pseudonym 'Amanda Cross'. They are modern novels, yet they have the erudition and intelligence of the early masters of the donnish detective novel, and like Dorothy L. Sayers she can write a comedy of manners which is nonetheless a gripping mystery. The amateur detective is Kate Fansler, Professor of English Literature, and the professional is her fiancé, Assistant District Attorney Reed Amhearst. In one of the best,

Cross, Amanda
Poetic justice
New York: Knopf, 1970; Gollancz, 1970
Kate becomes embroiled in the internal politics and academic rivalries of her university, which come to a head with the death of a professor. Aspirin, to which he is allergic, has been substituted for his usual headache pills. Kate and Reed investigate, amid suspicions that murder has taken place – and amid plentiful quotations from the poetry of W. H. Auden, who even makes a fleeting personal appearance in the book.

Harry Kemelman (b. 1908) set out to write novels of the Jewish suburban community, and found that the rabbi's accepted function as a judge and as a legal interpreter placed this central figure in an ideal position to play detective. Thus Rabbi David Small was born, and he has appeared in a successful series of detective novels beginning with

Kemelman, Harry
Friday the rabbi slept late
New York: Crown, 1964; Hutchinson, 1965

The rabbi, independent and uncompromisingly honest as well as very young, has not yet gained the full approval of his congregation. On the Friday in question, when the handbag of a strangled girl is found in his car, their confidence seems even less likely to be achieved.

Kemelman has also demonstrated his skill in short stories, as an exponent of pure armchair detection. Previously published in *Ellery Queen's mystery magazine*, the stories contained in

Kemelman, Harry
The nine mile walk: the Nicky Welt stories
New York: Putnam, 1967; Hutchinson, 1968

are models of the art. In an introduction the author explains how they came to be written, and a little of his philosophy of the detective story. Nicky Welt is a Professor of English Language and Literature, and the storyteller is a modern 'Watson' who dines or plays chess with Welt while marvelling at his reasoned solutions to the latest murders.

The Roman Catholic equivalent of Rabbi Small is Father Robert Koesler, created by William X. Kienzle (b. 1928). Kienzle was himself a priest for twenty years, before turning to mystery fiction with

Kienzle, William X.
The rosary murders
Mission, Kansas: Andrews & McMeel, 1979; Hodder & Stoughton, 1979

Father Koesler is a young priest working in Detroit, where for weeks a killer has been terrorizing the Catholic community by murdering priests and nuns alternately. Adding a further touch of the macabre, each corpse is left clutching a rosary. When a suspect provides important information in the confessional, Father Koesler is placed in the classic dilemma of his calling.

The several excellent mysteries by Kienzle to date have all been amusing and puzzling, as well as being informative about the Church in an urban society. Specially recommended is

Kienzle, William X.
Mind over murder
Fairway, Kansas: Andrews & McMeel, 1981; Hodder &
Stoughton, 1981

Monsignor Thomas Thompson is head of the tribunal concerned
with couples who wish to marry in church when one or both of
them have been married before, and he is despised for his misuse
of power and the apparently sadistic pleasure this gives him.
Ranged against him are not only the couples whose future happi-
ness he threatens, but also his fellow priests. It is a situation
which can lead to murder, and when Monsignor Thompson disappears it seems to Koesler that someone has reached breaking-
point.

There is one further book, the inclusion of which in this survey
might be criticized, on the grounds that it is a 'mainstream'
novel, a story of politics and violence and contemporary issues
rather than a crime novel. It is nevertheless suggested that Martin
Cruz Smith (b. 1942) has produced a major novel which is also
one of the most significant detective stories to have come out of
the USA for decades.

Smith, Martin Cruz
Gorky Park
New York: Random House, 1981; Collins, 1981

was many years in the writing, and has enjoyed phenomenal
success. It begins with the discovery of three frozen bodies in
Moscow's Gorky Park, and their secrets immediately set up a
conflict of interests between the policeman Arkady Renko and
the KGB officer Major Pribluda. It is a story of violence, and
other deaths occur as the investigation proceeds, but it is also a
story which analyses the character and beliefs of the central
detective in a way that few other mystery novels have done.
Above all, however, it is a story of Moscow – the miseries, the
touches of warmth, the intrigues and the cynical bureaucracy.
The final quarter of this lengthy novel is set in New York where,
in spite of its freedoms, there is still much to hide. Crime, corruption and ruthlessness are shown to be universal.

POSTSCRIPT

This guide to the best in crime fiction is now as up to date as author and publisher can make it. It is nevertheless a field which constantly attracts new talent, and each year brings a fresh crop of writers who are as yet impossible to place in context. The crime story in its many guises remains in good hands, and there is no doubt that in years to come there will be other names to place beside the leaders in the field.

Already there are some writers on both sides of the Atlantic who, having entered on the scene in comparatively recent years, now show clear evidence that they will soon be listed among the best. It might be invidious to risk making a selection at this stage, but one thinks of British authors like Sarah Caudwell, James Melville, Jack S. Scott, Sheila Radley, Liza Cody, Dorothy Simpson and Andrew Taylor. Turning to the USA, high standards have been displayed by Mary Higgins Clark, Andrew Coburn, Lucille Kallen and Jonathan Valin.

If ever there is a temptation to think of the crime story as being in decline, it must also be remembered that many of the experienced practitioners mentioned in these pages are still producing new material. While this book bears little resemblance in size and scope to its predecessor *Best detective fiction*, the closing sentences of that earlier book may be confidently repeated here without qualification. Over ten years later, it may still be said that the genre has a deal of life in it. Or alternatively, to borrow a phrase from Mark Twain, any reports of its death are greatly exaggerated.

Checklist Of Books Featured

INDEX

This index consists of one alphabetical arrangement of AUTHORS, *Titles* and Series characters.